The Failure of China's "Democratic" Reforms

Challenges Facing Chinese Political Development

Series Editor: Sujian Guo, Ph.D.
San Francisco State University

In an attempt to reflect the rapidly changing political environment of the People's Republic of China, editor Sujian Guo has assembled a book series to present specialized areas of research in current Chinese political studies. Incorporating theoretical, empirical, and policy research on contemporary Chinese politics both domestically and internationally, this series contemplates the Chinese past, present, and future by utilizing interdisciplinary perspectives to approach issues related to Chinese politics, economy, culture, social development, reform, the military, legal system, and foreign relations. Aimed at bringing a greater understanding of the current Chinese political climate to Western audiences, this series is focused on the emerging voices of Chinese scholars and their perspectives on the ever-changing Chinese diaspora.

Recent titles in the series are:

The Dragon's Hidden Wings: How China Rises with Its Soft Power, by Sheng Ding
"Harmonious World" and China's New Foreign Policy, by Sujian Guo and Jean-Marc F. Blanchard
China in Search of a Harmonious Society, edited by Sujian Guo and Baogang Guo
Greater China in an Era of Globalization, edited by Sujian Guo and Baogang Guo
Toward Better Governance in China, edited by Baogang Guo and Dennis Hickey
Dynamics of Local Governance in China during the Reform Era, edited by Tse-Kang Leng and Yun-han Chu
Dancing with the Dragon: China's Emergence in the Developing World, edited by Dennis Hickey and Baogang Guo
Online Chinese Nationalism and China's Bilateral Relations, edited by Simon Shen and Shaun Breslin
Multidimensional Diplomacy of Contemporary China, edited by Simon Shen and Jean-Marc F. Blanchard
Thirty Years of China-U.S. Relations: Analytical Approaches and Contemporary Issues, edited by Sujian Guo and Baogang Guo
Environmental Protection Policy and Experience in the U.S. and China's Western Regions, edited by Sujian Guo, Joel J. Kassiola, and Zhang Jijiao
China's Quest for Political Legitimacy: The New Equity-Enhancing Politics, by Baogang Guo
New Frontiers in China's Foreign Relations, edited by Allen Carlson and Ren Xiao
The Failure China's "Democratic" Reforms, by Zaijun Yuan

The Failure of China's "Democratic" Reforms

Zaijun Yuan

LEXINGTON BOOKS
Lanham • Boulder • New York • Toronto • Plymouth, UK

Published by Lexington Books
A wholly owned subsidiary of The Rowman & Littlefield Publishing Group, Inc.
4501 Forbes Boulevard, Suite 200, Lanham, Maryland 20706
http://www.lexingtonbooks.com

Estover Road, Plymouth PL6 7PY, United Kingdom

British Library Cataloguing in Publication Information Available

Library of Congress Cataloging-in-Publication Data

Library of Congress Cataloging-in-Publication Data Available

ISBN 978-0-7391-6694-9 (cloth : alk. paper)
ISBN 978-0-7391-7089-2 (electronic)

™ The paper used in this publication meets the minimum requirements of American National Standard for Information Sciences—Permanence of Paper for Printed Library Materials, ANSI/NISO Z39.48-1992.

Printed in the United States of America

Contents

Contents		*v*
Tables and Figures		*vii*
Foreword		*ix*
Preface		*xiii*
Acknowledgments		*xv*
Chapter 1	Introduction	1
Chapter 2	"Direct Elections" for Township Executives	9
Chapter 3	"Inner-Party Democracy" and the Experiments of Direct Elections for Township Party Secretaries	29
Chapter 4	Another Form of "Inner-Party Democracy": the Party Congress Reform	55
Chapter 5	The Experiments with "Deliberative Democracy"	73
Chapter 6	Independent Candidates in China's Local People's Congress Elections	103

Chapter 7 Conclusion 143

Bibliography 151
Index 173
About the Author 177

Tables and Figures

Table 2.1	Six Types of Township Executive Election Reforms and Their Important Cases	12
Table 3.1	Eleven Cases of "Direct Elections" for Township Party Secretaries	38
Table 3.2	Criteria for Eligible Candidates in Some Cases of "Direct Election" for Township Party Secretary	40
Table 4.1	Result of a Survey on the Relations between the Party Members and the Party Congress Members	61
Table 5.1	Five "Deliberative Democracy" Reform Cases in Wenling City	81
Figure 5.1	Strength of the Deliberation Session and Congress Session in the Reform Cases	88
Table 7.1	Party's Attitude to the Reforms	146
Table 7.2	The Numbers of Media Articles Regarding the Reforms	147

Foreword

I first met Zaijun Yuan on 4 October 2005 in my office at Monash University. Zaijun had wanted to talk to me about possible PhD research because when he was a postgraduate student in Nanjing he had read a 1991 article I had written about China's elections.[1] Such meetings rarely yield a harvest, but this one proved to be different.

On 15 August 2006 Zaijun formally became my PhD student. He originally did focus on China's elections and that ancestry shows in this book, for example, on the experiments with direct election of township government executives and in the chapter on independent candidates in people's congress elections. But soon Zaijun's work evolved into the much more important topic of the failure of China's "democratic" experiments.

From a supervisor's perspective, Zaijun's development as a scholar during the four years from the commencement of his PhD candidature until the successful examination of his PhD thesis was wonderful to observe. His co-supervisor, Dr. Dennis Woodward, and I observed a person increasingly breaking free of the constraints of his Chinese education and becoming more and more aware of alternative approaches. Thus, for example, he learned that the word democratic had quite different meanings in China as compared with the West. More and more, he began to use quotation marks around the word democratic when using the term in a Chinese context. During these four years, his written and spoken abilities in English also improved until he became virtually fluent in English.

In this book, Zaijun examines five types of so-called "democratic" reform experiments in China. The first four types of reform all share several characteristics. First, they were all initiated and instituted by the local party. Second, they

---

[1] J. Bruce Jacobs, "Elections in China," *The Australian Journal of Chinese Affairs*, No. 25 (January 1991), pp. 171–199.

were all limited in their geographical scope. Third, in each case, there was a "black box" that enabled the party to manipulate and control the outcomes. Thus, none of these reforms was democratic. In many cases, the party terminated even these very limited experiments.

The first experiment, the subject of Chapter 2, was direct popular election of township government executives, who normally are chosen by the township people's congress. In his analysis of these experiments, Zaijun writes:

> [E]ven though the procedures of the reform experiments were improved in some aspects, each of these experiments had major flaws that reduced the "directness" of the elections and hindered the voters from participating in some procedural steps. In every experiment, there was at least one stage where the power holders played a dominant role and the grass roots voters were excluded. This stage was critical in the whole process to decide the final candidate list.

Chapter 3 examines the second experiment, attempting to implement "Inner-Party Democracy" and direct election of township party secretaries. Zaijun shows how some party thinkers believe "inner-party democracy" is essential for China's future, but how this reform is essentially conservative rather than progressive in nature. As a case study, Zaijun examines the direct election of township party leaders. He finds these experiments are an improvement on the traditional party elections, but they have a flaw very similar to the experiments in the government elections in that they "were actually not so 'direct.'"

Chapter 4 examines another case of "Inner Party Democracy," reforms of the Party Congress. Again, Zaijun demonstrates that such reforms have not been implemented. "[R]eformed party congresses still could not genuinely elect the local party leaders." And, despite attempts to elevate party congresses in the system, they have remained subordinate.

The fourth experiment, discussed in Chapter 5, differs from the previous experiments in that foreign scholars were more deeply involved. Several prominent Western scholars have worked on "deliberative democracy" and some have made attempts to introduce this process into China. Zaijun conducted interviews with one of the key Western supporters of "deliberative democracy," Professor Baogang He of Deakin University, a sister university here in Melbourne, Australia. Zaijun also went to Zhejiang Province where he conducted extensive interviews with participants in China. Zaijun found that the Chinese experiments departed significantly from the Western ideas of "deliberative democracy." In addition, he found that such experiments were initially supported by the local party organization and then were subverted by the local leaders. Thus, in fact, the reform experiments in Zhejiang "do not fully meet the criteria for deliberative democracy."

Zaijun's last case study differs greatly from the previous case studies in that the party did not initiate or promote the candidacies of independent candidates in local people's congress elections. Chapter 6 shows how the local authorities repeatedly intervened at every stage of the electoral process to prevent independent candidates from winning local elections. Such interventions sometimes even broke Chinese law such as changing the boundaries of electorates and even changing the previously announced day of the election without giving advance notice. This chapter makes explicitly clear that local Chinese elections are far from democratic.

In preparing this book, Zaijun has extensively consulted Chinese documents and publications as well as Western publications relevant to his case studies. In addition, he has conducted extensive field research within China. The result is a stark description and analysis of China's so-called "democratic" reform experiments that makes clear China does not have a democratic political future as long as the present political power holders in the Chinese Communist Party remain in control. Thus, Zaijun's book both expands the frontiers of research on this topic and it clearly undermines the arguments of those who hold an optimistic view of China's short-term prospects for democracy.

I commend this important book to you.

J. Bruce Jacobs
Professor of Asian Languages and Studies
Monash University
Australia

February 2011

Preface

In its propaganda, the Chinese Communist Party does not deny the value of "democracy," but it insists that democracy in China can be only "socialist democracy with Chinese characteristics." The most essential nature of such "democracy" is that it is under the single-party system and it excludes multi-party politics and competitive elections. In recent years, "Chinese democracy" has won more support because of achievements the party has made in developing economy. This raises a question: does this "efficient" authoritarian political system in China, even if it is not democratic, deserve applause because it can facilitate economic development? The party also insists that it is "democratic." But, is the party's theory of "democracy" compatible with western democracy?

Since 1998, the party has organised some political reforms, such as "direct elections" for township executives, "direct elections" for township party secretaries, township party congress reform and "deliberative democracy" experiments, while maintaining single-party politics. In the party's propaganda, some of these reforms have become party achievements in improving "socialist democracy with Chinese characteristics." In addition to these four kinds of party-organised reforms, another "reform" originated from the grassroots, the participation of independent candidates in a few local people's congress elections.

This book examines these five local political reforms. It demonstrates that the four reforms instigated and organised by the party were tightly controlled and manipulated by the party. Although some reform measures may possibly liberalise parts of China's political mechanism, it is highly unlikely that the four reforms will eventually lead to political democratisation in China. In the fifth "reform," which was motivated from outside the bureaucratic system, the party took drastic measures to repress the political participation of grassroots power. As a result, nearly all independent candidates in the local people's congress elections failed in their attempts to gain office. The prospects for this "reform" are also poor. This book argues that all five reforms have failed and that none will lead to China's democratisation in the near future. The book concludes that the party's authoritarian regime in China is by nature anti-democratic and that so called "socialist democracy with Chinese characteristics" is not democratic.

Acknowledgements

I am heartily thankful to my PhD supervisor, Professor J. Bruce Jacobs of Monash University in Australia, whose encouragement, guidance and support from the initial to the final stage enabled me to develop an understanding of the subject and to accomplish the research. I also owe my deepest gratitude to my other supervisor, Dr. Dennis Woodward of Monash University, whose guidance and persistent help has greatly assisted me in this endeavour. I would also like to thank Professor He Baogang of Deakin University in Melbourne for his suggestions and assistance for parts of my research.

I am grateful to Professor J. Teufel Dreyer of University of Miami and Professor Edward Friedman of University of Wisconsin. Their comments and suggestions on the manuscript helped me to improve this work.

I owe my gratitude to Professor Guo Sujian of San Francisco State University. His enthusiastic recommendation facilitated publication of this work. He also provided encouragement and assistance while I revised and edited the manuscript.

I would like to extend my sincere thanks to those who I have interviewed, who must remain anonymous.

I thank the staff at Rowman & Littlefield-Lexington Books for their careful production of this book.

I dedicate this book to my patient and understanding wife, Wang Bing, and our son, Yuan Xuzhi. Their support has sustained me throughout this undertaking. This book is for them, with my love and affection.

Chapter 1

Introduction

After painstaking efforts in economic reforms over the past two decades, China's achievements in economic development have astonished the world. Chinese political reforms, however, have lagged far behind its economic reforms. The basic polity of China, with the Chinese Communist Party's authoritarian rule and leadership in most political and social spheres, has changed little. Specifically, there have been no obvious improvements in such areas as political power decentralisation, elections and expression of public opinion.

Although the party always avoids comprehensive political reform and refuses to loosen its control over key parts of the political structure, it frequently uses "democracy" in many central party documents and the propaganda articles written by senior party theorists. More interestingly, several kinds of political reform experiments have occurred in a few places at the local levels. This book examines these reform experiments and assesses whether or not they are leading China towards democratisation.

What are Local Political Reform Experiments and Why Study Them?

There are five levels in the Chinese political structure.[1] The reform experiments studied in this book are at the two lowest levels: township and county (or district in urban areas which equals the county in rural areas).[2] Furthermore, the book is focused on the reform experiments which happened inside China's official political system. In other words, the selected experiments are directly related to such basic institutions as party committees, governments or people's congresses.

Defining the term "local political reform experiments" as above, the book will exclude the political changes (mainly direct elections) which have taken place in villages in rural areas or in resident communities in urban areas. These are not official government institutions as they are below the township level. Chapter 6, however, will discuss the village and urban community elections as they are related to the local people's congress elections. On the other hand, no reform experiments discussed in the book happened at the levels above the county. In fact, no such cases exist. However, the reactions of high-level political institutions to the local political reform experiments are analysed in chapters 2, 3, 5 and 6.

There are five categories of political experiments discussed in the book. First, the "direct elections" for township executives are examined in chapter 2. Second, the "direct elections" for township party secretaries are examined in chapter 3. Third, the experiments of township party congress reform are examined in chapter 4. Fourth, the experiments of "deliberative democracy" reform are analysed in chapter 5. Fifth, the independent candidates in local people's congress elections are analysed in chapter 6.

The experiments are processes whereby the targeted political spheres can hopefully be reformed and improved by the reformists.[3] The reform experiments will be studied from different dimensions. Specifically, the following dimensions of local political reform experiments will be examined in the subsequent chapters to assess the status of the experiments in each category and to anticipate the future development of these reforms.

1. Instigations and instigators of a reform. In China, a reform of any part of the institutionalised political system is sensitive even if it happens at local levels. It is useful to discover who initially instigated a reform and who possibly benefited. Answering these questions helps to explain the questions arising in the research of other dimensions such as the quality and impacts of the reform.

2. Organisers and designers. In some experiments, the organisers who carried out a reform and the designers who designed the reform were not the people who instigated it. To know who they were and their attitudes towards the reform helps to understand more about the questions mentioned above.

3. Normal system. Profiling the normal system provides a basis for comparison, which will enable the reader to identify whether or not a reform experiment improved parts of the political system.

4. Relevant laws and rules. Laws and rules are normally not very important in the case studies of Chinese politics as the power holders often tend to ignore them. However, the laws and rules may become powerful weapons for the conservatives to abort reforms. Therefore, to check if the reforms conform to the laws and rules or to analyse how broad the space allowed by the laws and rules for the future development of reform is valuable for examining the reform's sustainability and thus enables the researcher to anticipate the impacts, if any, the reform will have on the Chinese political system.

5. Procedures. The reform experiments at local levels, even when they seem similar, may have different procedures from case to case. The book tries to restore details of these reform experiments in order to analyse and comment on them.

6. Improvements and defects in a procedure and the value of an experiment. Based on the description of a reform procedure, the comparison between it and the normal system and then further analysis, a conclusion can be drawn on the improvements and defects of the procedure of each experiment and the overall quality of the experiments in each category. This forms the foundation for the final conclusion of the book.

7. Sustainability and possible impacts. Based on the research results, a general conclusion will be drawn on the sustainability of the reforms and the possible impacts they may have. Comparing this conclusion with "socialist democracy with Chinese characteristics" and the "political reforms" in the context of the party's propaganda, the book will enable the reader to have an in-depth understanding of China's current political situation and perhaps will enable them to anticipate the future tendency of political developments in China.

The Chinese Communist Party does not deny the value of "democracy" but insists that democracy in China can be only "socialist democracy with Chinese characteristics." In the party's theory, the most essential nature of such kind of "democracy" is that it is under a single-party system. That is to say, this "democracy" excludes multi-party politics and competitive elections. This "democracy" deprives the Chinese people of such basic human rights as freedom of the press, speech, assembly, association, demonstration and religious belief, which would effectively liberalise the social spheres and thus pave the way for liberal democracy. Adhering to single-party politics, the party has still instigated and organised some political reforms[4] for various reasons. In the party's propaganda, some of the reforms have become the achievements the party has made in improving "socialist democracy with Chinese characteristics," which further indicates that "political democratisation" will be finally achieved in the Chinese one-party authoritarian state. Some western researchers, who believe that the fast economic growth and the established social middle class in some regions in China have become ripening conditions for China's democratisation, put hopes in the local political reform experiments (Dittmer & Liu, 2006; He, 2006a; Leib & He, 2006; Perry & Goldman, 2007). Creating political-economic concepts like a "Chinese model," "Beijing consensus" or believing China is moving toward "soft authoritarianism," some western researchers argue that the governments of under-developed countries should accept the values that the Chinese Communist Party has been promoting for nearly thirty years: fast economic growth is the ultimate goal for a government and it can finally help the government to solve every problem in the country (Jacques, 2009; Naisbitt & Naisbitt, 2010; Ramo, 2004). According to them, the authoritarian politics in China facilitates the rapid growth of the Chinese economy and under-developed countries should follow this route to develop their economy. This suggests that liberal democracy should give way to authoritarian politics in order to achieve economic development.

The book will not study any possible correlation between politics and economic development. Instead, it will focus on the nature of the Chinese political system and the so-called "socialist democracy with Chinese characteristics" under such a system. Within the context already discussed, an important objective of this study is to examine if the party's view is true that in China political democracy[5] is compatible with the single-party authoritarian political system. To be specific, the book tests whether the political reform experiments carried out in the single-party system are really democratic. If the answer is positive, the book then assesses how democratic they are.

Among the reform experiments discussed in the book, some reform experiments were instigated and organised by the local party committees. The central party dislikes and has prohibited some of them, such as "direct elections" for township executives, or shows an ambivalent attitude to some such as "deliberative democracy" reform. As for these reform experiments, the objective of the book is to discover the reasons why the central party has such negative or ambivalent attitudes. The analysis of these reasons is based on in-depth comparative analysis of the instigations, procedures and impacts of the reform experiments. The book then checks if the prohibitive attitudes are caused by the conflicts between the reforms and the single-party principle. The "reform" of the participation of the grassroots power in local people's congress elections has experienced increasingly severe suppression. The analysis of the reforms and of the party's strong negative attitudes can lead to conclusions on how likely mass democratic activities will appear in China's current political system. The answers to all these questions will be summarised and analysed in the last chapter to form the final conclusion, which describes the nature of the political reforms and anticipates their possible future development.

There has been some research on the reforms of "direct elections" for township executives, "direct elections" for township party secretaries, and township party congress reform and "deliberative democracy" reform. Research on the independent candidates in local people's congress elections is comparatively rare. Most research focuses on only one category of reform. The lack of previous research which views various categories of reform experiments in an integrated way means such fundamental questions as what these experiments are and how they might change the political system remain largely unanswered. This study aims to address this lack by examining political experiments as a whole and asking key questions about the changes and impacts the experiments as a phenomenon have brought on China's politics. In addition, the existing case studies of the reform experiments were mainly conducted by researchers from mainland China, who often had "blind spots" because of political ideology or censorship. This research, which uses these case studies as well as my own field research, allows contemporary political reform in China to be better understood from an evidence-based viewpoint.

Why choose to study these reform experiments that occurred in the period beginning in 1998? Some researchers place their hope for China's democratisation on a "bottom up" democratic movement, which starts from "village elections" fully carried out throughout China and became institutionalised in 1998 when the *Organic Law of Village Committees* was enacted (He, 2007; O'Brien & Li, 2001; Pastor & Tan, 2001; Tan, 2006). In the "bottom-up" perspective, the local political reform experiments, especially the election reforms instigated by the party, are naturally viewed as the growth of "village elections" extending upwards to the higher levels of the Chinese official system. These scholars even expect that such an "upward extension" will be sustainable to achieve democratisation of the nation's entire political system. Considering this, it is important to study the nature of the local reform experiments that have occurred since 1998 and the possible impacts they may have on the political system.

Methodology and Sources of Materials

In this study, I am committed to the value of liberal democracy. I have employed political science methods, analysis of facts and data and comparative methods to conduct the research. In mainland China, mainstream studies of this subject are not built on democratic values and are inclined to be over-optimistic, though they provide us with useful data. The critiques from overseas address less specific cases so their theoretical hypotheses are generally weakly supported. This study tries to overcome these problems.

The materials in this book come from both archival and field research. Most materials in chapters 2, 3 and 4, which respectively study the reform experiments of "direct elections" for township executives, "direct elections" for township party secretaries and the experiments of the party congress reform, were obtained from archival research because the collected archives have been able to provide a large quantity of data regarding these experiments. In fact, the "direct elections" for township party secretaries and party congress reform are the focus of the party's propaganda, while the "direct elections" for township executives were reported by the media or discussed in Chinese researchers' papers because of their special political significance.

I did field research for the data regarding the reforms of "deliberative democracy" and independent candidates in local people's congress elections, which are respectively discussed in chapters 5 and 6. The party has banned press coverage and academic research on the independent candidates in local people's congress elections, trying to hide the truth from being exposed to the outside world. Although a little data can be viewed from the work of some independent researchers or from some overseas online media sources, field research is important and it is perhaps the only means to gain sufficient factual evidence for the subject. I conducted field research on the "deliberative democracy" reform because, compared with other kinds of reforms, it has interested overseas academics. Different from the "direct elections" for township party secretaries and the local party congress reform, the "deliberative democracy" reform is believed by some western researchers to be a true "democratic" model compatible with China's single-party political system.[6] In addition, the higher provincial and central levels of the party have ambivalent attitudes to this reform. Field research is perhaps an efficient way to acquire the information regarding their real standpoint and considerations.

Field research includes both interviews and the collection of original documents. Interviews have been the major activity of my field research, mainly with lay participants, local cadres, party theorists, government researchers and independent observers or public intellectuals. These interviewees have been chosen on the basis of previous archival research and from other people's recommendations.

While doing archival research for the book, I tried to collect data from a variety of sources to ensure a variety of perspectives. However, regarding the independent candidates in local people's congress elections, most information was available from sympathetic overseas news media as well as interviews. In the process of my research, I heard the doubts about reliability of such information sources because "they are run or sponsored by alien governments." To strengthen the research conclusion, it is important to clarify the question as to whether evidence collected from these sources is reliable. Like all sources, they must be tested, but they can be a valuable source of information.[7]

Central Argument and Hypothesis

This book argues that the reform experiments fall well short of being truly democratic. As such, they do not hold out the prospect that China will move towards a western style liberal democracy in the near future.

Notes

1. According to article 30 of *The Constitution of PRC*, the five levels of the Chinese political structure from high to low are the (1) *zhongyang* [centre], (2) *sheng* [province]/*zizhiqu* [autonomous region]/*zhixiashi* [municipality], (3) *shi* [city]/*zizhizhou* [autonomous prefecture], (4) *xian* [county]/*qu* [district], and (5) *zhen* [town]/*xiang* [township] (NPC, 2004b).

2. In all chapters except chapter 3, both the township/town and the county/district are defined as local levels. The party committees, governments and people's congresses at the town/township and county/district levels are generally called the local party committees, governments and people's congresses. Only in chapter 3, a town or township is defined as the primary level and a county or district is defined as a local level based on two party laws (see p. 37 and note 16 in chapter 3 for details).

3. I do not exclude the possibility that some reform experiments were deliberately designed to be ineffective or were carried out carelessly for propaganda purposes.

4. These reforms include the "direct elections" for township executives discussed in chapter 2, the "direct elections" for township party secretaries in chapter 3, the township party congress reform in chapter 4, and the "deliberative democracy" reform in chapter 5.

5. Political democracy here refers to the genuine political democratisation of any part of China's five-level bureaucratic system such as the governments, party committees and people's congresses. The elections or participatory institutions at the village or resident-community level are not in the scope of the subject discussed in this book.

6. The researchers include James S. Fishkin (Fishkin, He, & Siu, 2006), Ethan J. Leib (Leib & He, 2006), Baogang He (He, 2006b), Shawn Rosenberg (Rosenberg, 2006), John Dryzek (Dryzek, 2006), Daniel A. Bell (Bell, 2006) etc..

7. For example, Radio Free Asia, which is in the category of such questionable media, does seek to confirm from those involved, details of every event before they report it (Lin Hui, 2009).

Chapter 2

"Direct Elections" for Township Government Executives

Introduction

Of all party-instigated political reform experiments in China, the "direct elections"[1] for township government executives, which were held in some localities between the years of 1998 and 2004, are perhaps the most significant. Different from other party-instigated reform experiments, such as the inner-party reform, which is of an obviously narrower scope, or the "deliberative democracy" reform, which has no impacts on the voting system, the experiments with "direct elections" for township government executives aimed at the political power in the local level of Chinese government and tried to expand the voters' participation in the process of election. The first part of this chapter analyses the laws related to the election procedure and the party's control in the traditional elections of this kind. The second part of this chapter examines, analyses and comments on the six most important reform cases. In the third part, on who instigated the experimental elections, the local and central party's attitudes and their influence on the reform are discussed. The fourth part examines whether the reform experiments have had impacts on the current Chinese political system and if the reform is likely to appear again in the future.

The Related Law Articles and the Conventional System

The laws related to the elections for township government executives include *The Constitution of the People's Republic of China* (NPC, 2004b) and *The PRC Organisation Law for Local People's Congresses and Local Governments at All Levels* (NPC, 2004a). The specific articles are:

Article 101 of the Constitution says:

> Local people's congresses at their respective levels elect and have the power to recall governors and deputy governors, or mayors and deputy mayors, or heads and deputy heads of counties, districts, townships and towns

It is clear in the Constitution that a township government executive should be elected by the people's congress of that township.

This point is confirmed by Article 8 of the Organisation Law:

> Township, minority nationality township, and town people's congresses will exercise the following functions and powers: . . . They will elect their township leaders and deputy leaders and town leaders and deputy leaders

According to the constitution and laws, the people's congresses are China's legislative bodies and the organ of state power. The elections in China are divided into two categories, "direct" and "indirect." Voters directly elect the members of the people's congresses at township and county level, while the members of the township and county people's congresses elect the executive, legislative and judicial heads in their own administrative district. The county people's congress members also elect the next higher-level people's congress and the members of these higher-level people's congresses elect the government executives, legislative and judicial heads at the same level. In this system, the voters only directly elect the members of the people's congress at the township and county level. All other elections are indirect. In fact, the party tightly controls the direct elections for the members of the local people's congresses, a topic fully discussed in chapter 6. Compared with the direct elections, "both congress delegates at various levels and Chinese social scientists studying the topic find China's indirect elections much less democratic than its direct elections" because the "party plays a much more obvious role in China's indirect elections" (Jacobs, 1991). In general, the forms of both direct elections and indirect elections have remained unchanged in China for the three decades since the new Electoral Law became effective in January 1980. The party committees of various levels actually hold absolute power in the elections at their level. "At the township level,[2] the party organisation dominates all other political organizations. . . . Regarding the elections for government executives held in the congress, the party committee nominates the candidates . . . decides the subject and agenda of the congress election meetings. The congress becomes a rubber stamp and the elections are just a formality" (Huang Weiping & Zou Shubin, 2003:63–64). Therefore, neither direct nor indirect elections enable the voters to elect their own political leaders. These elections are "little more than opportunities for the communist leadership to conduct propaganda among the citizenry" (Wu Guoguang, 2000).

In the Chinese political system, the township government is at the lowest level. It deals directly with villagers who account for the biggest proportion of China's population. In China today, *sannong wenti* [the three problems of agriculture, villages and peasants],[3] urgently need to be solved. In addition, there is increasing tension between the masses and local governments in many places of China. Mass riots[4] have increased yearly from 8,709 in 1993 to 11,000 in 1995, 15,000 in 1997, 32,000 in 1999, 40,000 in 2004 and 90,000 in 2006 (Chung, 2004; Yu Jianrong, 2009). The increasing tensions between the masses and local governments have brought instability to Chinese society. An important reason for such problems is that the local cadres gain their political powers from the higher-level party committee rather than from the local voters. Accordingly, they need to be responsible to the higher levels, not to the voters. Thus, two problems may arise in local governance. First, the local government cadres work to please the higher levels and much of their work is done only to gain credit for future promotion.[5] This "looking upward" working style is quite popular among local cadres and it keeps the relations between the masses and local governments tense. Nowadays in China, local taxes collected from villagers financially support the township and county governments. When villagers do not believe the local governments are working in their interest, inquiries on the governments' legitimacy are naturally raised. However, the party does not allow such a topic to be discussed in public. Second, there is also insufficient inspection of local government executives, who are using illegally-gained political powers. The unrestricted powers of the party and government leaders often lead to their corruption which worsens the relationship between the government and the people.

In my view, the ultimate purpose of political reform is to return political power into the people's hands. Local government executives elected by direct elections will be more responsible to the electorates, carefully control budgets, work for what people really need and genuinely represent people's interests.[6] On this basis, holding direct elections for local government executives is a first important step towards China's political democratization. In practice, to directly elect local government executives and to allow more local self-governance is an effective solution to ease the tension between the masses and local governments.

Case Studies of Six Types of the Experiments

From 1998 to 2004, the reform in the elections for government executives was conducted in a few townships. The reform processes varied from place to place but there were still similarities. Accordingly, this book categorises these experiments into six different types, which can be seen from Table 2.1.

Table 2.1 Six Types of Township Executive Election Reforms and Their Important Cases

Type	Locality	Time	Election for
(1) Direct Election	Case 1: Buyun Township, Shizhong District, Suining City, Sichuan Province	December 1998	Township government executive
	Case 2: Buyun Township, Shizhong District, Suining City, Sichuan Province	December 2001	Township government executive
	Case 3: Seven townships of Shiping County, Honghe Yi and Ha'ni Minority Autonomous Prefecture, Yunnan Province	February to April 2004	Township government executive
(2) Three Ballot System, etc.	Case 4: Dapeng Township, Longgang District, Shenzhen City, Guangdong Province	January to April 1999	Township government executive
(3) Two Ballot System	Case 5: Zhuoli Township, Linyi County, Yuncheng City, Shanxi Province	April to May 1999	Township government executive, party secretary and people's congress speaker
(4) Open Nomination	Case 6: Yangji Township, Jingshan County, Jingmen City, Hubei Province	August to September 2002	Township government executive and party secretary
(5) Self-Nomination and Test System	Case 7: More than eighty townships in Sichuan Province	1998	Township government executive
(6) Nomination by People's Congress Delegates	Case 8: Eleven Townships of Mianyang City, Sichuan Province	November 1998 to February 1999	Township government executive

Important Cases and Their Procedures

Experimental elections of the same type had similar procedures. The following part selects the most important cases for each type and examines their major procedural steps.

There are three cases to be examined in "direct election" type.

Case 1:

The best known direct election for township executive was held in Buyun Township, Sichuan Province in December 1998. The main procedural steps were (Li Fan, 1999):

1. The higher-level party committee nominated one candidate and the voters nominated (through a joint nomination from at least 30 voters) fifteen candidates.

2. A committee was established[7] to elect two candidates from the fifteen ones who were nominated by the voters in the first step. Before the election of this round, the fifteen candidates gave campaign speeches before the committee. The candidate nominated by the higher-level party committee automatically entered the next round without going through the election in this step.

3. The three candidates campaigned for one week in all villages.

4. Voters directly elected the township executive from the three candidates in this step. The candidate nominated by the higher-level party committee won the election.

Case 2:

The township executive, who was elected in case 1, left his position at the end of 2001. Another experimental election was held in Buyun in December 2001. Feeling the pressures from conservatives in the party, the organisers added two final steps to the procedure, in which the party committee regained the power to "nominate" one candidate and the township people's congress regained the power to vote on the candidate. The newly-added two final steps were just a formality which did not affect the election result.[8] Such an arrangement, however, enabled the experiment to be more easily accepted by the higher-levels. The major steps are described below (Tang Jianguang, 2002):

1. Self-nomination was allowed in this election. Fourteen candidates were self-nominated. The party did not nominate candidates but it secretly supported the incumbent township executive who stood for the election. Two of the fourteen candidates were assessed as not qualified and another two were removed for unknown reasons.[9] Whereas nearly thirty percent of the candidates in 1998 were villagers, all of the candidates in the 2002 election were government cadres or employees.

2. The ten candidates gave campaign speeches before a committee, and then the committee voted to elect two from the ten candidates. The committee was established in the same way as in 1998.

3. Voters directly elected one candidate from the two candidates to enter the last round.

4. The township party committee nominated the winner of the direct election in step 3 to be the candidate on the final list (only one candidate at this step) for the last round of voting held in the township people's congress.

5. The township congress members voted to elect this person to be township executive.

Case 3:

In April 2004, "direct elections" for township government executives were held in seven townships of Shiping County, Yunnan Province. The elections involved eight steps (Gao Yingxiong, 2004):

1. Voters elected township people's congress members, who then examined and approved the direct election procedure.

2. The township congress made criteria for candidate nomination and elected a panel which would be responsible for checking the eligibility of the nominated candidates in step 5 (see step 5 below) based on the pre-set criteria.

3. The township congress approved the formation of an election committee.[10] The committee members would vote to elect final candidates in step 6 (see step 6 described below).

4. The township congress was adjourned and the members went back to their electorates to organise the elections there.

5. Voters nominated (through joint nomination from at least 30 voters) candidates. The panel elected in step 2 examined the eligibility of the nominated candidates and published the list of the eligible initial candidates.

6. All initial candidates made campaign speeches to the committee formed in step 3. The committee voted to elect two final candidates from the initial candidates.

7. The two final candidates made campaign speeches in villages. Voters directly elected township executive.

8. The township people's congress resumed its session to check the whole procedure. The congress members then ratified the result of the direct election in step 7.

Case 4:

One case of "three ballot system" is examined, the election for township executive held in Dapeng Township, Guangdong Province in January 1999. The major steps are described as below (Huang Weiping, 2000):

1. The township party committee declared that every voter should nominate a candidate by casting a secret ballot. The nomination (the first ballot) lasted for seven days. A total of 5,048 voters (around 97 percent of all voters) nominated 76 candidates.

2. According to the method which the township party committee made in advance, candidates who gained more than 100 nominations could enter the next round. Five candidates out of the 76 then entered the next round.

3. The five candidates made campaign speeches before the 1,068 voters' representatives[11] and the representatives voted to elect one final candidate from these five candidates. This is the second ballot.

4. The township party committee nominated the winner of step 3 as the only candidate for township executive. The township people's congress members voted to approve him to be the township executive, the third ballot.

Case 5:

We now examine one case of the "two ballot system" held in April 1999 in Zhuoli Township, Linyi County, Shanxi Province. There were five steps in the procedure (Shi Weiqin, 2003):

1. The higher-level county party committee nominated the incumbent township government executive, the incumbent township party committee secretary and the incumbent township people's congress speaker as the only candidates for the positions they were currently holding.

2. The three candidates reported their work to some voters at a meeting that was broadcast live by the county's TV station. Nearly 1,000 voters attended the meeting and about 8,000 voters watched the meeting on TV.

3. The three candidates were voted in a public poll in accordance with the higher-level party committee's policy: a candidate who won more than 85 percent support in the poll would enter the second vote, a candidate who won 60 to 70 percent support would still enter the next round but would be investigated by the county government, while a candidate who obtained less than 60 percent of the vote would not enter the next round. In addition, he would be warned and moved to a lower-rank position. A candidate who received less than 50 percent of the vote would be dismissed from the party, government or people's congress system.

4. A total of 9,240 of all 9,445 eligible voters cast ballots in the poll. The township government executive, party secretary and congress speaker all won high rates of support, respectively 88.84 percent, 92.02 percent and 88.17 percent. This round of voting was called "the first ballot."

5. The three candidates then entered the second round of voting, which was held as "institutionalised elections." Specifically, the township people's congress members voted to elect the township government executive and congress speaker, the township party congress members voted to elect the secretary of the township party committee. There was only one candidate for each position in these elections. This round of voting was called "the second ballot."

Case 6:

The procedure of an "open nomination" was held for the election of township government executive and party secretary in September 2002 in Yangji Township, Hubei Province. The procedural steps were as follows (Government of Yangji Township, 2003):

1. In the nomination round, all voters could nominate candidates for township government executive and party secretary. In both government and party elections, the three candidates who won the most nominating votes entered the next round.

2. In the second round of the election for government executive, the members of the committees of all villages and urban residential communities voted to elect two candidates from the three candidates. In the second round of the election for party secretary, all township party members voted to elect two candidates from the three candidates.

3. In the last round of the government election, the township people's congress members voted to elect the township government executive from the two

candidates elected in the second round. In the last round of the election for party secretary, the township party congress members voted to elect the township party secretary from the two candidates elected in the second round. Before the voting in both people's and party congress meetings, the candidates made campaign speeches.

This case is similar in procedure to case 4. The difference will be discussed in the analysis part.

Case 7:

One case using the "self-nomination and test" method is described as below:

The elections in this case were held in more than eighty townships in Sichuan Province in 1998. The major steps are as the following (China Innovations, 2003):

1. The township government published the positions (various positions including government executive, deputy executive and party secretary) and the criteria for candidature. Self-nomination was allowed.

2. The township government organised a written exam in this step. Normally, the top six in the exam would proceed to the next round.

3. An oral test was held at a meeting. The six candidates needed to answer the randomly selected questions as well as the questions raised by the meeting participants.[12] After the test, the meeting participants voted on the six candidates. Among the candidates for township party secretary, the one who won most supporting votes was appointed to the position in this step. Among the candidates for township government executive, the two who were most supported entered the next round.

4. The township people's congress members voted to elect the township government executive from the two candidates.

Case 8:

"Nomination by people's congress members" was used for township government executive elections held in 1998 and 1999 in ten townships of Mianyang City, Sichuan Province. In these elections, the higher-level party committees did not nominate or recommend any candidates. Only ten or more people's congress members could jointly nominate candidates (Yang Xuedong, 2003). Although according to the Constitution voters can directly elect township people's congress members, as shown in chapter 6, the party tightly controls the local people's congress elections so the local party committee might still be able to manipulate the nomination in this case.

Analysis of the Cases

Some conclusions can be drawn from the above eight cases.

First, compared with the "traditional" party-controlled elections, the reform experiments had procedures which were more open to grassroots voters. In some cases, voters could participate in one procedural step to "directly elect" the township government executive or "directly elect" candidate(s) for the next round, such as step 4 in case 1, step 3 in case 2 and step 7 in case 3. In step 4 of case 5, voters could vote on the candidates in a public opinion poll and the result might decide if the candidates could enter the next round. In some cases, voters could nominate candidates and those who won most nominations entered the next round, such as in step 1 of cases 4 and 6. In addition to the voters' participation, there are some other reforms such as self-nomination in cases 2 and 7. Candidates were encouraged to make "campaign speeches" in step 3 of case 1, step 2 of case 2, steps 6 and 7 of case 3, step 3 of case 4, step 2 of case 5, step 3 of case 6 and step 3 of case 7. Written and oral tests helped select candidates in steps 2 and 3 of case 7. The party seemingly did not interfere in the candidate nomination in case 8. These reforms made the elections more liberal compared with traditional elections.

Second, even though the procedures of the reform experiments were improved in some aspects, each of these experiments had major flaws that reduced the "directness" of the elections and hindered the voters from participating in some procedural steps. In every experiment, there was at least one stage where the power holders played a dominant role and the grassroots voters were excluded. This stage was critical in the whole process to decide the final candidate list. For example, two were selected from the fifteen candidates in step 2 of case 1, two were selected from ten in step 2 of case 2, two were selected from around eleven in step 6 of case 3,[13] and one was selected from five in step 3 of case 4. By setting one or more such "stage(s) under control" in an experiment, the local power holders were able to change the election result to meet their desires. The stage was like a "black box" that no one understands. In addition to the above-mentioned black box step, some experiments have other specific flaws. The party-nominated candidate in case 1 had a privilege of directly entering the next round without going through step 2. In case 5, the number of candidates was equal to the number of positions (only one candidate for each position). Even worse, all the candidates were nominated by the party and they were all incumbents. In cases 4 and 6, the grassroots voters could participate in the elections by nominating candidates in the initial step but their nomination votes tended to be scattered among too many candidates.[14] In these two cases, considering the fact that the unofficial election campaigns were strictly prohibited before the nomination step and that the grassroots voters had no opportunities to participate in the steps after the nomination, the participation of grassroots voters in the first initial step could barely affect the final election results. The party still held absolute powers in the procedural steps after the nomination to control the election result. In addition, the power holders in nearly all cases preset some criteria for candidates which in fact deprived some citizens of their right to stand for elections. For example, there were conditions of age, education, job and political background for becoming the candidates in cases 1, 2, 3, 4, 6 and 8.[15] The measures which the local power holders took to control the elections seemed very effective. According to the existing documents regarding all eight cases, no candidates from the grassroots appeared in any of the eight cases except for case 1. Four years later, when a similar experimental election (case 2) was held in the same township, grassroots candidates did not appear even in the first step. Even worse, in case 2, none of the township cadres self-nominated perhaps because they knew that the party would manipulate the election to guarantee the winning of the party-preferred candidate. In order to make the election look "competitive," the local party organisation had to persuade eleven cadres to "self-nominate" and "compete" with the party-preferred candidate in the election (Wang Yi, 2003). Furthermore, the winners of the elections in all cases, according to the data available, were the candidates whom the party preferred and expected to win.

Third, other special problems remained in some cases. In case 4, even though ninety-five percent of the 5,259 eligible voters, who were all local residents, participated in the election, more than 30,000 migrant workers living at the locality were deprived of their voting right (Huang Weiping, Zou Shubin, Zhang Dinghuai, Yang Longfang, 2001). That the majority of eligible voters were absent from the election devalues the reform.[16] In fact, such a problem was quite common in elections or other political activities[17] held in eastern developed areas where migrant workers had largely moved (Renminwang, 2006). After cases 1 and 2, which were thought to be the more advanced election reform compared with other cases, the elected township executive had troubles in his political career because of the conflicts between the reform and traditional systems. In the centralism-featured political system in China, the ultimate goal of most cadres is to be promoted. The elected township executive in cases 1 and 2, however, lost the opportunity to be promoted by the higher-level because he was "directly elected" by voters, so he complained he was a "victim" of the reform. Unlike all his colleagues, who were appointed by the higher-level party committees, worked only for higher-levels and would get promoted by the higher-levels, the elected township executive in cases 1 and 2 had to be responsible to his voters. Being responsible to different groups of people, the directly-elected township executive can advocate very different policies from his appointed colleagues (Wang Yi, 2003).

Conditions, Prospects and Conclusion

Local Economy

It is widely believed that a developed local economy, an established middle class and a sophisticated education system help to increase democratic awareness of citizens (Acemoglu & Robinson, 2006; Przeworski, Alvarez, Cheibub, Antonio & Limongi, 2000). According to this theory, "democratic" elections are feasible only in places with better economic development. However, the results of the comparative analysis of cases 1, 2 and case 4 are not in accordance with this theory. It appears that the willingness to conduct a political experiment, which was designed to open the political process for public participation, has little to do with the level of economic development in a locality.

Among China's electoral political experiments, case 1 in 1998 is considered the most "democratic" one. Three years later in 2001, case 2 was held at the same locality. Comparatively, the election in case 4 held in 1999 was much less "direct" and less "democratic." In addition, no further electoral experiments were held at that locality after 1999. The economy in the locality of case 4 (Dapeng Township), however, is far more developed than the locality of cases 1 and 2 (Buyun Township). The statistical data show that the annual per capita income in Buyun Township in 2003 was 2,180 *yuan*, while it was 7,717 *yuan* in Dapeng Township (Hu Jiajia, 2006). The average annual income for the Chinese agricultural people in that year was 2,622 *yuan* (National Bureau of Statistics of China, 2004). Obviously, the economic development in the locality of case 4 was much higher than the national average level while the locality of cases 1 and 2 was close to the average. On the other hand, the voters in cases 1 and 2 held more positive attitudes than those in case 4. A survey result clearly shows that the voters in cases 1 and 2, compared with those in case 4, had more expectations from the election reform and were acting with more confidence in the process. After the events, their evaluations on the elections were much higher than those of case 4 (Cai Dingjian, 2003). It might be the comparatively liberal nature of the experimental elections that made the cases 1 and 2 voters more positive about the experiments and more active in their participation.

Such an analysis might not refute the hypothesised positive correlation between economic and democratic development because of insufficient sample size. The analysis of the cases, however, clearly indicates that democratic or liberal reforms can be made in less developed places. In my view, only if there is genuine democratic reform are people able to build up their confidence and learn to enhance their democratic awareness and capability in the process of their participation. The party's claim that the direct elections should be delayed because of the "unripe conditions" such as a less-developed economy, education and other social factors is poorly grounded and misleading.

The Party's Attitudes

It was the county or city level party committees that instigated and organised most of these local election reform experiments. Party committee secretaries, the absolute power holders at the locality, were normally the leading reformers who designed and conducted the reform in one or more subordinate townships. The instigations of these local power holders to start the experiments are not clearly defined and perhaps vary in different cases. The biggest incentive appears to be to gain a reputation in order to be promoted by their higher-level.[18] Even though we cannot exclude the possibility that reformers in some cases had some "democratic" awareness so that they started the reform to allow more public participation in local politics,[19] it is a fact that none of these experiments were truly instigated or initiated from the grassroots. On the other hand, the nature of the instigators explains why the experiments were still tightly controlled by the party. The analysis of the instigations indicates that the local power holders could never give up complete political power to the grassroots voters if their purpose was to win credits for a brighter future in their political career.

It is clear from the above analysis that the local power holder, who was normally the higher-level party committee secretary, was decisive in most aspects of the reform. An aborted experimental election in Pingba Township, Chengkou County, Chongqing Municipality in 2003 proves from another side the higher-level party secretaries' dominant role in such a reform. Possibly due to a more liberal design of the election[20] and the bad communication with the immediate higher-level party committee,[21] the township party secretary Wei Shengduo, who was the instigator and organiser of the experiment, received the punishment of *Shuanggui*,[22] demotion in his career and was even illegally deprived of his people's congress membership. The experimental election was then aborted while it was in progress (Chou, 2005). There is another example to demonstrate the local power holders' authority in reform. In spite of the pressures from the conservatives, the reformers still organised the case 2 election at the same locality three years after case 1. The case 2 reform, however, was obviously less liberal than case 1 with the steps especially added to emphasise the role of the party and people's congress.[23] Even though the case 2 election was changed to please the higher-levels, the township people's congress dared not vote on the candidate in step 5 because of "the opposing opinions from some higher-level cadres who were insisting that the reform should be completely stopped and the election should be in the thoroughly traditional way" (Zou Shubin, Huang Weiping, Liu Jianguang, 2003). Not until a photo of the voting scene was published in the newspaper of the provincial party committee, which indicated the approval of the provincial party leaders, did the township people's congress go through with step 5 to "legitimate" the election result (Zou Shubin, Huang Weiping, Liu Jianguang, 2003).

While the local power holders played a crucial role in the local election reform, the central party's attitudes towards reforms determined their fate nationally. As analysed above, the reformers conducting the reform experiments and their higher-level supervisors agreeing to the experiments were mainly aiming to win credits for a future promotion. In the current centralised Chinese political system, the "biggest boss," the central party, tightly controls the political careers of reformers and their higher-level supervisors. Therefore, the central party's attitudes to the reform are good indicators to the ups and downs of a reform.

The first encouraging signal was from Jiang Zemin's report to the party's 15th National Congress in 1997. The document says, the party "shall extend the scope of democracy at the grassroots level to make sure that people directly exercise their democratic rights" (Jiang Zemin, 1997). The local reformers thought the central party's abstract and propaganda-like expression provided a guideline and the theoretical basis for the election experiments held afterwards (Zou Shubin, Huang Weiping, Liu Jianguang, 2003). Also, after the party's 15th national congress, according to an informant, the central party was considering the reform of the elections for township government executives. This message was disclosed with the central party's seeming approval to some researchers and local cadres through channels and then through reform case 1, which was believed the most open and liberal election.

However, the central party's attitudes towards the existing reform experiments remained unclear for a couple of years. The central party released neither affirmative nor negative views to the experiments during this period, while relevant reports from the party-controlled media or some overseas media, which claimed to have sources,[24] demonstrated the top-level's uncertain or even contradictory viewpoints on the reform.

An editorial of *The Legal Daily* on 15 January 1999, which is the official organ of the Ministry of Justice, criticised the case 1 election as unconstitutional and said such elections were not the right "democracy." The article, however, argued that "the experiment was demonstrating people's awareness of democracy and such awareness should be protected" (Zha Qingjiu, 1999). However, just a few days later on 23 January 1999, an article in the same newspaper compared the case 1 election to the Xiaogang Village Event[25] and highly commended it as "a milestone for Chinese political reform." On 26 February of that year, CCTV commented in a news program regarding the case 1 election that the election was a new step towards further rural reform. A high ranking officer who had been working on village elections told *The Washington Post* that this program showed the central party's affirmative view to the case 1 election (Liu Yawei, 2002). Such a conclusion was too optimistic. On 4 November 1999, an article published in a Singaporean newspaper, *Lianhe Zaobao*, said that the central party was against such an election as case 1 even though it did not negate the election result. In the article, four points regarding the central party's attitude were clarified: first, such elections as case 1 were unconstitutional; second, the election did not comply with the party's organisation rule since the local cadres did not gain approval from the provincial party committee before starting the process; third, the election result could be ratified because the winner was the right cadre nominated and preferred by the higher-level party committee; and fourth, no more such experiments would be allowed in the future (Zhou Ruipeng, 1999).[26] According to the article, it was the provincial people's congress that made the four-point decision and the National People's Congress (NPC) approved it. Normally, the NPC did not make a decision or a policy on a certain issue at the local level. However, as for such an important political reform experiment as case 1, which drew attention from all sides, it was very possible that the NPC (actually the central party) made the decision and then instructed the provincial people's congress to publish and carry it out. According to a research paper, in 2001 the NPC standing committee published in a document[27] its opinions on the experimental reform elections for township government executive held in some localities. The document clarified that the "direct elections" for township government executive were unconstitutional and against the organisation law, and should not be held in the future (Zou Shubin, Huang Weiping, Liu Jianguang, 2003). The real signal stopping election reform was an article published in *Qiushi*, the organ of the central party, in August of 2006. Sheng Huaren, the vice chairman of the NPC Standing Committee, wrote:

> In previous elections in some localities voters directly elected township government executives, which some people thought were experiments to improve

> local democracy. These elections, however, were unconstitutional and unlawful. In the future, the procedure of the elections for township government executives must strictly comply with the constitution and the organisation law. No such direct elections will be allowed (Sheng Huaren, 2006).

With the change of the central party's attitude from ambivalent and uncertain to firmly negative, the reform in elections for township executives gradually went into eclipse. After case 3, which was held in early 2004, such election experiments became very rare.

Premier Wen Jiabao's talk on the local election reform also provides evidence for the central party's changing views. On 6 September 2005, the former British Prime Minister Tony Blair visited Beijing as part of the European Union (EU) presidency programme. In Beijing, Wen Jiabao held a joint press conference with Blair and EU Commissioner José Manuel Barroso. At the press conference, Wen made a promise for China's local election reform:

> In terms of the electoral system in China we have the People's Congress system. For the village level units in China we have adopted direct elections, and for the People's Congress Deputies at the county and urban district level we also have direct elections, but for those above the district level, up to the central government, we have a system of indirect elections. That is decided by the current state of affairs in the Chinese economy, society and political conditions, but I can assure you that China will press ahead with its development of democratic politics, that is political restructuring in an unswerving and firm way including direct elections. Since the Chinese people can well manage a village, at the current stage I believe in several years they can manage a township, so that will be an evolving system (Wen Jiabao, 2005).

Normally all activities and words of the Chinese top leaders become headlines in the party-controlled press. The above speech of Wen regarding local election reform, however, has never been in any Chinese media and thus remains unknown to most people in mainland China. One year later in September 2006, at a meeting with three European journalists before his trip to Europe, Wen talked about the local election reform again but this time he became cautious and conservative. He emphasised this time that the conditions for direct elections at the township or above levels were not ripe. The unripe conditions, according to Wen, included "China is a big country with a large population, the Chinese economy is not developed, the economic development in various regions is unbalanced" (Wen Jiabao, 2006). There is not sufficient evidence to judge whether Wen's talk in September 2005 was a real expression of his reform intention or just propaganda to the outside world. His talk in September 2006, however, was most probably an excuse for the central party's decision not to allow further local election reform. This again proved the central party's negative and prohibitive attitude to the reform, which had been clarified in the above-mentioned article in *Qiushi* in August 2006.

Prospects

As seen from the above analysis, it was some local cadres who started, designed and organised the township government election reform experiments and their instigation was mainly to win credit for future promotion in their political career. Within the nearly five-year period when the central party's attitudes to the reform were uncertain and unclear, experiments with various "reform election methods" were carried out in some localities. These experiments became fewer and they were generally degraded in their "democracy" as the pressure from the conservatives gradually accumulated. The experiments finally disappeared after the central party clarified its negative and even prohibitive attitude to such a reform. Considering that first, the original instigation was from inside the party system, second, the party system is authoritarian with power centralised, and third, the central party has clarified its negative and prohibitive attitude to the reform, it is hard to see new experiments of this kind in the future unless the above-mentioned three facts, especially the last two, have changed. Thus, it is highly unlikely that the reform of "direct elections" for township executives will lead to China's political democratisation in the near future.

The party never denies the value of "democracy" but it emphasises in all its propaganda that the "democracy" it pursues is "a socialist democracy with Chinese characteristics." [28] Different from the "liberal democracy" in western political systems, Chinese "democracy" strictly excludes a multi-party system or even competitive elections to ensure the authoritarian party-state polity in China. The direct elections for government executives or even genuine direct elections for local people's congress members,[29] are "competitive" to some extent and thus are against the nature of "a socialist democracy with Chinese characteristics." Naturally the party keeps trying to avoid such reform elections which might "endanger" the current single-party system. However, mostly for propaganda purposes, the party had to present the public another blueprint of its "socialist democracy" after it prohibited the local government election reform. It then sought other kinds of "political reform" which contain neither competitive elections nor will lead to multi-partism. In this instance the "inner-party democracy" reform and "deliberative democracy" reform became the best choice of the party because they were "safe" enough not to reduce the party's monopolistic political power while enabling the party to continue its "democratic" propaganda. As a senior party theorist told a journalist, inner-party democracy and deliberative democracy would "become two major breakthroughs in China's democratization" (Hua Yangsheng, 2007). The experiments of these two kinds of reform are discussed in the next three chapters.

Notes

1. As for the "direct elections" for township executives discussed in this chapter and the "direct elections" for township party secretaries in chapter 3, the analysis shows that in

some of the reform experiments there was no direct election, or the direct election was in only one step rather than the whole procedure in the other experiments. Thus, the accurate names of the reforms discussed in this chapter and in chapter 3 should be "reform of the elections for township executives" and "reform of the elections for township party secretaries." However, these two reforms are generally called "direct elections" in the collected Chinese documents. In this book, I call the reforms "direct elections" for township executives and "direct elections" for township party secretaries too but I apply a quotation mark on the term "direct elections" in order to show that they are different from the direct elections in the western political system.

2. In fact, the party's dominance exists not only at township level but throughout the political system of China.

3. It needs to be pointed out that the very concept of *sannong* is a concept peculiar to the Chinese and not commonly used outside of China. *Sa nong* involves (1) *nongye* [agriculture], which can best be discussed by agricultural economists in terms of productivity and supply and demand, (2) *nongcun* [villages], which can best be handled by sociologists in terms of social change and migration, and (3) *nongmin* [peasants], which is basically a broad, inter-disciplinary term involving politics, sociology and economics. The whole question of *san nong* is therefore an immensely complex issue. The problems in these three dimensions have been one of the burning issues with which the CCP must come to grips. If they remain unresolved for a long time in the future, they could become a potential time-bomb for the Chinese leadership (Wong & Wang, 2007: 160).

4. The party calls the riots the *qunti xing zhi'an shijian* [mass security incidents] and defines them as groups of people who gather to disturb public order and destroy public property.

5. In the field and archival research, I found that even the political reform experiments, which the local cadres claimed strengthened the voters' participation, were actually instigated by the local cadres trying to gain credit for future promotion. This will be discussed in this and the following chapters when the instigators for the experiments are analysed.

6. I admit that what I describe here is the most ideal result which can be achieved in a genuine democratic voting system. I understand such a best result perhaps cannot be fully or immediately achieved due to some social and cultural factors. Other problems may possibly arise along with the democratic elections. The occurrence of political machines is one of these problems and they actually have existed in China because of the direct elections held at the village level. However, no system is flawless and no system can be designed to solve all problems in China instantly. In spite of its side effects, holding democratic elections is still the quickest way to China's political democratization and the most effective solution to many problems in China. As for the possible political machines in China, even though they are undemocratic, they are the products of a democratic system. At least, they are more responsive and efficient than an unlegitimized and authoritarian ruler. I also believe, with the establishment of a more advanced legal system, the side effects of the democratic election system such as political machines will be gradually diminished.

7. According to the election method, the committee was composed of the party secretaries of all villages and urban communities, the heads of all villages and residential communities, the office secretaries of all villages, the heads of all *cunmin xiaozu* [villager groups] from every village, two villager representatives from each village or residential community who were appointed by the village or community heads, the chief officer of each township government department and the township election officers (Government of Buyun Township, 1999).

8. Some researchers worried that the majority of congress members would vote against the "directly elected" candidate, which would create conflict between the people's congress and the grassroots voters. Fortunately such a situation did not come about.

9. In some collected papers, the reasons are described as the candidates moved to work in another place or they themselves chose to give up their candidatures before the election (Li Changping, 2002; Ma Shengkang, 2002).

10. In the collected news reports on this experiment, the committee was made up of the township people's congress's presidium members, village cadres and villager representatives (Tian Shubin, Li Ziliang, Wang Yan, 2004). Three villager representatives were elected from each village to attend the committee (Renmingwang, 2004).

11. These "representatives" comprise all party members in the township, all township government cadres and employees, and villager representatives (Ji Zhilong, 1999). To be specific, there were around 430 party members, nearly 160 village heads and village party committee secretaries, and nearly 150 government cadres. The rest of the seats, which were obviously the minority, were occupied by the real "representatives" of the villagers (Huang Weiping, Zou Shubin, Zhang Dinghuai, Yang Longfang, 2001).

12. The participants were mainly the village heads and village party secretaries, the party and government leaders at the township and county (the immediate higher) levels (China Innovations, 2003).

13. Eleven is the average figure by calculation. There were altogether seventy-seven initial candidates in the seven townships of Shiping County where the experiment was held. The exact number of the initial candidates in each township cannot be found from the available documents.

14. In case 4, 76 candidates were nominated in the first step. In case 6, 17 candidates were nominated.

15. In cases 1, 2 and 3, the qualified candidates had to be between 25 and 45 years old and they had to have a high school or a higher diploma (He Baogang, Lang Youxing, 2002; Tian Shubin, Li Ziliang, Wang Yan, 2004). In case 4, the candidates had to be younger than 50 and have obtained a university or higher diploma (Huang Weiping, 2000). In case 6, the male candidates had to be younger than 50 and the female younger than 48 and all of them had to have a university or higher diploma (Government of Yangji Township, 2003). In addition to age and education, there were conditions of political background and job experience in some cases: only party members could become candidates in case 4, only government cadres could gain candidature in case 6 (Government of Yangji Township, 2003). In case 5, only the incumbent was appointed by the party committee as candidate for the position, so no criteria were needed to hold back the competitors from outside the system. The relevant information cannot be obtained from the existing documents for case 7. However, compared with other cases, its whole procedure was less open to the grassroots voters and thus it was more like a reform in the selection round which was held within the government and party system. The party theorists argued that this reform experiment "provides the cadres, especially the young cadres an opportunity to demonstrate their abilities and to compete for the higher positions" (China Innovations, 2003). In case 8, no age nor education were required for being a candidate but there was a "political condition" (Research Team of the Organization Department of the CCP Committee of Sichuan Province, 2003). In case 8, compared with the nominated candidates in other cases, the candidates who were nominated by the local people's congress members in case 8 were obviously fewer. In the eleven elections of case 8, there were only twenty-three candidates "freely nominated" by the people's congress members. In some of the elections, only one candidate was nominated (Huang Weiping, Zou Shubin, Zhang Dinghuai, Yang Longfang, 2001). In my opinion, there were two possible reasons. First, some candidates had an obvious advantage over others and thus they were strongly sup-

ported by the majority of the people's congress members. Second, the party secretly supported some candidates and made "black box" in the nomination procedure which made the nominations of other candidates impossible. For lack of evidence, the reason for why the nominated candidates in case 8 were fewer than other cases remains unknown.

16. According to the National People's Congress, a migrant can either entrust a voter with a proxy vote in the electorate where he/she registered his/her residence or vote in the electorate where he/she currently resides (NPC, 1983). In fact, most migrants do not vote by proxy in the electorates where their *hukou* [registered residence] is. Thus, they are eligible to vote in the places where they reside. Unfortunately, the election organisers tend to neglect the migrant voters in the elections.

17. The same problem occurred in the "deliberative democracy" experiments in Zhejing Province discussed in chapter 5.

18. Zhang Jinming, the instigator and organiser of cases 1 and 2, is a good example. She was the incumbent county/district-level party secretary who instigated and organised the experimental elections. After that, she soon became a "star reformer" and was then promoted to be a city-level party secretary.

19. Before the Central Party declared its negative attitude towards the reform, this is described as the chief instigation in most propaganda reports by the party-controlled press media.

20. The election would have three major procedural steps: self-nomination, campaign speeches and direct election. In addition, in Wei's design, the elected township government executive would have had the right to choose cadres to form a township government cabinet. If such a reform were to come into being, it would be the most liberal one among all experimental elections.

21. According to a document, Wei started the experiment without reporting it to the immediate higher-level county party committee. He even thought the county party leaders must have known his reform plan and had given him tacit approval (Chou, 2005). Another document reveals that the central party did not know the suppression: "When answering an enquiry call from a journalist, the Discipline Inspection Department of the central CCP expressed that they did not know this matter and they would not comment on it." In addition, an informant revealed that the central CCP later criticised the party cadres of Chongqing Municipality and Chengkou County for their illegal deprival of Wei's congress membership (Ma Ya, 2004a, 2004b). Based on the analysis of this information, it was most probably the county party committee secretary who suppressed the reform and punished the reformer while the municipality party leaders approved of this action.

22. *Shuanggui* is a disciplinary measure outside the regular legal system under which party members are detained and interrogated.

23. The details were as steps 4 and 5 of case 2 on pp. 13–14.

24. A senior researcher in Chinese journalistic studies revealed to me in an interview that in some cases the party purposely released some information on sensitive issues to "friendly" overseas media to test the public reaction. The party-controlled media would then confirm some of the news afterwards.

25. In the spring of 1979, farmers in Xiaogang Village, which was one of the poorest villages in Anhui Province, secretly distributed the collective farm land and farming tools to each family. The village then started a new type of agricultural production with each family as a basic working unit. This reform became the prototype of the "family responsibility system," which has been adopted by nearly all Chinese villages from the early 1980s. Xiaogang Village was then thought as the cradle of the economic reform in China.

26. This news in *Lianhe zaobao* has never been confirmed by any party-controlled media so it may not be as reliable as the above-mentioned information which was published in the Chinese official media.

27. The original text of the document cannot be obtained.

28. Such a view has commonly appeared in the party's important documents such as the reports to the CCP's national congresses, the top leaders' articles and the important party's theorists' essays (Hu Jintao, 2007; Jiang Zemin, 1997, 2002; Wen Jiabao, 2007; Yu Keping, 2006).

Please refer to note 2 in chapter 3 for the explanation of "socialist democracy with Chinese characteristics."

29. Different from the elections for local government executives which are unconstitutional and unlawful, the direct elections for local people's congress members are guaranteed by the electoral law. Nevertheless, the party manages to control every step of the elections to exclude the grassroots power from the congresses and to make sure every "elected" congress member is a party-preferred one. The sixth chapter of this book will discuss this subject.

Chapter 3

"Inner-Party Democracy" and the Experiments of Direct Elections for Township Party Secretaries

Introduction

In the map of political reform which the CCP draws, the party boasts that "inner-party democracy"[1] will be a quick and "safe" path to China's democratisation. In this larger reform, inner-party electoral reform forms an important component. This chapter analyses "inner-party democracy" and examines some important electoral experiments within the party. In the first part, the chapter analyses some influential articles which party theorists wrote to propagandise the party's self-reform. Based on these articles, the chapter researches the instigations for the reform, the reason why the party prioritises this reform rather than others, what reform contents are preferred and planned by the party, whether and how the inner-party reform will affect the party's organisation and China's political system. The second part of the chapter focuses on the inner-party experimental elections, which is an important part of the party's self-reform. In this part, the chapter analyses the articles of *The Party Constitution* and other party laws regarding the party's local elections, trying to explain what the traditional elections are like and to discover if the reform experiments are "lawful." The third part studies the procedures of eleven most important election cases. This aims to allow the local party election reform to be understood from an evidence-based viewpoint. The last part analyses the election cases and the prospects of "inner-party democracy." This chapter will provide scholars a basis from which to evaluate the prospect of inner-party reform as well as its effects on China's political development.

Can "Inner-Party Democracy" Push Forward "People's Democracy"?

"Inner-Party Democracy" in the Party's Propaganda

While China gains huge profits from its capitalist economy, the Chinese Communist Party seems very reluctant to step forward towards political democratisation. Except for a few individual local reform cases carried out in some special circumstances, the main authoritarian political system has been kept unchanged for nearly thirty years.

In contrast to its practical reluctance in carrying out "people's democracy,"[2] the CCP has theoretically prioritised "inner-party democracy" in recent years. Researchers believe the CCP chose inner-party reform as a breakthrough to China's political democratisation only because this form of "democracy" is both "safe and controllable."[3]

The theoretical boost for inner-party reform has intensified in recent years. The frequency of the term "inner-party democracy" in *The People's Daily*, the official newspaper of the central party, has obviously been increasing since 2003 (Qian Gang, 2007). Some senior party theorists have written in the party's top-level journals or newspapers to promote "inner-party democracy."

For example, Zhen Xiaoying, the president of the Central Socialist Academy, jointly published an article in *Qiushi* with his PhD student Li Qinghua on 16 June 2003, which immediately attracted attention from the western media and researchers. In the article, they stated:

> Inner-party democracy is the lifeblood of the party. It leads the way and pushes forward the people's democracy. To develop inner-party democracy is necessary not only for the party's self-building, but also for pushing forward people's democracy and improving socialist political civilization. It is a great strategy that we should push forward people's democracy by developing inner-party democracy, thus achieving the Chinese-style socialist civilization. It is also a practical and efficient path to the Chinese-style political democratisation (Zhen Xiaoying, Li Qinghua, 2003).

Zhen and Li also said, "just like there is no way out if we do not develop the economy to improve people's living standard, we will reach the same impasse if we do not reform the political system and do not develop people's democracy." Many overseas researchers and observers believed the article was a signal to possible political reform in the near future, which would be started with the party's self-reform.

Another influential article, written by Xu Yaotong, professor at the China National School of Administration, was published in *The Study Times*, the journal of the Central Party School, in 2005. In the article, Xu said because the former Russian communist party leaders failed to fulfil the task of building up inner-party democracy that there was neither people's democracy nor inner-party democracy in the former Soviet Union. Xu also said:

> Inner-party democracy must be prioritised because it is tightly connected with people's democracy. In western countries, political parties were established after the foundation of democratic countries. In these countries, on the social condition that citizens can actively participate in political activities, democracy within political parties was gained naturally and easily. However, the situations are different in the culturally and economically underdeveloped countries. The communist parties were established and developed in revolutions and inner-party democracy was impossible in severe struggles against the reactionaries. After the success of a revolution, when there is no democracy both inside and outside the party, democracy must be practised inside the party at first and it will push forward the people's democracy. This is a practical and effective way [to achieve democratisation] (Xu Yaotong, 2005).

In the article, Xu criticises the political system of the former Soviet Union and highly praises western democracy, a viewpoint rarely seen in the previous party-controlled media. The argument of Xu to prioritise "inner-party democracy" is then understandable if it is a tactic to fully develop democracy in the authoritarian Chinese political system. Xu's other argument reveals the party's intention to prioritise "inner-party democracy." Xu said in the article, "in economically and socially underdeveloped countries, it is very crucial to practise inner-party democracy. People's democracy is bounded or even deteriorates if no inner-party democracy exists. If we develop people's democracy before inner-party democracy, an uncontrollable and messy situation will possibly occur" (Xu Yaotong, 2005). This statement of Xu, who is a senior party theorist, indicates that the party insists on strengthening its ruling power even in reform and it lacks confidence that people are capable of managing their state.

Similarly, on 16 December 2006, *Renminwang* [*The People's Daily* online] established a web page which included a group of passages promoting "inner-party democracy."[4] The passages stated why "inner-party democracy" should be prioritised and how it can be achieved. One passage illustrated some possible paths to "inner-party democracy" and an important path was to reform inner-party elections. Another passage studied and highly evaluated the township party-cadre election experiments in Luxi County, Yunnan Province in 2004, which was a "very rare case of large scale inner-party election reform at the township level." One of the passages researched the procedure of recalling party cadres at a party conference and argued that such recalling, which is an important function of party conferences, should be strengthened. The passage also concluded that "inner-party democracy" would be improved by doing so.

In addition to the above articles, there were many other propaganda articles for "inner-party democracy." Some important ones include an article published in *Liaoning Ribao*, the organ of the Liaoning provincial party committee, emphasised the relationship between "inner-party democracy" and the party's "advanced characteristics" (Tang Xiaoqing, 2006). An article in *Liaowang* argued that to build up a more sophisticated inner-party inspection system on political powers was essential to expand "inner-party democracy" (Li Jie, 2006).

The CCP's "Inner-Party Democracy": Being Conservative rather than Progressive

In recent years, there has been a unanimous voice from all sides that inner-party reform should be carried out, but what that reform should be like remains controversial. Generally, there are two different opinions.

Some researchers hold progressive views.[5] They argue for the legal position of rival factions within the CCP. According to them, allowing free competition inside the party is an effective way to achieve inner-party democracy. According to them, genuine representative democracy should be implanted into inner-party politics. In that case, various interest groups can be represented by different factions within the CCP. Only in this way, they argue, can the quality of the party and its leadership be improved and the increasing tension between social classes possibly be relieved.

By contrast, most other researchers, theorists and party cadres hold conservative views.[6] They argue that there should be more democratic elements in every sphere of the party's activities to protect the grassroots party member's political rights and to decentralise power from the few party leaders. They also propose establishing a more powerful inspection system on the party cadres. With these methods, they expect authoritarian politics and corruption to be avoided. On the other hand, they oppose establishing inner-party factions because that view goes beyond the party's ideology and thus makes no sense in China's current political circumstances.

The central party is strongly against the progressive reform proposals which allow inner-party rival factions. They believe that rival factions and free competition inside the party do not comply with the party's organisation principle and challenge the party's centralised political power. Article 3 of *The Party Constitution* clarifies that one duty, which all party members must fulfil, is to "uphold the party's solidarity and unity . . . firmly oppose all factions and small-clique activities" (CCP, 2002b). Although most probably there are always invisible factions inside the CCP, the central party has strictly prohibited such factions and internal-struggles from becoming institutionalised. Once the factions and struggles change from "invisible" to "obvious," the leaders of the factions are accused of "breaking up the party." The party's top leaders from the first to the fourth generation, unexceptionally, have all been centralising their ruling power and prohibiting challenges from inner-party factions. Considering this, I do not expect the central party leaders to allow distinct inner-party factions and competition, nor will they institutionalise them (Lin Jialong, 1999:48). The central party disallows such viewpoints published in the press and it even uses government power to prevent the views from being spread through other channels (Xiao Gongqin, 2004).

In contrast, the central party theoretically agrees with most of the conservative reform methods such as strengthening the inner-party inspection system, decentralising power from individual cadres and improving inner-party elections.[7] The central party also loudly propagandises its "strategy" that it will develop "inner-party democracy" to push forward people's democracy. Against such a background, a large number of articles promoting "inner-party democracy" were published in the party-controlled media.

Party General-Secretary Hu Jintao's report to the 17th National Party Congress once again confirmed that the proposed inner-party reform is generally in accord with the views proposed by the conservative researchers. Hu stated in his report:

> We will expand intra-Party democracy[8] to develop people's democracy and increase intra-Party harmony to promote social harmony. . . . We need to respect the principal position of Party members, guarantee their democratic rights, increase transparency in Party affairs and create favourable conditions for democratic discussions within the Party. . . . We will improve the working mechanisms of local Party committees at all levels and their standing committees and let the Party committees make decisions on major issues. We will strictly implement democratic centralism, improve the system that combines collective leadership with division of responsibilities among individuals, and oppose and prevent arbitrary decision-making by an individual or a minority of people. We will introduce a system of voting for use by local Party committees in discussing and deciding on major issues and appointing cadres to important positions. . . . We will reform the intra-Party electoral system and improve the system for nominating candidates and electoral methods. We will spread the practice in which candidates for leading positions in primary Party organisations are recommended both by Party members and the public in an open manner and by the Party organisation at the next higher level, gradually extend direct election of leading members in primary Party organisations to more places, and explore various ways to expand intra-Party democracy at the primary level. . . . Adhering to the principle that the Party is in charge of cadre management, we will establish a scientific mechanism for selecting and appointing cadres on the basis of democracy, openness, competition and merit. We will standardize the cadre nomination system, perfect the cadre assessment system in accordance with the requirements of the Scientific Outlook on Development and a correct view on evaluating cadres' performances, and improve the procedures for open selection, competition for positions and multi-candidate election. We will expand democracy in the work related to cadres and make democratic recommendation and assessment more scientific and authentic. We must enforce stricter oversight over the whole process of selecting and appointing cadres. We will improve the tenure system and the recusal system for leading cadres as well as the system for transferring them between different posts, the public servant system, and the system of dual administration of cadres. . . . (Hu Jintao, 2007).

Even though these minor patchwork reforms may possibly be empty talk, this part of Hu's report may also have set maximum goals for inner-party reform.

However, some other words in Hu's report seem to set clear boundaries on the reform:

> Party members must firmly uphold the centralized and unified leadership of the Party, conscientiously abide by the Party's political discipline, always be in agreement with the Central Committee and resolutely safeguard its authority to ensure that its resolutions and decisions are carried out effectively. . . . Adhering to the principle that the Party is in charge of cadre management, we will. . . . (Hu Jintao, 2007).

Analysis of the Nature of the CCP's "Inner-Party Democracy"

Based on the analysis of the background of inner-party reform and the central party's attitude to the reform, some conclusions can be drawn:

First, the reason why the party broadcasts powerful propaganda on the "inner-party democracy" is that the reform is "safe" and controllable. This consideration indicates that the ultimate purpose of the reform is to stabilise or even strengthen the party's authoritarian ruling power. As Juan L. Linz states, "the ruling party's democratization, if it is undertaken in an undemocratic nation, is possibly able to revitalise the party and to extend the single-party's authoritarian rule" (Linz, 1999: 8).[9] The prospects for China's thorough democratisation are pessimistic if we understand this original motive for inner-party reform.

Second, "inner-party democracy" only includes liberal reform measures the CCP might possibly take up to patch the procedures of some of the party's political activities that are narrow in scope. Even if the party can change the reform blueprint into reality and achieve the goals set out in Hu's report, these measures will only just slightly liberalise the policy-making procedure and the mechanism of selecting or evaluating cadres at the primary levels. The reform will not change the party's centralised organisation system. Specifically, the following facts will not be changed after inner-party reform: (1) all power is centralised in the central party, (2) the party is in charge of cadre management, and (3) CCP cadres occupy almost all important government positions. In that case, inner-party reform, which is seen as an important breakthrough to China's democratisation, will most probably have no impact on the current authoritarian party-state regime of China.

Third, even if inner-party liberalism is attained at a higher level, for example, inner-party factions are allowed to exist and competitive elections are held at all levels, and the primary and local level party committees or even the Central Party's Political Bureau make decisions based on the opinions of the majority of the party members, inner-party democracy still theoretically would have nothing to do with people's democracy. The CCP, a party with all China's political power centralised in a minority group of party leaders, can hardly represent the fundamental interests of the overwhelming majority of the Chinese people, even though it has nearly seventy-six million members.[10] Some party theorists rate highly the importance of "inner-party democracy" because they believe that party members must be of higher quality compared with the non-party people and China's democratisation should begin from the democratisation of this elite group. According to them, people's democracy will come easily if the CCP, which is the "ever-lasting" single ruling party in the current China's one-party authoritarian political system, has been democratised. By this logic, to accept the theory that inner-party democracy will push forward the people's democracy, we have to admit the legitimacy of China's current party-state authoritarian system. This point, however, is obviously problematic. In fact, no matter how thoroughly inner-party liberal reform has been conducted and what high achievements of such elite democracy has been made, the existence of China's party-state authoritarian system will still make China an undemocratic country.[11] A genuine democratic political system must have some basic features such as free political parties and competitive elections between them, which are obviously lacking in a party-state authoritarian system.

The Reform of Elections for Township Party Leaders

Having examined calls for "inner-party" democracy, I will now examine whether it has been carried out. In particular, I will focus on the reform of elections for township party leaders.

An article published in *The Study Times* explains the meanings of "inner-party democracy" from four perspectives: (1) all party members enjoy equal political rights, (2) follow the principle that the minority is subordinate to the majority, (3) decentralise power and inspect power, and (4) democratically elect leading groups.[12] Among these four dimensions in which "inner-party democracy" is possibly carried out, the election reform is most primary. While the other three points focus on liberalising the process of utilising power, the election section decides the source of the power and how it is formed. The following two sections examine inner-party election reform, which may provide a basis for an in-depth understanding on "inner-party democracy." In my view, just as free elections form an important component of political democracy, the reform in the elections for party leaders, cited as the fourth point of the above-mentioned principles, is a valuable research subject regarding inner-party reform. Thus, research on the party's election reform may provide a basis for an in-depth understanding of "inner-party democracy."

The reform Hu Jintao proposed in his report to the 17th National Party Congress involves two important sections on electoral procedure: nomination and voting.[13] On March 1 of 2006, Ouyang Song, deputy director of the central party's organisational department, declared at a press conference held by the State Council Information Office that *gongtui zhixuan* [open nomination and direct election][14] for township party cadres had been held in two-hundred and seventeen townships of thirteen provinces. Ouyang Song also stated that the central party supported this kind of reform (Li Yajie, 2006). An article published in

The Study Times in 2008 shows that the reform of elections for township party committee secretary had taken place in more than two thousand townships across China (Cai Xia, 2008). The existing documents show that the experimental elections for party secretaries were mainly held at the township level. Although the reform methods varied from place to place, the general form of the experimental elections allowed self-nomination and direct voting by all township party members.[15] What is a traditional party election like? What do *The Party Constitution* and other party laws say about the elections? Are the reformed electoral methods legal or not? The answers are important because they decide how difficult furthering the reform can be.

Conventional Party Elections and the Relevant Party Law Articles

The procedure of a traditional election for a township party secretary usually involved three steps: (1) the township party members elect the township party congress members (normally 100 to 200, no more than 300), (2) township party congress members elect township party committee members (5 to 9 members), and (3) party committee members elect the township party secretary and deputy secretaries (1 secretary and 1 or 2 deputy secretaries). In a special township where the party members number less than five hundred, or where they are more than five hundred but live comparatively closely to each other, they can directly elect township party committee members. This means in these special townships, the above-mentioned first step can be omitted. The township party members elect the township party committee members and the township party committee members elect the township party secretary and deputy secretaries in these townships.

A township is at the most primary level in the party's organisation structure but the party goes through three steps (or two steps in special townships) to elect party secretaries at this level. Obviously, in even the lowest-level party elections, the direct participation of the grassroots party members is low.

Candidate nomination was poor too. In the traditional elections for township party secretaries, according to article 16 of *The Provisional Ordinance of the CCP's Organisational and Electoral Work at the Primary Level*, candidates are nominated by the previous township party committee and their candidacies should be examined and approved by the higher-level party committee (CCP, 1990). Obviously, grassroots township party members or even township party congress members, if they are not the township party committee members, have no right to nominate candidates. Only a few people including members of the party committees at the township or above levels can nominate. In practice, such an important power as nominating candidates of party secretaries is normally held by the secretaries of the higher-level party committees because of two strict party organisational disciplines: (1) the lower level must be subordinate to the higher level, and (2) power is centralised in the *yibashou* [top leader] of a party committee.

To summarise, the traditional elections for township party secretaries are controlled by one or several party leaders in the higher-level party committees. The elections lack the essential elements a true election must have such as equality, representation and competition.

In contrast, the reformed party elections normally involve open or self nomination and direct voting of grassroots party members. Are they lawful or party-constitutional? The legal documents relevant to inner-party elections include: (1) *The Party Constitution*, (2) *Several Regulations about Inner-party Political Activities*, (3) *The Ordinance of the CCP's Local Organisational and Electoral Work*, and (4) *The Provisional Ordinance of the CCP's Organisational and Electoral Work at the Primary Level* (CCP, 1980, 1990, 1994, 2002b). Documents 3 and 4 specify the inner-party election procedures. Since the party election reform has been restricted to the township level, only document 4, which applies to township party elections, is directly relevant to the reform.[16] One thing clarified in these two documents is that a party committee at the township level is defined as a primary-level party committee while the party committees at the levels from county to provincial are the local party committees. Understanding these definitions, we can check the party laws to see whether self-nomination and "direct voting" in township party secretary elections are within party ordinances.

In *The Party Constitution*, articles 29 and 30 are directly relevant to township party elections:

> Article 29: . . . A primary Party committee is elected by a general membership meeting or a delegate meeting.
>
> Article 30: . . . Results of the election of a secretary and deputy secretaries by a primary Party committee, general branch committee or branch committee shall be reported to the higher Party organisations for approval.

Analysing these two articles of *The Party Constitution*, I find they convey neither the exact meaning that the township party secretaries must be elected by primary (township-level) party committees nor the meaning that all party members directly electing township party secretaries is banned. That is to say, the non-rigorous expression in *The Party Constitution* leaves some space for holding direct elections at the primary (township) level.[17]

The real obstacle is in article 16 of *The Provisional Ordinance of the CCP's Organisational and Electoral Work at the Primary Level*:

> Article 16: Candidates for secretaries and deputy secretaries of party committees at the primary level are nominated by the party committee members of the last term and approved by the higher-level party committee. Secretaries and deputy secretaries of party committees at primary level are elected at the plenary sessions of their party committees.

The open or self nomination and direct voting are unlawful in township party elections according to this party legal document. Regarding this breach, an article published in *The Study Times* argued: "to reform we have to be in breach of some existing regulations. We cannot negate the value of a reform just because it is a breach" (Wang Yongbing, 2006).

Eleven Important Experiments

This part examines eleven primary-level inner-party electoral experiments held at various localities, which were mostly reported by the Chinese official media. I choose to study these cases for two reasons. First, these experiments most frequently mentioned in the party's propaganda articles may represent the highest level of the inner-party reform. Therefore, to do research on them enables us to understand how deeply such reform has gone. Second, the large amount of news reports and a few research papers on each single experiment can provide sufficient information about these cases. In this chapter, the primary-level inner-party election reform is researched as an integrated subject and is understood from an evidence-based viewpoint. Some conclusions are drawn based on the analysis and comparison of the procedural steps of the experiments.

Table 3.1 summarises the time, localities and reform contents of the eleven cases.

Table 3.1 Eleven Cases of "Direct Elections" for Township Party Secretaries

	Locality	Time	Reform contents
Case 1	Lianhua Township, Dongchan Township, Shizhong District, Suining City, Sichuan Province	September to November 1998	Elections for township party committee secretaries
Case 2	Nancheng Township, Qingshen County, Meishan City, Sichuan Province	December 1998	Elections for township party committee secretaries and members and party disciplinary committee members
Case 3[18]	Yangji Township, Jingshan County, Jingmen City, Hubei Province	August to September 2002	Elections for township executives and party committee secretaries

Case 4[19]	Pingba Township, Chengkou District, Chongqing Municipality	August 2003	Elections for township executives and party committee secretaries, establishing standing committee of people's congress and party congress at the township level
Case 5	Mulan Township, Xindu District, Chengdu City, Sichuan Province	November to December 2003	Elections for township party secretary
Case 6	Nine townships of Pingchang County, Bazhong City, Sichuan Province	January 2004	Elections for township party secretaries and party committee members
Case 7	Thirteen Townships of Muyang County, Suqian City, Jiangsu Province	February 2004	Elections for township party secretaries
Case 8	Longxin Township, Yubei District, Chongqing Municipality	May to July 2004	Elections for township party secretaries
Case 9	Ten townships of Luxi County, Honghe Yi and Ha'ni Minority Autonomous Prefecture, Yunnan Province	July to August 2004	Elections for chief township party cadres including secretaries, party committee members and party disciplinary committee members
Case 10	Xiangshui Township, Nanzheng County, Hanzhong City, Shaanxi Province	April to May 2005	Elections for township party secretaries
Case 11	Yongxing Township, Chuanshan District, Suining City, Sichuan Province	December 2005	Elections for township party secretaries and party committee members

The main procedures of the experiments are as follows.

Step 1: Nomination

Normally, the first procedural step of these experimental elections was "self-nomination" and "qualification-check," which happened in cases 1, 2, 4, 5, 6, 7, 8, 10, and 11. In these cases, the election organisers (normally the immediate higher party committee) published the criteria for eligible candidates and allowed the grassroots party members to nominate themselves. The organisers then assessed the qualifications of these self-nominated people using the published criteria and decided the list of the eligible candidates. The exceptions were cases 3 and 9. In case 3, all local voters (including both the party members and the masses) nominated candidates. The three candidates who won most nominating votes entered the next round. In case 9, the local party members and the masses nominated the candidates but the nomination method was different from that of case 3. In case 9, inside the party, the party members were organised into *dangzhibu* [party branches] to nominate candidates, while outside the party, more than thirty non-party member voters in agreement were able to nominate a candidate.

In this step, it is interesting to study the criteria. The criteria indicated the preferences of the election organisers (the higher-level party committee). They enabled the organisers to exclude those whom they disliked from entering the elections. Even though the criteria were slightly different from case to case, they have many common points. They usually involved four aspects: age, education, work experience and official rank. The specific criteria in some of the cases can be seen from Table 3.2.

Table 3.2 Criteria for Eligible Candidates in Some Cases of "Direct Election" for Township Party Secretary

	Age	Education Background	Length of Party Membership or Working Experience	Official Rank
Case 1	< 45	Tertiary Education	At least 5-year working experience in a government or a party department	Being at the deputy *Ke*-level[20]
Case 4	> 25 and < 40	Tertiary Education	Data not obtained	Data not obtained
Case 5	< 45	Tertiary Education	At least 3-year party membership	Having been at the deputy *Ke*-level for at least 3 years or being at the *Ke*-level

Case 6	None	Tertiary Education and at least 2 month training at party schools or (governmental) administration schools	At least 3-year party membership and at least 3-year working experience in a government or a party department	Having been at the deputy *Ke*-level for at least 2 years
Case 7	Data not obtained	Data not obtained	Data not obtained	Being at the deputy *Ke*-level
Case 8	< 45	Tertiary Education	At least 3-year party membership	Having been at the deputy *Chu* level for at least 2 years or being at the *Chu*-level[21]
Case 11	< 45	Secondary Education	At least 3-year working experience in a government or a party department	Having been at the deputy *Ke*-level for at least 2 years or currently being at the *Ke*-level

Notes for Table 3.2:

1. The method of "self-nomination" and "qualification-check" was not utilized in cases 3 and 9 so there were no criteria set in the step of these two cases.
2. The data of criteria in cases 2 and 10 cannot be obtained from the existing documents.
3. The data in cases 4 and 7 are incomplete in the existing documents.
4. In cases 6 and 11, the elections were held to elect other township party cadres besides the township party secretaries. The "official rank" criteria listed in the Table were applied to the selection of the candidates for only township party secretary positions.
5. Some exemption situations were found in cases 6 and 11. In case 6, an incumbent township party cadre was exempted from the requirements if he/she was to compete for his/her current position. In case 11, the village or *shequ* [urban community] (urban citizens' unit at the most primary level, similar to a village in rural area) party secretaries with outstanding working achievements were exempted from the requirements of age, education and work experience.

Step 2: Selection of Final Candidates

The next step was the selection of final candidates. The selection methods of the eleven cases varied but they can be generally divided into the following four categories:

(1) Election. In cases 3, 4, 5, 6, 8, 9, and 10, the final candidates were elected from these initial self nominations. However, who was allowed to vote in such an election varied in different cases. In case 3, all township party members voted to select the two final candidates from the three initial candidates. In case 4, according to the election method, the election for final candidates involved two steps: (1) all township party congress members elected some candidates from the initial ones,[22] and (2) all registered voters in the township (including both party-member voters and non-party voters) elected a number of final candidates from the candidates elected in the first step.[23] In case 4, however, after the step of "self-nomination and qualification-check," the experiment was actually aborted and the planned following steps (including the above-described election) were not carried out.[24] In case 5, two-hundred and twenty-two people, including all township party and governmental cadres, party secretaries and heads of the subordinate villages, heads of the villager groups (the units subordinate to a village), entrepreneurs in the township, township party congress and people's congress members, and delegates of the democratic parties and non-party members, formed a conference to elect the two final candidates from the eleven initial ones. In case 6, the elections for township party secretary, deputy secretaries and party committee members were held. All township party members and some delegates of the masses, who were less than thirty percent of the total township party members, all voted to elect two final candidates from at least three initial candidates for one secretarial position, four final candidates from at least five initial candidates for two deputy secretarial positions, and some candidates (population decided upon the vacancies) for committee members.[25] In case 8, altogether eighty-five people including the district cadres responsible for organising the election, all township party and government cadres, heads and party secretaries of the subordinate villages, heads of the township government-owned factories and schools, members of the township party congress, people's congress and people's political consultative conference, and delegates from the democratic parties and non-party members, all voted to elect two final candidates from the eighteen initial ones. In case 9, a joint electoral conference was held to elect the final candidates (the number of the final candidates was normally one more than the vacant positions in that township).[26] In case 10, two-hundred and ninety-one people including township party and government cadres, villages' party secretaries and heads, township party congress, people's congress and people's political consultative conference members voted to elect two final candidates for township party secretary and another two final candidates for deputy secretaries from forty-two initial candidates.

(2) The party making the decision. In cases 2 and 7, the county (immediate higher-level) party committee decided the list of the final candidates. In case 2, the county party committee decided the list based on the pre-fixed ratio of the vacant positions to the final candidate number. In case 7, which included the

elections held in thirteen townships, the selection in this step involved two stages: First, the county party committee's standing committee selected a certain number of candidates (three times the vacancies, approximately forty-five persons and an average three for each township) from the sixty-five initial candidates. An existing document shows that the county party committee selected these candidates based on the result of a survey it made (Yu Jindong, 2004).[27] The three candidates in each township needed to write working proposals and make campaign speeches in front of a group of people including the heads of the county's party disciplinary committee, the township cadres and delegates of party members.[28] These people then marked each candidate and the two candidates getting the highest marks entered the next step.

(3) Tests. Written and oral tests were used to select final candidates in case 1. The initial candidates first took a written test and the top six went into the oral test. In the oral test, the examiners were made up of the leaders of the district party committee and government, the heads of the district party and governmental departments, the heads of the district people's congress and political consultative conference, the election panellists (mainly the district cadres), the township party and government cadres, the village heads (who had to be party members) and the delegates of grassroots party members. After the oral test, the examiners voted to elect two final candidates from the six examinees.

(4) Evaluation and Election. In case 11, the method of selecting final candidates was somewhat complicated. It involved two steps: evaluation and election.

The evaluation had two parts. In the first part, the election organisers held a public poll on each candidate in his/her current working unit. Only if a candidate won more than sixty percent approval votes, could he/she enter the next part. The number of the approval votes each candidate received was counted as ten percent of the final evaluation mark. In the second part, the examiners were divided into four groups. Group one consisted of the members of the township party congress, people's congress and people's political consultative conference as well as delegates from villages and urban communities (two delegates from each village or community). Members in group two included party secretaries and heads of all villages and communities, party secretaries of the township government-owned enterprises. Members in group three were incumbent and previous township party secretaries. Group four was made up of the election officers who were mainly the cadres from the district. The marks on a candidate made by groups one and two were respectively counted as twenty percent of the candidate's final evaluation mark. The marks made by groups three and four were respectively counted as twenty-five percent of the final evaluation mark. When the final evaluation marks for candidates came out, those candidates who received the highest marks entered the next round.[29]

In the following election round, the twenty district (the immediate higher-level) party committee members voted to elect two final candidates for one township party secretarial position from the four candidates who won out in the above-mentioned evaluation, and all township party members voted to elect six township party committee members from the eight winners of the evaluation round.

In this step in cases 4, 5, 6, 7, 8, 9, 10, and 11, the candidates made campaign speeches. In addition, some other reform methods were adopted. In cases 4, 7, and 10, the initial candidates needed to write and hand in their working proposals. In case 4, they were also required to lodge their asset statements. In cases 5, 8, 10, and 11, the initial candidates were organised to spend several days of field study in the townships.

Step 3: Final Selection

The last step in all eleven cases was to select township party secretaries from the final candidates. In cases 2, 6, 9, 10, and 11, other township party leaders such as the party committee members and the party disciplinary committee members were also selected in the last step.

In the last step of cases 2, 4, 5, 6, 8, 9, 10, and 11, all township party members voted to elect township party secretaries (and other township party leaders in the cases mentioned in the last paragraph) from the final candidates. In cases 3 and 7, it was the township party congress members who voted to elect township party secretaries. In case 1, the standing committee of the district (the immediate higher-level) party committee selected one from the two final candidates as the township party secretary.

As mentioned in the above paragraphs, other township party leaders, in addition to township party secretaries, were elected in the last step of cases 2, 6, 9, 10, and 11. In cases 2 and 9, the township party members voted in two unrelated elections to elect the party secretary and other party leaders. In case 11, the township party members elected the township party secretary from two candidates.[30] The elected township party secretary was then authorised to appoint one from the six township party committee members[31] to be the township deputy party secretary.

The procedures of final election in cases 6 and 10 were special. The final election involved a series of related rounds in which the township party secretaries and other township party leaders were elected successively. In case 10, the township party members elected the township party secretary from the two final candidates in the first round. Then the loser of the first round entered the second round to compete with the other two candidates for the two deputy party secretarial positions. In the second round, the voters elected two deputy party secretaries from the three candidates. In case 6, the procedure was similar but the election involved three rounds. In the first-round voting, all party members voted to elect one township party secretary while the losers entered the second round. In the second-round voting, all party members voted to elect the deputy secretaries, while the losers entered the third-round voting for party committee members. In the third-round voting, all party members elected the party committee members from the remaining candidates. The party secretary and deputy secretaries elected in the first and second rounds, according to the electoral rule, automatically became party committee members. They and the party committee members whom were elected in the third round formed the township party committee. Unlike case 10, all final candidates in case 6 were able to compete for the party secretarial position, which seemed to be a more open and liberal reform.

The methods adopted in the step of final election in cases 6 and 10, especially the method in case 6, were highly rated by some party theorists as an improvement in inner-party elections.[32] The sequence of the traditional inner-party elections in a locality is normally from the elections for lower positions to those for higher positions. In such a system, along with the elections for the positions from lower to higher, the range of voters becomes smaller and smaller. Taking township elections as an example, all township party members (normally from hundreds to thousands) elect township party congress members (normally one hundred to three hundred), township party congress members elect township party committee members (normally five to nine), township party committee members elect township party deputy secretaries and secretary (normally two to three). Such a multi-step indirect election system greatly reduces the effectiveness of the grassroots party member's participation in deciding the party leaders and other inner-party issues in that locality.[33] In the view of these party theorists, compared with the traditional electoral method, the reform in the final election of case 6 enabled all township party members to directly elect one township party secretary (the party's top leader at the township level) in the first-round voting. Then in the second-round voting, all township party members directly elected the township deputy party secretaries (they were ranked lower than the township party secretary who was elected in the first-round voting) from the candidates who just lost in the first-round voting. In the third-round voting, all township party members directly elected the township party committee members (they were ranked lower than the township deputy party secretaries whom were elected in the second-round voting) from the remaining candidates. Such an unconventional arrangement to elect from higher to lower positions did attract researchers' attentions, but is it effective to make all the elections genuinely democratic? I will discuss this in the following section.

Analysis of the Cases

Some conclusions can be drawn based on the analysis of the above cases.

First, compared with the traditional elections, these experimental elections are more open and liberal. The grassroots party member in the localities can participate more fully in the experimental elections. In some of these cases, one procedural step was open to grassroots party members, allowing them to "directly" elect township party leaders. Such a step of "direct election" can be found in cases 2, 3, 4, 5, 6, 8, 9, 10, and 11.[34] In case 6, the reversed sequence of the elections in the final step looks more scientific and enhances the grassroots party members' participation in deciding who would occupy the township party's leading positions.

However, having a flaw very similar to that in governmental reform elections, these reform elections were actually not so "direct." In the process of nearly all cases, there was at least one stage where the power holders played a dominant role and the grassroots party members were excluded. This stage was normally critical in the whole process to decide the final candidates. For example, the final candidate list was decided by the county party committee in case 2, two final candidates were selected from eleven in case 5, final candidates (only one more than vacant positions) were selected from the initial candidates in case 6, the final candidate list was decided by the county party standing committee in case 7, two final candidates were selected from eighteen in case 8, five final candidates were selected from sixty-one candidates in case 9, four final candidates were selected from forty-two candidates in case 10, in case 11, four final candidates were decided after winning out from the evaluation but the district party committee selected two of them for the next round. In practice, one or more "step(s) under control" existed in nearly all experiments to enable the power holders inside the primary and local level party committees to change the election result according to their desires. This can also be demonstrated by the failure of case 4. When the higher-level party committee found the upcoming elections in case 4 were too liberal, they aborted the experiment instead of letting it go "out of control."

In the last step of case 6, a seemingly more "scientific" reversed sequence of the final elections was adopted, but this reform implied the elections were "party-controlled" and undemocratic. In a democratic election, the candidates represent various interest groups and they conduct their distinctive electoral campaigns and attract voters with their unique political plans. After the election, the winner takes the power to fulfil his political promises while the loser becomes the opposition to inspect the power. Oddly enough in case 6, the losers became the winner's subordinate after the election and the rivals worked together in one team. Such an arrangement was even able to "improve the quality of the township party committee's leadership" (Zhou Hongyun, 2007). Based on this analysis, we perhaps can draw the conclusion that the elections in case 6 still lack the essential elements which a democratic election must have, such as genuine representation and competitiveness. The harmonious working relationship among these rivals after the election shows us evidence of the party's arrangement and control of the elections. As a party theorist commented, the election reform in case 6 "strengthened the township party committee's leading position" (Zhou Hongyun, 2007).

Second, in cases 1, 4, 5, 6, 8, 9, 10, and 11, some non-party people could participate in one step (normally the step in which final candidates were elected). In cases 6 and 9, there was even a requirement for a minimum proportion of non-party members in that step (thirty and twenty percent respectively). However, the existing documents show that these non-party people who were allowed to vote in one step of these elections were obviously local elites, such as members of the people's congresses or the people's political consultative conferences, heads of villages or village groups, heads of government-owned enterprises and schools. On the other hand, these non-party people who could participate in the elections were without exception appointed by the county-level party committees, which were normally the election organisers. Considering these facts, it is doubtful whether these non-party people, whom the higher-level party committees selected to participate in the inner-party elections, can fully represent the vast majority of the masses living in the localities.

Third, compared with the party nominated candidates in the traditional elections, the open-nomination or self-nomination was more open and liberal. However, the requirements for an eligible candidate, such as having received tertiary education and having been at *ke*-level for at least two years, excluded most grassroots party members, i.e. party members not working in governmental or party departments, from becoming candidates.[35] In some governmental election reform cases studied in chapter 2, there were a few school teachers or business owners who could self-nominate to be candidates and then went further in several of the following rounds. In the inner-party election reform cases of this chapter, however, no grassroots party members could be found. According to the criteria, qualified candidates must be party members who are also holding posts in the party's or governmental departments. In practice, on the condition that the whole authoritarian political system remains unchanged, it was not "safe" for a party or government cadre to participate in such local and incomplete reform experiments, if he/she was not the candidate preferred by higher-level party committee. No matter whether he/she succeeds or fails in the election, the fact that he/she once challenged the party-preferred candidates in a "party-controlled election" could endanger his or her future political career.

Fourth, in the step of "direct" election, some grassroots party members[36] could not vote because they were working elsewhere as migrant workers. In some of the above cases, according to the method, the election result was valid only if the number of voting party members reached a certain proportion of all registered township party members. For example, in cases 6 and 9, the voters must be more than eighty percent of all registered township party members. However, as it was difficult to carry out the policy in the elections which were held in the places where migrant labourers largely move out, the central party's organisation department made a regulation to allow the local election organisers to remove the migrant party members from the list of registered voters (Bao Yajun, 2007). The regulation provides a legal basis for depriving these migrant party members of their voting rights, which was an obvious flaw in these experimental elections. In contrast, those party members who were working as professional party or governmental cadres took advantage of voting at their working localities. They were actually members of the bureaucratic system. Their guaranteed participation and the absence of the migrant party members, who were outside the bureaucratic system, enabled the party to strengthen its control in the "direct voting" round.

Based on this analysis of these most influential cases, we find that the inner-party election reform was instigated, organised and tightly controlled by the higher-level party committees. Although some stages of the elections were open to grassroots party members or even a small amount of the "masses" who were actually the "party-nominated" local elites, the elections were still not democratic nor were they truly direct. In these elections, different from these traditional ones, the power holders did not directly decide who would occupy the positions. Instead, they furtively managed to control the election process and the result. In this meaning, as a distinguished independent political researcher commented in an interview, "the inner-party election reform is thoroughly deluded."[37]

Prospects and Impacts of "Inner-Party Democracy"

It is not very possible to hold such kind of "direct elections" reform at levels higher than the township. Hu Jintao, in his report to the party's 17th national congress, only promised to extend direct election of leading members in primary party organisations[38] to more places. The relevant articles in *The Party Constitution* and laws all assert that, at the levels above township, only the local or the higher-level party committees have the power to select party leaders at the locality.[39] These laws allow no space for inner-party "direct" elections to be held at the county or above levels. In addition, since the inner-party election reform is instigated by the party's higher-levels, it will most probably be restricted within the township level if the central party does not have an intention to push it to the higher levels. Currently and normally, the local[40] party leaders are decided by the immediate higher-level party committee. Hu stated in his report that "we will introduce a system of voting for use by local Party committees in discussing and deciding on major issues and appointing cadres to important positions" (Hu Jintao, 2007). The voting system Hu praised in his report as an improvement in "inner-party democracy," however, is still like a "black box" in the whole process of appointing party and governmental cadres. In article 13 of *The Method of the Party's Local Committee Voting on the Candidates of the Chief Leaders of Its Direct Subordinate Party Committee or Government*, all party committee members who participate in the voting are required to "obey the party's discipline of secrecy, to not release any news to outside about the nomination, discussion and voting." At this stage, to guarantee the party's absolute control, "in the process of the party committee members voting, any such behaviour as criticising rivals, colluding and campaigning are prohibited" (CCP, 2004a). Under such a regulation, the voting process Hu praised in his report obviously lacks free competition and open inspection. No one knows what happens in the "black box."

The inner-party elections at the central level, including the elections for the Central Party Committee members, the elections for the Central Party's Political Bureau and the elections for the Central Party's Political Bureau Standing Committee are thoroughly closed to the public. The party-controlled media released the news that some reform had taken place in the elections at the CCP's 17th National Congress, such as increasing the ratio of candidates to congress seats to 1083:1000 in the election for Central Party Committee members (the ratio was 1050:1000 in the election at the party's 16th national congress)[41] and conducting "public" polling on the candidates of the Party's Political Bureau members among nearly four hundred high ranking party cadres,[42] though the public still does not have access to such detailed information as how many votes each candidate won and who lost in the election. In the elections for the Central Party Committee members, the elected members were listed in an order according to the stroke number of their surnames, thus to avoid ranking the members from high to low votes. A professor from the central party school even justified this method as a good means to keep the party united and to maintain the equality of each elected member (Yang Lin, 2007). The elected members of the Political Bureau and the Political Bureau Standing Committee are listed in an order from higher to lower positions, which also avoids disclosing any voting information to the outside. In fact, these two elections for the highest rank of the Chinese leaders are usually the state's top secret. It is normally impossible for an outsider to obtain information about the nominating method, electoral procedure, and voting result. At the press conference which was held at the party's 17th national congress, when asked by a foreign journalist if the election for the political bureau members would adopt the "differential quota" method and how many positions there would be in the political bureau, the party's news officer answered "you will get to know how many positions the political bureau has when the election result comes out."[43] In such inner-party elections, even the number of vacant positions is kept secret. It is not difficult to understand that there is a very long way to go before inner-party elections become genuinely democratic.

Now we look back to examine the question whether such "inner-party democracy" will push forward people's democracy. A Taiwan political researcher summarised four possible routes to China's political democratisation: (1) reform from inside the party to outside the party, mainly by expanding inner-party democracy, (2) reform from outside the party to inside the party, mainly by establishing opposition parties and allowing free competitive elections, (3) reform from the higher level to the lower level, mainly by separating the party's power from the government's administration power, and (4) reform from the lower level to the higher level, mainly by promoting democratic elections from the local to central levels (Lin Jialong, 1999: 47–55). Viewing the existing inner-party reform, I found it is different from the "reform inside the party" which the researcher means when describing route one. In route one, the "reform inside the party" is explained by the researcher as to allow rival factions and free competition inside the party. The existing inner-party reform, which mainly involves the measures to improve selecting-cadres and other policy-making procedures at the primary level, is more like the fourth route rather than the first route according to the definitions of the researcher. However, according to the researcher, if democratic local elections cannot be promoted to the higher levels, China's democratisation will be a very difficult and time-consuming process. Based on the analysis in the above paragraphs, the inner-party elections at the central level are far from open, not to mention liberal or democratic. In addition, it seems that the central party has no plans to carry out reform in inner-party elections at the levels higher than township. By analysing the existing cases, I realise that the procedures of even the township-level inner-party reform elections have just liberalised some procedural steps. They have not democratised the party, which still remains "safe and controllable." Considering all these factors, a conclusion can be drawn that the existing "inner-party democracy" will not be able to lead China to democratisation.

The CCP will not easily give up its power and any intention to promote self-reform is to strengthen its authoritarian rule. In my opinion, the genuine inner-party democracy can be achieved only when the party can truly represent a group or groups of Chinese people's interests and compete equally with other political parties in real democratic elections. This, however, can only happen after political democratisation is completed in China.

Notes

1. In the existing documents, *dangnei minzhu* [inner-party democracy], a term that has been established and widely used by the party in its propaganda and by Chinese scholars in their research, involves only liberal measures the party takes to patch up some procedures of its political activities. These measures are far from the value of liberal democracy. In order to avoid confusing the theories, I will try to use the terms "inner-party reform," "the party's self-reform," or "inner-party liberal reform" rather than the party's self-propaganda term "inner-party democracy" in this book. If the term "inner-party democracy" has to be used to keep the translation consistent with its original meaning, a quotation mark will be applied to indicate such "democracy" is different from liberal democracy in the western political system.

2. *Remin minzhu* [People's democracy] or *you zhongguo tese de shehuizhuyi minzhu* [socialist democracy with Chinese characteristics] are terms created by the CCP to distinguish "Chinese democracy" from the liberal democracy in western political science. "Chinese democracy" theoretically includes such fundamental elements as the people's congress system, the system of multi-party cooperation and political consultation led by the CCP, people's electoral rights and supervision rights, which form the foundation of China's polity. Political researchers, however, cast great doubts on the value of such "democracy" which excludes the multi-party system or even a competitive election. Even worse, the mechanism of this party self-defined "democracy," such as the systems of people's congress and political consultation, do not genuinely function in reality. Thus, the goals of "socialist democracy with Chinese characteristics," which frequently appear in the party's propaganda, have never been achieved.

3. Deliberative democracy, the second "breakthrough," has the same feature of "safe and controllable." This cautious attitude, from another aspect, proves the CCP carries out the reforms to relieve itself from pressures from both inside and outside. The aim of these reforms is to help the CCP grip political power more tightly rather than giving it back to the Chinese people.

4. The web page is at http://theory.people.com.cn/BIG5/40555/3948952.html.

5. The researchers holding such progressive views are mainly public intellectuals and overseas researchers such as Yang Jisheng (Yang Jisheng, 2007), Zhang Boshu (Zhang Boshu, 2007), Hao Wang (Hao Wang, 2005), Hu Wei (Hu Wei, 1999), Wang Feiling (Wang Feiling, 2000) etc. Articles with such opinions, however, do not get published in the Mainland China's media because of the party's repression. When writing this chapter, the BBC published news about a retired professor of Peking University writing a letter to the central party. In the letter, the professor urged the party to carry out the political reform in China. An important reform content that he suggested in his letter is that the central party should allow rival factions inside the party and free competition between them. The news is at http://news.bbc.co.uk/chinese/simp/hi/newsid_7340000/newsid_7341000/7341057.stm.

On 23 December 2009 when this chapter was revised, Zhang Boshu, one of the above-listed researchers, who promoted progressive party reform, was dismissed by the state-sponsored Chinese Academy of Social Sciences for publishing articles calling for political reform (Clem, 2009)

6. The holders of that conservative view are mainly researchers from universities inside mainland China, theorists from the party's academic institutes or publicity departments of various levels, and some party cadres, such as Li Yuanchao (Li Yuanchao, 2007), Wang Xiugui (Wang Xiugui, 2002), Zhang Shulin (Zhang Shulin, 2007a), Xiao Gongqin (Xiao Gongqin, 2004), Li Dongming (Li Dongming, 2008), Li Shenming (Li Shenming,

2006) etc.. In fact, nearly all articles pro "inner-party democracy" published in Mainland China have such conservative opinions.

7. This does not mean the party would actually like to carry out such reform. See the conclusion to this chapter.

8. "Intra-party democracy" is the official translation of *dangnei minzhu* in the English version of Hu Jintao's report released by the CCP, though I use the term "inner-party democracy" in this book.

9. Specifically referring to "inner-party democracy" of the CCP, Juan L. Linz made this statement in his keynote speech at the Conference on the Party-State Reform and Democratization in China and Taiwan, which was jointly organised by the Fairbank Center for Chinese Studies, Harvard University and the Taiwan Research Funds in February of 1998. Linz's speech was translated into Chinese and compiled into the conference proceedings (Lin Jialong, Qiu Zeqi, 1999). The original English manuscript of the speech, however, could not be obtained from the archival research.

10. The "*sange daibiao* [three represents] theory," created by the party's former General-Secretary Jiang Zemin, has been written into *The Party Constitution* as the party's important principle. In the theory, the CCP represents the fundamental interests of the overwhelming majority of the Chinese people, advanced productivity and advanced culture.

The number of the party members was according to a statistic made by the CCP Organisation Department at the end of 2008: http://news.xinhuanet.com/politics/2009-06/30/content_11626985.htm.

11. In fact, there is so far no evidence that the limited proposals for "inner-party democracy" have been actually achieved.

12. The original article has not been found. Some contents of the article are from http://www.chinanews.com.cn/n/2003-08-20/26/337230.html.

13. The relevant contents can be found in the quoted part from Hu's report on p. 33.

14. *Gongtui zhixuan* [open nomination and direct election] is the most frequent term in academic papers and news reports to describe the reform of township-level party cadre elections. These methods actually varied from place to place, but they are generally called "open nomination and direct election."

15. According to the existing documents, direct voting by all township party members happened in only one of the several rounds of the whole procedure. The word "direct voting" or "direct election" in the context of this chapter refers to the direct one round, which is different from the direct elections held in democratic countries.

16. The 2nd article of document 4 states that the document applies to the elections at township level. The 2nd article of document 3 states that the document applies to the elections at the levels from county to provincial (all levels excluding the centre and township).

17. Interestingly, in *The Party Constitution*, different from the non-rigorous expression of the electoral method at the primary (township) level, the expression of the article regarding elections at the local (from county to provincial) levels is very clear. Article 27 of *The Party Constitution* clearly states: "Local Party committees at various levels elect, at their plenary sessions, their standing committees, secretaries and deputy secretaries and report the results to the higher Party committees for approval." According to this article, the inner-party direct elections at the local levels are obviously unlawful.

18. Case 3 in this chapter is case 6 examined in chapter 2. This reform experiment involved elections for both township executive and township party secretary so it is studied in two chapters of the book which respectively research township executive election reform and township party secretary election reform.

19. In this case, the reform was aborted for both township executive and party secretary. Some information about the case has been introduced in chapter 2 on p. 20 and in notes 20 and 21 in chapter 2.

20. *Ke*-level is the primary level in the five-level cadre system in China: *Ke*, *Chu/Xian*, *Ju/Ting/Si/Shi*, *Bu/Sheng*, Central (from lower to higher). Each level has its deputy level which is a half level lower. Normally, township party secretaries are *Ke*-level cadres. According to the criteria for candidates, a qualified candidate must attain the deputy *Ke*-level, which is a half level lower than the *Ke*-level and is the lowest level in cadres' ranking system.

21. In this election, the lowest rank a qualified candidate must attain is the deputy *Chu*-level, which is one-level higher than the normal requirement in other experimental elections. This is because of the special status of Chongqing Municipality in China's governmental system. Chongqing Municipality, the same as the municipalities of Beijing, Shanghai and Tianjin, is a unit at the *Bu/Sheng* level, which is one level higher than normal cities. All governmental and party units subordinate to Chongqing Municipality are accordingly one-level higher than the units in other cities. Specifically, Longxin Township, Yubei District, Chongqing Municipality, the township where the election was held, is actually a *Chu/Xian*-level unit.

22. The exact number cannot be obtained from the existing documents.

23. The exact number cannot be obtained from the existing documents.

24. Some details about the aborted experiment in Pingba Township, Chengkou District, Chongqing Municipality (case 4) are described in chapter 2 on p. 20 and in notes 20 and 21 in chapter 2.

25. In case 6, the experimental elections were held in nine townships. The numbers of the voters in this step varied in different townships.

26. In case 9, the elections for township party secretaries were held in one hundred and twenty-six townships. The exact numbers of the final candidates varied in different townships.

27. The information regarding what kind of survey it was and how it was conducted cannot be obtained from the collected documents.

28. The participant numbers and the proportion between the groups could not be obtained.

29. In this case, the elections for township party secretary and other township party leaders were held. In the evaluation step, the candidates were categorised into groups according to their desired position. The exact number of the winners from each group was not clear in the existing documents, but seemingly four candidates for the secretarial position and eight candidates for party committee members won the evaluation and could then enter into the following round of election.

30. The two final candidates for township party secretary were elected by the twenty district party committee members from the four candidates who won out in the previous evaluation round. Refer to p. 43 for the detailed information.

31. These six township party committee members were elected by all township party members from the eight candidates who won out in the previous evaluation round. Refer to p. 43 for the detailed information.

32. They are party theorists such as Bao Yajun (Bao Yajun, 2007), Chen Xuelian (Chen Xuelian, 2007), Li Jiajie (Li Jiajie, 2007), Li Meiling (Li Meiling, 2007) and Zhou Hongyun (Zhou Hongyun, 2007).

33. In reality, even these indirect elections are meaningless and deceptive. Power is centralised in a higher level and this power enabled them to decide who can take the lower-level positions.

34. In case 4, the planned "direct election" step had not been carried out before the higher-level party committees aborted the experiment.

35. In article 4 of *The Party Constitution*, "to stand for election" is a right a party member has (CCP, 2002b).

36. The grassroots party members here refer to the party members who are not holding positions in the party's or governmental departments.

37. The interviewee's name is undisclosed for his or her safety.

38. "Primary" means the township level. Please refer to p. 37.

39. The laws include *The Party Constitution* (CCP, 2002b), *The Ordinance of the CCP's Local Organisational and Electoral Work* (CCP, 1994), *The Method of the Party's Local Committee Voting on the Candidates of the Chief Leaders of Its Direct Subordinate Party Committee or Government* (CCP, 2004a), *The Ordinance for Electing or Appointing Party and Government Cadres* (CCP, 2002a), and *The Provisional Regulations for the Open Selection of Party and Government Cadres* (CCP, 2004b).

40. "Local" here means the levels from county to provincial. Please refer to p. 37.

41. The data can be found from http://www.chinanews.com.cn/gn/news/2007/10-22/1054906.shtml.

42. The information is from http://news.xinhuanet.com/politics/2007-10/25/content_6939939.htm.

43. The information is from http://news.ifeng.com/special/zhonggong17da/zuixinbaodao/200710/1014_2077_258116.shtml.

Chapter 4

Another Form of "Inner-Party Democracy": the Party Congress Reform

Introduction

As discussed in chapter 3, the CCP boasts about the achievements of its party electoral reform, which the party believes will pave the way for China's political democratisation. The reform of the elections for township party secretaries and other leaders, in the party's propaganda, forms the most important component of such "inner-party democracy." In addition to these electoral experiments, a reform named *dangdaihui changrenzhi* [the permanent tenure system of party congresses],[1] which the party believes can strengthen the power of local party congresses, has become another emphasis in the party's self-reform. This chapter focuses on this reform. The first part introduces the origin and contents of the reform.[2] It also analyses the party's attitudes to the reform based on publications of some party theorists. The second part illustrates the traditional work and organisation of the party congresses, which can provide a basis for comparison with the reformed system. The third part of the chapter uses case studies to examine the reform measures and their effects. This aims to allow the reform to be understood from an evidence-based viewpoint. The conclusion analyses the reforms. This chapter is to provide the reader with an appropriate basis from which to observe and evaluate this kind of reform. Based on the analysis and conclusion made in this chapter, readers can further understand the nature of "inner-party democracy" and judge whether such "democracy" will lead to China's political democratisation.

Contents and Origin

Briefly, "the permanent tenure system of party congresses," a "new" and "important" party self-reform in the party's propaganda to achieve "inner-party democracy," is instigated by the central party and designed and carried out by the party committees of the localities. The reform aims to strengthen the role of the local party congresses and of the congress members in many spheres of the party's politics. Thus, it should also reduce the power of the local party secretaries. Some specific measures include (1) holding a plenary meeting of the congress members annually (in contrast to normally only one plenary meeting in the first year of a party congress's five-year tenure), (2) establishing commissions (inside a party congress) on certain party issues such as the party organisation and disciplinary inspection, and (3) setting up offices (inside a party congress) to tighten the links between the party congress members and grassroots party members. In addition, there are reforms in other party congress activities such as the elections for party congress members, training and organising party congress members to inspect the local party committee's work, and organising party congresses to evaluate the local party leaders. The reform methods vary in different localities but the local reformers and the party theorists categorise all of them into "the permanent tenure system of party congresses" reform if the reform method is to strengthen the power of a local party congress. On that basis, "the permanent tenure system of party congresses" is actually a reform of the party congress system, although the reform measures vary in different localities. In some cases, the reform involves some changes in the organisational structure of local party committees, which has also been included by party theorists into "the permanent tenure system of party congresses" reform. The third part of this chapter will fully discuss the specific reform measures and the effects of the reform.

Some party theorists try to justify the reform and detail reform methods in their publications. They discuss the reform from different perspectives. For example, an article published in *The People's Daily* defines the reform comprehensively:

> The permanent tenure system of party congresses is a complete set of reform methods to facilitate the party congress members and the relevant institutions[3] to play their roles during their whole tenure. The establishment of the system aims to insure a party congress as the leading and inspection institution for other party organisations [of that level]. The measures include: during the tenure of a party congress, a plenary meeting for all congress members is held annually to strengthen the role of the congress, a party congress member can fulfil his responsibility during the whole [five-year] tenure of the party congress, [which is different from the normal situation that a congress member does nothing and can do nothing before and after the plenary meeting which is held only once during the five years] (Sheng Ruowei, 2008).

As discussed in the first paragraph of this part, the reform involves many other aspects of a local party congress such as elections for congress members, congress members' duties, inner-congress commissions or offices for special purposes, and local party committees (actually local party leaders). There are propagandistic articles published in the party's media which focus on these aspects.

Some theorists call the reform *dangdaibiao renqizhi* [the permanent tenure system of party congress members] in their articles, which contextually emphasises the role of the party congress members in the reform. Although the focus of these articles is on the party congress members, the reform they talk about has little difference from "the permanent tenure system of party congresses." As a party theorist stated in his article, a party congress functionally provides a platform for its members to fulfil his/her duties (Gao Xinmin, 2007).

Another party theorist more precisely discussed the relations between the party congress, party congress members and the party committee:

> On one side, once a party congress member is elected through the procedure which is written *in The Party Constitution*, he/she obtains the congress membership during the same tenure as that of his/her party congress. He/she has the rights and bears the responsibilities [of a party congress member] during the tenure. On the other side, during the tenure, a party congress which is made up with these congress members should hold the ultimate leading and inspection power at the level. The party committee elected by the congress has only administrative power and it should be responsible to the party congress [by which it was elected] (Han Lei, 2006).

Some researchers argue that the reform should not be restricted to such formalistic things as plenary meetings and tenure of a party congress. Instead, the reform should be carried out to improve the party congress members' quality and to strengthen their power. A senior party theorist stated in his book that "the elections for party congress members should be genuinely democratic, the party congress members can freely discuss and vote on the party's issues at the congress meetings, a decision must be made on the basis of the voting result" (Gao Fang, 2006). Another party theorist believed that the reform should be an institutionalised system comprising the comprehensive measures to ensure a party congress's leading and inspection position among all party organisations at that level (Zhang Shulin, 2007b). A few of these proposed measures were carried out in some reform experiments, which will be discussed in the third part of this chapter.

Xu Jiqing and Ma Bingjun historically studied the development of the permanent tenure system of party congresses (Xu Jiqing, Ma Bingjun, 2007). Their research showed that the party adopted some measures of this reform in its organisational and political activities at a very early stage of the party's history. After the founding of the People's Republic of China, the first-generation of the top leaders seemingly had the intention to re-adopt these measures but that never occurred. In April 1956, at a meeting of the party's Political Bureau, Mao Zedong suggested establishing the permanent tenure system of party congresses to strengthen the role of the party congress (Mao Zedong, 1956).[4] In September, Deng Xiaoping re-affirmed the decision and proposed some specific reform measures including establishing permanent party congresses[5] at the national and local levels, reforming the party congresses to be the party's ultimate leading and inspective institution, and increasing the party congress members' power in collecting suggestions and opinions from the grassroots party members and the masses (Deng Xiaoping, 1956). These proposals of Deng were later approved by the CCP's 8th National Congress and were written into *The Party Constitution (1956)* (CCP, 1956). In 1958, according to the newly-added party constitution articles, the plenary meeting of the CCP's 8th National Congress was held in the second year of its five year tenure. After that, however, the reform was not carried out in the following decades even though it should have been done according to *The Party Constitution*. In 1982, just before *The Party Constitution (1956)* was to be amended at the CCP's 12th National Congress, some party theorists argued that the party should resume the reform but the head of the central party's publicity department rejected the proposal so that the permanent tenure system of party congresses was not written into *The Party Constitution (1982)* at the 12th congress (Hu Qiaomu, 1982). Other decades have passed since then. Nowadays when the central party theoretically has prioritised "safe and controllable" "inner-party democracy" to alleviate the pressures from both inside and outside the party, it seems to remember the reform. In November 2002, Jiang Zemin stated in his report to the party's 16th National Congress: "The system of party congresses with regular annual conferences should be tried out in more cities and counties. We should explore ways to give play to the role of delegates when party congresses are not in session" (Jiang Zemin, 2002). Hu Jintao also included this point in his report to the 17th CCP National Congress: "We need to respect the principal position of party members, guarantee their democratic rights, increase transparency in party affairs and create favourable conditions for democratic discussions within the party. We will improve the system of party congresses by adopting a tenure system for their delegates and implementing a system of party congresses with a fixed term on a trial basis in selected counties, cities and districts" (Hu Jintao, 2007).

Traditional Party Congress System

Articles 10 and 25 of *The Party Constitution* state a party congress's political status and its power.

> Article 10: . . . The highest leading body of the Party is the National Congress and the Central Committee elected by it. The leading bodies of local Party organisations are the Party congresses at their respective levels and the Party committees elected by them. Party committees are responsible, and report their work, to the Party congresses at their respective levels.
>
> Article 25: The functions and powers of the local Party congresses at all levels are as follows:
> (1) To hear and examine the reports of the Party committees at the corresponding levels;

(2) To hear and examine the reports of the commissions for discipline inspection at the corresponding levels;
(3) To discuss and decide on major issues in the given areas; and
(4) To elect the Party committees and commissions for discipline inspection at the corresponding levels (CCP, 2002b).

These party constitution articles clarify that a party congress has the highest leading, supervision and inspection powers at its level. The party committee is elected by the party congress and is responsible to the party congress. Article 27 of *The Party Constitution* states how a party standing committee, which is a party organisation with the most centralised leading power at the level, is elected.

> Article 27: Local Party committees at various levels elect, at their plenary sessions, their standing committees, secretaries and deputy secretaries and report the results to the higher Party committees for approval. The standing committees of local Party committees at various levels exercise the powers and functions of local Party committees when the latter are not in session. They continue to handle the day-to-day work when the next Party congresses at their levels are in session, until the new standing committees are elected (CCP, 2002b).

These articles of *The Party Constitution* clearly state the relations between the party standing committee, the party committee and the party congress in a locality. The party congress elects the party committee and the party committee elects the standing committee. The standing committee is responsible to the party committee and the party committee is responsible to the party congress. However, the party's organisational principle of "centralism"[6] turns the power structure upside down. In such a structure, the party standing committee and party committee are not the units to exercise the power on the party congress's behalf. Instead, they become the leading party organisations in a locality. Under the principle of "power centralism" and "the lower-level party organisations being subordinate to the higher-level party organisations,"[7] political power is centralised in the party committee, its standing committee and even the party committee secretary. They dominate all other "subordinate" party organisations in the locality including the party congress. While declaring the "leading position" of the party congresses, *The Party Constitution* also has articles 18 and 24 which clarify the leading position of a party committee in organising the party congresses at the locality and controlling the party congress members.

> Article 18: The National Congress of the Party is held once every five years and convened by the Central Committee. . . . The number of delegates to the National Congress of the Party and the procedure governing their election shall be determined by the Central Committee (CCP, 2002b).

> Article 24: Local Party congresses are convened by the Party committees at the corresponding levels. . . . The number of delegates to the local Party congresses at any level and the procedure governing their election are determined by the Party committees at the corresponding levels and should be reported to the next higher Party committees for approval (CCP, 2002b).

Articles 13 and 14 of *The Ordinance of the CCP's Local Organisational and Electoral Work* and article 10 of *The Provisional Ordinance of the CCP's Organisational and Electoral Work at the Primary Level* specify that a party committee has the power to determine the procedure of the elections for party congress members of that level and it has the power to examine a candidate's qualifications and to decide if he/she is eligible (CCP, 1990, 1994).

In addition, the party committee decides what issues are to be discussed at the party congress. In the elections held inside a party congress for party committee members, some procedural steps such as candidate nomination and voting are controlled by the incumbent party committee (Peng Jianjun, Mao Zhengxiang, 2007).

It is even worse that the political power tends to be centralised in few party leaders, especially the party committee secretary. With absolute power in his hands, the secretary is the real "big brother" in the locality. When the small group of party leaders or even the party secretary is able to decide nearly everything about the party congress, the party congress can be nothing but a political "rubber stamp."

The above analysis shows that the party's political structure greatly weakens the party congresses. The following part confirms this conclusion by analysing the role of the party congress members. In the system of "representative democracy," the congress members are elected to represent the voters' interests in such activities as making policies and inspection. The party congress system, according to the party's propaganda, "was designed under the representative democracy theory." [8] An analysis of party congress members' background, their representation of the grassroots party members and their duties in a party congress, however, demonstrates that the party congress system still is far from genuine representative democracy.

First, the majority of the party congress members are power holders rather than grassroots party members. Data indicate that the party congress members at various levels account for only one percent of all party members, yet around seventy-five percent of the party congress members are professional party or government cadres (Peng Jianjun, Mao Zhengxiang, 2007). Han Lei specifies in his paper that this proportion at the provincial party congresses is approximately seventy-five percent. As for the party congresses at the county level, he says, this proportion is around sixty percent (Han Lei, 2006). The data of a survey on a county party congress show that only fifteen members were not professional cadres, accounting for only 4.63 percent of three-hundred and twenty-four members in that county party congress (Peng Jianjun, Mao Zhengxiang, 2007). There might be a hypothesis that a party congress which is made up of more party and governmental power holders should be more capable of carrying out its functions. However, this is not the reality. On the contrary, the bureaucratic background of most congress members may possibly restrain them from fulfilling their duties of representing grassroots party members in their locality. With *zuzhixing jiluxing* [the sense of organisation and discipline] and the principle "the lower-level party organisations being subordinate to the higher-level party organizations" deeply rooted in their mind, these members who are from the bureaucratic system and occupy most seats of party congresses at various levels virtually transform the party congresses into a subordinate organisation to the party committees and party standing committees at that level. Thus, the status of a party congress as the "leading body" of its level, even if it is clarified in *The Party Constitution*, is not possible in practice.

Second, the communications between the party congress members and the grassroots party members are insufficient. A survey on the relations between the party members and the party congress members they "elected" was conducted in seven localities of four provinces (Peng Jianjun, Mao Zhengxiang, 2007). One-thousand seven-hundred and ninety-seven party members participated in the survey and their views are shown in Table 4.1.

Table 4.1 Result of a Survey on the Relations between the Party Members and the Party Congress Members

Question 1: Do you know who the party congress members in your locality are?

Yes, I know	No, I don't know	I don't care
42.52%	52.70%	4.29%

Question 2: Do you think the party congress members in your locality can represent you?

Yes, they can	No, they can't	Not sure
20.26%	33.44%	45.58%

Question 3: Have you ever communicated with the party congress members in your locality?

Yes, often	Sometimes	Never
6.07%	20.37%	64.33%

Question 4: Do you seek assistance from the party congress members in your locality when it is necessary?

Yes, I do
1.07%

Notes for Table 4.1:

1. As for question 4, the 1.07% interviewees who were positive to this question include the relatives or friends of the party congress members and those who themselves were party congress members. The datum of the interviewees who were negative to this question could not be obtained from the available documents.
2. According to the surveyors, some participants in the survey possibly confused people's congress members[9] with the party congress members so that the real situation might be worse than these survey data indicate.

The communications between the grassroots party members and their "delegates" in the party congresses were obviously poor as shown from the above survey data. In practice, such a poor relationship between the party members and the party congress members shows that the party congresses can hardly function as organisations of "representative democracy."

Third, during the five-year congress tenure the duties of a party congress member are not clear. In the traditional party congress system, the whole work for a party congress member in the five year tenure of the party congress was to attend one plenary meeting which lasted three to seven days.[10] Except for attending this plenary meeting, the party congress members had no other specific duties to fulfil in the rest of the time of the congress tenure. Unlike the rights of a party member which are clarified in *The Party Constitution* and other relevant party laws (even if the party members can hardly practise these rights in reality),[11] the duties and rights of a party congress member are not stated in these legal documents of the party. In summary, the oddly-designed system does not provide the platform for the party congress members to fulfil their responsibility during their tenure. The lack of support in the party constitution and laws clearly weakens their capability of "democratically representing" the grassroots party members in political activities. The data of a survey conducted in the eighteen districts and counties of Beijing may possibly support this conclusion. In the survey, 1,233 participants agreed that "the party congress members did not fully fulfil their duties or they did not fulfil their duties at all," accounting for 54.6 percent of all surveyed people. Ironically, seventy-three percent of the district and county *yibashou* [top leaders] agreed with that point in the survey (Research Institute of the Beijing Municipality Party Committee, 2004).

Reform Localities and Measures

Perhaps to solve the problem of centralised power, the central party started reform in the 1980s. In 1988, the central party's organisation department chose twelve localities to make reform experiments.[12] By the CCP's 16th National Congress in 2002, the experiments in seven of the localities had been aborted because the local party committees lost interest and became reluctant to carry them out.[13] As the party's 16th National Congress "re-emphasised"[14] the importance of the reform, the local authorities of the twelve places were ordered to further or resume the experiments. Since 2002, the central party has also chosen some new localities to conduct experiments.[15] In 2005, the reform was expanded to even more localities.[16]

The reform experiments at these localities are generally termed "the permanent tenure system of party congresses." However, they involve various measures to reform the different aspects of a local party congress. The following section analyses the reform measures on the basis of case studies.[17]

The reform measures can be divided into several categories:

Reform of Elections for Party Congress Members

Normally the party committees dominate the elections for party congress members by nominating almost all candidates and deciding the ratio of the candidate number and the congress seats (normally 1:1). The collected documents show that the reform aiming to "democratise" such elections happened in Xingjing County and Yucheng District, Ya'an City, Sichuan Province in December 2002, in Luotian County, Hubei Province in February 2003, in Yidu City, Hubei Province in 2003 and 2006, in Jiaojiang Distrct, Taizhou City, Zhejiang Province[18] and in Huizhou City, Guangdong Province in 2003.

In the experimental elections for party congress members held in Yucheng Distrct and Xingjing County, the grassroots party members were allowed to nominate themselves to be candidates. In these two localities, more than 2,000 party members nominated themselves to be candidates and competed in the elections for the 325 seats in the local party congresses. After the procedural steps of a qualifications check[19] and preliminary election, all party members in the two localities voted in their electorates to elect the party congress members. Both preliminary elections and final elections were held in the electorates. An electorate was usually a township of the county or a *jiedao* [urban community] of the district. In Yucheng District, for example, there were eighty-two electorates (urban communities). A researcher states in his article that "a county party secretary cannot be guaranteed to win a party congress seat if he or she has to be voted in an electorate at the primary level"[20] and "the events that some party leaders 'unexpectedly' failed in the voting held at the primary-level electorates demonstrate the value of the reform" (Li Ling, 2006). In Xingjing County, an incumbent township party secretary "unexpectedly" failed in the election.[21] In Yucheng District, five *ke*-level cadres failed too.

In the reform experiment in Jiaojiang District, most electorates were a township or an urban community. However, the reform was not as thorough as that in Yucheng Distrct and Xingjing County. According to the existing documents, some of the electorates in Jiaojiang District were still the party branches of some party and governmental departments, in which some incumbent local party leaders won election. Their success in the election was much more guaranteed in this way. In addition to the measure of setting up more primary-level electorates, there were some other minor reforms in Jiaojiang District such as increasing the candidate quota in the elections (the ratio of candidates to congress seats was increased to 153:100) and assigning some congress seats to the *jiebie* [special groups of local party members] such as women party members and party members who were retired cadres.

In Luotian County, the grassroots party members could nominate candidates for their own electorate and the minimum ratio of candidates to congress seats was increased to 130:100. In the elections held in Yidu City, the procedure was similar to that of the elections in Yucheng District and Xingjing County, involving the steps of self-nomination, preliminary election and final election held in the primary-level electorates.[22] Also in Yidu City, the candidate number was increased (the ratio of candidates to congress seats was increased to 140:100) to make the elections "more competitive."

In the experimental election held in Huizhou City, the electorates were set up at the townships and urban resident communities. All party and governmental leaders must be voted by the grassroots party members in these primary-level electorates. However, the election organisers made some other methods to enhance their probability of winning. First, after the number of congress seats was assigned to an electorate, an extra congress seat was added if a party or governmental leader would participate in the election in that electorate. Second, unlike other candidates who must go through the procedural steps of preliminary election and qualifications check, the party or governmental leaders directly entered the final election. The election procedure for normal candidates was different. The election organisers arranged the preliminary election first and then checked the qualifications of the candidates who won the preliminary election. Only after that, the election organisers decided the number of congress seats for each electorate and then added the extra seats for party or governmental leaders (Research Institute of the Huizhou Party Organization Department, 2004). The election organisers claimed that they made such an arrangement to "balance the seats for various groups," but most probably they hoped to insure the party or governmental leaders won by manipulating the candidatures and congress seats of the electorate.

Theoretically, reforming the election for party congress members can be the most fundamental step to liberalise the party congress system. The analysis of the above five cases, however, shows the existing reform of elections was still not very liberal. The most distinguished reform was that the local party and governmental leaders, in some cases, had to participate in the election held at the primary-level electorate such as a township or urban resident community so that the grassroots party members could vote on them, but this reform happened in only the two cases of Yucheng District and Xingjing County. In the case in Jiaojiang District, some electorates were set up in townships and urban resident communities but some local leaders could still be voted in an electorate inside the party and government departments. In the Huizhou case, the local leaders were voted by the grassroots party members in the primary-level electorate but the unjust "dual procedure," which hindered the normal candidates while promoting the candidates who were incumbent party leaders, degraded the reform. The method of self-nomination or open nomination was adopted in some cases as a kind of "reform," but the party's relevant laws clarify that such nomination methods must be used in the elections for the primary and local level party congress members.[23] Such a comment in some news reports and research papers that the self or open nomination is a "reform" or "creative" method possibly reveals the fact that some basic election methods, which are obligated by the party's laws to ensure the minimal "democracy" of the party congress elections, are not carried out. On the contrary, "centralism" is actually the overwhelming principle for all the party's activities. Other reform measures, such as increasing the candidate number, actually had little impact on the party congress system. As analysed in note 21, under the current party organisation system, party secretaries, as well as other important party and governmental leaders, must win party congress elections to become party congress members or their political career is in danger. That is to say, in the party congress elections, these leaders who "must" be party congress members were guaranteed their seats in the party congresses. On the other hand, even if in the reformed elections there was competition, it could exist only among the candidates who were grassroots party members. Therefore, the effect of increasing candidate positions is merely to allow more competitions among the grassroots candidates, which does not even slightly weaken the bureaucratic power inside the party congress. The data of the surveys on the elected party congress members support this conclusion. Candidate numbers increased in the election held in Luotian County, but still more than 70 percent of the party congress members were local party or governmental cadres. The grassroots party congress members accounted for only 3.5 percent of all party congress members (Ruan Siyu, 2007).[24] After the elections in Yucheng District and Xingjing County, which are generally thought to be the most "liberal" cases of this kind, the party and government cadres still occupied 60 percent of the party congress seats (Social Science Academy of Sichuan Province, 2004).

Holding Plenary Meetings Annually

Holding an annual plenary meeting, probably the most common measure in the party congress reform, happened in most experimental localities. An important agenda of the meeting, according to the existing documents, was an opinion poll on the local party leaders. Such a poll was carried out in Yucheng District, Xingjing County, Luotian County, Yidu City and ten townships of Shanghai Municipality.[25] In Luotian County, if more than thirty percent of all party congress members cast disapproval votes on a party committee member, he/she must be dismissed.[26] In some of these reform cases, the plenary meeting had other agendas, such as party congress members examining the reports of the party committee and the party disciplinary committee, raising motions and discussing them, questioning party committee members about their work or other questions. According to a report, in the reform localities in Sichuan Province, party issues and the important economic and social issues must be discussed at the annual meeting of the party congresses. Resolutions were made on the basis of the discussion results to guide the party's and the government's future work. In Xingjing County, the local people's political consultative conference members were invited to attend the annual meetings. In Taizhou City, Zhejiang Province, grassroots party members were allowed to audit the annual meetings of the party congresses but they needed to make an application to the local party and await approval.[27]

Special Offices or Commissions

In some cases, special offices or commissions were set up to link the party congress to the party committee or to the grassroots party members. In Yucheng

District, Xingjing County and Luotian County, a *ke*-level office was set up under the party committee's organisation department. It was responsible for making reports to the party congress about the work of the party committee and the party disciplinary committee. Another function of it was collecting the congress members' feedback. In Huizhou City, the office also provided training to the congress members about how to do field research and how to write proposal reports to the party committee. In Jiaojiang District, an office was set up under the party congress that organised and coordinated the activities of the congress members. In addition, it received visiting party members, recording their suggestions and delivered them to the party congress. In the ten townships of Shanghai, the office under the party congress connected the congress with both the party committee and grassroots party members. According to a report, with the establishment of such an office, the connections between the party committee, party congress members and grassroots party members were tightened in Gao County, Yibin City, Sichuan Province (Social Science Academy of Sichuan Province, 2004). In the propaganda articles by party theorists, the reform in the townships of Shanghai and Gao County was called *sanlian zhidu* [the three-liaison system], which linked the party congress to the party committee and grassroots party members. In addition to the liaison offices, commissions for special purposes were established inside some party congresses to strengthen their capability in some aspects. In Yucheng District, for example, three commissions were set up. The inspection commission, made up of the party congress members who must not be party committee or disciplinary committee members, was responsible for inspecting and assessing the committees' work, warning and reproving the party leaders who had misbehaved and proposing impeachment. The organisation commission was in charge of the congress's administrative work. The consultative commission organised public surveys on the party and social issues and they also collected suggestions from specialists. In Jiaojiang District, three commissions were established. Their functions were the same as those in Yucheng District. In Yidu City, in addition to the inspection and consultative commissions, there were two other commissions respectively in charge of the party congress membership and the motions the congress members raised.

Another component of the party congress reform, which party theorists believed important, was the opinion poll carried out annually on the working performance of the party congress members. According to the existing documents, such polls were organised in Yucheng District, Xingjing County, Luotian County and Jiaojiang district. In all these localities, a party congress member who was disapproved by more than thirty percent of all interviewed party members in a poll, would lose his/her party congress membership.

The abolition of the party standing committee (normally five to ten members), which some party theorists boasted could decentralise power, was carried out in Luotian County and Jiaojiang District. According to these theorists, this reform widened the range of the local "leading body" to the whole party committee (normally ten to twenty members). In addition, when the party committee decided an important issue, every member of the committee cast a vote. This reform actually has little to do with the party congress but the party theorists normally label it as an important component of party congress reform. In some places, the activities of the party committee and party disciplinary committee were somewhat open to party congress members. According to the existing documents, in most reform localities of Sichuan Province, some party congress members were allowed to audit the meetings of the local party committee and its standing committee. This was thought a part of party congress reform.

Analysis of the Reform

The party congress reform, also called "the permanent tenure system of party congresses," involved various measures to decentralise the local party committees' power and to strengthen the local party congresses' role. It was probably not so effective in practice as the party theorists boasted in their propaganda articles. This conclusion is based on the following analysis.

First, in practice, the reformed party congresses still could not genuinely elect the local party leaders. All such power, according to *The Party Constitution* and other relevant party laws, is absolutely centralised in the party committees at the same or higher levels.[28] The polls of the local party leaders which were carried out at the annual meetings of some party congresses, though theoretically able to remove disqualified cadres from their positions, had little impact on the current cadre management system which has been institutionalised legally and practically. Furthermore, considering the fact that sixty to seventy percent of the congress seats in even these reformed congresses were still occupied by the members from the same bureaucratic system, there is doubt whether the polls can be fair and effective.

Second, the offices and special commissions which were set up to tighten the congresses' external links to party committees or to strengthen their internal functions, were not able to push the party congresses up to the "leading" position. On the contrary, the arrangement disclosed the truth that the congresses were still in a "subordinate" position even after the reform. In nearly all cases, the offices which were responsible for connecting the party congresses to the party committees and the grassroots party members were set subordinate to the party committee's organisation department, or were inside a party congress but under the *shuangchong lingdao* [double leadership] of both the party congress and the party committee's organisation department. This bureaucratised *ke*-level unit enabled the party committee to directly monitor all aspects of the party congress including the communications between the party congress and grassroots party members. The special commissions are without exception the same. In Yucheng District, for example, the inspection commission of the party congress was also directly subordinate to the party committee's disciplinary department. The organisation commission and the consultation commission were respectively under the party committee's organisation department and the party committee's research institute. Such an arrangement was obviously problematic. These commissions, which were set up inside the party congress but supervised and managed by the party committee, could expose any of the "leading" and "inspecting" activities of the party congress to the power holders. The seemingly "greater communications" between a party congress and a party committee actually put the party congress in a more dependent status, which further weakened its capability in fulfilling its duties. The problems were not only in the reform of the congress structure but also in the party congress members' political participation. The reform aimed to guarantee the party congress members' rights of raising motions and inspecting cadres. To accomplish these tasks, there must be tight links and sufficient communications between the party congress members. However, "small factions" and "colluding behaviour" are a "disciplinary offence" according to *The Party Constitution* and other party laws and thus are strictly prohibited.[29] Based on the above analysis, the party's organisation system (including the reformed party congress system) and the party's rule which prohibits and punishes "small factions" and "colluding behaviour" actually deprive the party congress members of their rights in local political activities. Even worse, if some inner-party dissenters insist on their rights, they may possibly be exposed to the danger of suffering revenge from the power holders because of the organisation system and rule. As some party researchers cautiously point out in a report, "after the field research, we feel that the party congress reform will finally be at an impasse, no matter how it is perfected" (Social Science Academy of Sichuan Province, 2004). The criticisms from other party theorists are more direct, "the reform [the permanent tenure system of party congresses] is meaningless unless it is supported by other more comprehensive reforms in the party's power structure.... The 'inner-party democracy' should begin from the reform of the cadre-management system" (Zhang Shulin, 2007b). In my view, these minor unimportant changes made by the party in the structure and working procedure of its congresses make the reform more like propaganda. They will definitely not achieve the goal of "separation of power" inside the party.

Third, even if the reform did genuinely strengthen the power of the party congress in local affairs, it could possibly reduce the power of the local people's congresses, which theoretically and practically represent a much wider range of the grassroots people.[30] In reality, the proposals party congress members raised and discussed at the annual meetings involved more non-party affairs rather than inner-party issues. In the annual meetings of the party congresses at Yucheng District and Xingjing County, for example, the proposals regarding inner-party issues accounted for only thirty-one percent and fourteen percent of all received proposals (Sheng Ruowei, 2008). In Baixia District, Nanjing City, Jiangsu Province, a highlighted reform case was that a party congress member raised a proposal regarding the problem of illegal parking in a street and urged the local authority to solve it (Xu Jiling, Guo Bensheng, 2008). Even though it has been a fact in China that the party's power can intervene in any context, it is definitely a negative signal that such intervening is theoretically justified under the name of inner-party reform. In addition, it is sad that party researchers are blind to this blurring of roles. In order to push forward party congress reform, some party theorists have proposed to utilize the resources of the people's congress system. According to them, "the party should learn to carry out its work inside the people's congress, changing the 'invisible influence' to the 'visible influence.' [The party] should set a permanent agent inside the people's congress to integrate these two systems. . . . [The party] should make policies to encourage party congress members to be elected as people's congress members, thus they can fully demonstrate the party congress members' good characteristics of advancement and representation" (Social Science Academy of Sichuan Province, 2004). While such a policy may strengthen the party congresses, it could also simultaneously weaken the people's congress system. Such a reform of "inner-party" democracy will not pave a way for China's political democratisation; on the contrary, it will hinder that from happening.

Fourth, tax payers have to pay more for "the permanent tenure system of party congresses" reform. In China's party-state political system, national and local revenue covers all expenses of the party. The party congress reform, which involves holding annual plenary meetings, establishing extra offices and commissions and organising more activities for party congress members, will certainly cause a heavier financial burden on the taxpayers. This problem is more serious in the under-developed rural townships where the peasants have already found it difficult to support the large, inefficient or even corrupted bureaucratic systems. The illegitimacy of China's party-state regime makes it illogical that the taxpayers pay the party's bill, especially when the bill is incurred by a reform which has no effect beyond propaganda.

Impacts and Prospects of the Reform

The party congress reform (or the reform called "the permanent tenure system of party congresses"), which aimed to decentralise the power of local party leaders but had its specific measures designed by the local party leaders and the whole process monitored and controlled by the local party leaders, has not been able to achieve the goal of "decentralising power" inside the party. On the other hand, the reform was carried out to liberalise parts of the whole party's power structure but it was not a component of a complete set of structural reforms so there were no other corresponding coordinated reform policies which could provide support for it. Under such circumstances, the party congress reform has not been very effective. Like the reform of "direct elections" for township party secretaries, discussed in chapter 3, there has been no theoretical or factual evidence to prove that such an inner-party reform, even if it could really achieve the goal of democratising the party system, might pave a way for China's political democratisation. In fact, the "democratisation" of an authoritarian ruling party has no relationship to the nation's democratisation, even if it has a huge number of members. On the contrary, as Linz stated, democratisation of an authoritarian party may possibly revitalise the party and extend its authoritarian rule (Linz, 1999:8). One possible trend of the party congress reform, which was suggested by some party theorists, may provide support for Linz's statement. That is, if the "democratised" and strengthened party congress system intervenes in more non-party affairs and even takes over the power of the people's congress system,[31] the party's authoritarian rule over China will be extended and China's democratisation will be delayed.

Notes

1. There are various English translations of *dangdaihui changrenzhi*, such as "the system of party congresses with a fixed term," "the system of permanent party congress," "permanent membership of party congress," "permanent in-house democracy mechanism" etc. The term adopted in this book, "the permanent tenure system of party congresses," was from the organ of the central party (Ouyang Song, 2007).

2. As this reform is comparatively less-known than the party's election reform in chapter 3, part 1 of this chapter will introduce some details of the reform contents before other information such as its origin, party theorists' arguments and the central party's attitudes are provided. Such a writing order may let the readers have an instant image of the reform so they will not get confused while reading other contents of this chapter. The specific reform measures will be fully discussed in the third part of this chapter.

3. "Relevant institutions" here refers to the various offices and commissions established within a local party congress.

4. Why Mao Zedong had an interest in the reform to strengthen party congresses and whether he had the true reform intention are questions in the area of the party's historical studies. The questions are not within the research scope of this book.

5. This means that a party congress exists and can play its role not only at the time of its plenary meetings, but at any time after it is formed and before a new party congress is elected. In practice, however, it was simplified to holding the plenary meetings annually (in contrast to only one plenary meeting being held immediately after the congress is just elected).

6. The party uses the term "democratic centralism" in its propaganda documents. In *The Party Constitution* "democratic centralism" is the party's fundamental organisational principle, which is explained as "a combination of centralism on the basis of democracy and democracy under centralised guidance" (CCP, 2002b). In practice, however, the power framework inside the party has been constructed to "ensure concerted action in the whole Party and prompt an effective implementation of its decisions" (CCP, 2002b). The centralism is excessively magnified while the democracy is always neglected and becomes empty talk.

7. "The lower party organisations are subordinate to the higher party organisations" is found in article 10 of *The Party Constitution* (CCP, 2002b).

8. The advocates of party congress reform especially hold such a view. For example, Wang Changjiang, a senior party theorist from the Central Party School, expressed such an opinion in his article (Wang Changjiang, 2009). Zhang Shulin, senior party theorist from *The People's Daily*, stated this view as well (Zhang Shulin, 2007b).

9. As the people's congresses are tightly controlled by the party, the people's congress members can hardly represent people's will too. Compared with the party congress members, however, they normally keep a "closer" relationship with the masses.

10. Even at the meeting, the elections as well as other political activities, as analysed on p. 60, are controlled by the party committee.

11. The most important one is *The Regulations for Protecting the CCP Members' Rights* (CCP, 2004c).

12. The twelve localities were (1) Jiaojiang Distrct, Taizhou City, Zhejiang Province, (2) Shaoxing City, Zhejiang Province, (3) Yongjia County, Zhejiang Province, (4) Rui'an

City, Zhejiang Province, (5) Lindian County, Heilongjiang Province, (6) Zhaodong City, Heilongjiang Province, (7) Mine Distrct, Datong City, Shanxi Province, (8) Hongdong County, Shanxi Province, (9) Yuci Distrct, Jinzhong City, Shanxi Province, (10) Heshun County, Shanxi Province, (11) Xinji City, Hebei Province, and (12) Hengshan County, Hunan Province.

13. The five localities where the experiments still went on were (1) Jiaojiang Distrct, Taizhou City, Zhejiang Province, (2) Shaoxing City, Zhejiang Province, (3) Rui'an City, Zhejiang Province, (4) Yuci Distrct, Jinzhong City, Shanxi Province, and (5) Heshun County, Shanxi Province.

14. Please refer to the information on pp. 57–58 regarding the central party's attitudes to the reform.

15. The experimental localities were nearly twenty counties, districts and cities of Sichuan Province, such as Xingjing County of Ya'an City, Yucheng District of Ya'an City, Da'an District of Zigong City, and Meishan City etc. Some localities in other provinces were Rushan City in Shandong Province, Shilou County in Shanxi Province, Xiangzhou County in Guangxi Zhuang Autonomous Region, Bao'an Distrct of Shenzhen City in Guangdong Province, Yangdong County of Yangjiang City in Guangdong Province, Huizhou City in Guangdong Province, Yidu City in Hubei Province, Luotian County in Hubei Province, Sheyang County in Jiangsu Province, Suining County in Jiangsu Province, Qindu District of Xianyang City in Shannxi Province etc.

16. In 2005, the experiments began in Xiangshui Township, Wanzhou District, Chongqing Municipality, and in Townships of Jiangping, Malu and Dongxing in Dongxing City, Guangxi Zhuang Autonomous region.

17. Due to the lack of first-hand data, the book uses the information which was collected from the existing documents including news reports and research papers. Most of the documents focus on individual cases or on certain kinds of reform measures and they provide enough factual evidence for in-depth and integrated research on the reform.

18. The time when the election reform happened in Jiaojiang District cannot be found from the existing documents.

19. The election organisers (local party committee) checked the candidates' qualifications.

20. Normally the party's institutions and governmental departments form an electorate and the cadres voted in this electorate to ensure that the party leaders win the party congress seats.

21. According to the party's organisation "principle," the party congress members elect the party committee and the party committee members elect the party committee secretaries. If this principle really operated, a party committee secretary must be an elected party congress member first and then an elected party committee member. However, the true situation is that the congress is a rubber stamp, the elections are meaningless and the party committee secretaries and committee members are all appointed by the higher-levels. In such a situation, to adhere to the above-mentioned "principle" means that the party secretaries appointed by the higher-levels "must be elected" as the members of the party congress and then the members of the party committee. Accordingly, the traditional party election system was designed to guarantee a local party secretary wins the elections. Considering this, an incumbent party committee secretary losing his membership in the local party congress greatly endangers his/her political career. It was said that the township party secretary in Xingjing County was probably the first party secretary who failed the election for party congress members in the CCP's history. Most ironically, before the experimental elections were held, the local party committees of Yucheng District and Xingjing County had taken pre-cautionary measures to prevent this from happening. The party congresses in these two localities respectively approved and published their

"provisional election method," saying "normally the party members should elect these county/district party committee members and disciplinary committee members as party congress members" (Research Team of the Organization Department of the CCP Committee of Sichuan Province, 2003).

22. The exact information about how the electorates were divided cannot be obtained from the existing documents.

23. Article 13 of *The Ordinance of the CCP's Local Organisational and Electoral Work* (CCP, 1994) and Article 9 of *The Provisional Ordinance of the CCP's Organisational and Electoral Work at the Primary Level* (CCP, 1990).

24. The rest are the local elites who do not work in a party or governmental department but have close connections with the bureaucratic system.

25. The townships in Shanghai Municipality were Ganxiang Township, Huajing Township, Wujiaochang Township, Gaoxing Township, Beicai Township, Qibao Township, Tongjing Township, Liugang Township, Zhaoxiang Township, Liuzao Township (He Jianping, Zhu Shuiqing, Ren Xueping, 2007).

26. The methods in other cases cannot be found from the existing documents.

27. In a case, around two hundred party members applied but only twenty were approved. http://www.zjwldj.gov.cn/shownews.asp?auto_id=1686.

28. The laws include *The Party Constitution, The Ordinance of the CCP's Local Organisational and Electoral Work, The Method of the Party's Local Committee Voting on the Candidates of the Chief Leaders of Its Direct Subordinate Party committee or Government, The Ordinance for Electing or Appointing Party and Government Cadres*, and *The Provisional Regulations for the Open Selection of the Party and Government Cadres* etc.(CCP, 1994, 2002a, 2002b, 2004a, 2004b).

29. Article 3 of *The Party Constitution* clarifies that one of the duties party members must fulfil is to "uphold the party's solidarity and unity . . . firmly oppose all factions and small-clique activities" (CCP, 2002b).

30. In reality, the people's congress system is thoroughly controlled by the party so it does not function as described in the constitution. However, compared with the party congress system, it represents a wider range of people and should have more power.

31. At the current stage, I find no evidence to prove that the existing experiments will lead to democratisation of the party congress system so "the trend of the party congress reform" and "the democratised and strengthened party congress system" are just a hypothesis. In fact, the current situation is worse than that in the hypothesis. A few party leaders or even only party secretary, who hold the centralised power, are intervening in any contexts and taking over the power of the people's congress.

Chapter 5

The Experiments with "Deliberative Democracy"

Introduction

Apart from "inner-party democracy," "deliberative democracy"[1] is another term which frequently appears in the Chinese Communist Party's propaganda materials. Some kinds of government reform experiments are labelled "deliberative democracy" and the party has boasted that such reforms have pushed China's political modernisation ahead. This chapter studies both western deliberative democracy and some important "deliberative democracy" experiments in China. Focused on its definitions and conceptions, the first part of this chapter introduces deliberative democracy in western political science. This part also tries to examine Chinese "deliberative democracy." Based on the comparison of the deliberative democracy in the two different contexts, the first part of this chapter discovers how the deliberative democracy theory is modified in China and why it is so prioritised by the party in its propaganda for "political reform." In the second part, the chapter studies five reform experiments in local township governments and people's congresses in Zhejiang Province, which are believed to be good examples and the most successful and influential cases of Chinese "deliberative institutions." In this case study part, such important factors of the experiments as the motivations, organisers, procedures, results and effects are examined. A general evaluation of the cases is made based on the analysis in this part. The third part researches some other local government reforms which are claimed by party theorists as forms of "deliberative democracy." The case studies in the second and third parts aims to allow the Chinese "deliberative democracy" to be understood from an evidence-based viewpoint. In the last part, a commentary conclusion is made on the basis of the previous analysis. This chapter will provide scholars with an appropriate basis from which they are able to evaluate the prospect of Chinese "deliberative democracy" as well as its possible impacts on China's political development.

A Brief Introduction to Western Deliberative Democracy Theories

Western theories of deliberative democracy have developed at a time when many in the west feel that the institutions of liberal democracy have become divorced from the premises of classical democratic theory. As a critique of liberal democracy, deliberative democracy usually presents principles to renew the deliberative project and practices to deepen democracy (He, 2006b:1). Deliberative democracy has been developed in Western countries within the context of some particular social problems, such as moral conflicts in multicultural societies, and the erosion of the citizenry's participation in public decision-making caused by the inequality of informational resources available to various racial and cultural groups. Most importantly, deliberative democracy is a theory attempting to remedy the institutional limits of electoral politics. It has emerged as a response to the limits of democracy advanced by representative democracy and proposes solutions for the legitimacy deficits produced by aggregative policies (Chen Shengyong, 2006a:162).

Since the theory emerged in the 1990s, western political researchers have explained deliberative democracy from different aspects. The elementary and commonly-accepted characteristics of such democracy are the following: (1) deliberative democracy is a democratic institution committed to a rational form of decision making, (2) decisions are made through a collective pursuit of discussion and deliberation, (3) the aim is to make important public policies, (4) participants in deliberative democracy are equal individuals, (5) they can express their opinions freely in discussion or deliberation, (6) they are willing to listen to opposing views, meaning they can finally pursue and realise applicable solutions that take into consideration personal preferences as well as the collective interests of the public (Gutmann & Thompson, 2004; Miller, 1992:74–92; Valadez, 2000).

The Party's Theory of "Deliberative Democracy"

In recent years, the party theorists claimed that deliberative democracy was an important component of "socialist democracy with Chinese characteristics" and was an "efficient" path to the "harmonious society."[2] In many of their articles, they strongly argued that there should be "deliberative democracy" in Chinese politics. Chinese "deliberative democracy," which was interpreted by the theorists in the context of the authoritarian politics, has added some "strange" meanings. "Deliberative democracy" as interpreted by party theorists has some features including:

First, according to these theorists, there must be an authoritarian organiser for Chinese "deliberative democracy," which can unify the different viewpoints in the deliberation and then make scientific and correct policies. The organiser must be the Chinese Communist Party because it is the ruling party with authoritarian power and it represents the interest of the whole nation rather than particular social classes or interest groups (Li Junru, 2006c, 2006d). More bluntly, "deliberative democracy in China is a form of democracy under the party's leadership" (Li Junru, 2006d) or the "nature of deliberative democracy is that the citizens participate in political affairs in good order" (Li Junru, 2006e).

Second, it is argued, while deliberative democracy still remains an academic theory in western countries, a form of "deliberative democracy" has been established and practised in China for decades (Li Junru, 2006f). The system of multiparty cooperation and political consultation, which is a basic political policy of China, is a form of "deliberative democracy." The Chinese People's Political Consultative Conference (CPPCC) is a "deliberative democracy" institution (Li Junru, 2005). The theorists believed that it is impossible to organise deliberation among the lay citizens in such a populous country as China. In their opinion, the CPPCC members, who are "vastly representative," can "directly and equally participate in deliberation." Therefore, according to the theorists, the CPPCC is a practical method to achieve Chinese-style "deliberative democracy" (Li Junru, 2005, 2006b). In the 1980s and 1990s when the westerners had just began their academic research on this kind of democracy, the Chinese people had already had some good experience but "we just did not study them" (Li Junru, 2006d).

Third, it is claimed, Chinese "deliberative democracy," which started in the 1940s, legitimated the regime of the People's Republic of China. More importantly, it is now leading China into a "harmonious society" (Chen Jiagang, 2007; Li Junru, 2006d). "The merits of the system of multi-party cooperation and political consultation under the party's leadership strongly proves that adopting such a form of [deliberative] democracy guarantees both democracy and unity, enabling harmony to be achieved between the various political parties, ethnic groups, social classes, Chinese communities at home or overseas, and thus keeps the solidarity of the whole society" (Li Junru, 2005).

Fourth, it is suggested, that although both electoral democracy (the voting system) and deliberative democracy should be improved in China, electoral democracy, which is an icon of western liberal democracy, has some obvious defects.[3] "Electoral democracy in western countries is the game played by only wealthy people" (Li Junru, 2006e). "The lay citizens who are not financially advantaged can vote but cannot participate in public administration after the voting . . . electoral democracy is unable to solve the conflicts existing in a multicultural society" (Li Junru, 2005, 2006e). "Western electoral democracy does not really guarantee the citizens' political rights or democratic politics [in these countries] (Li Junru, 2006a, 2006d, 2006f).

Fifth, it is posited, "to end the deficiencies of electoral democracy, we [the party] will combine electoral democracy and deliberative democracy to form 'socialist democracy with Chinese characteristics,' which shows the advantage of 'Chinese democratic politics'" (Li Junru, 2006f). It is argued that "in the U.S.A., the citizens have no rights to participate in policy-making after the elections, and all public policies are made by the politicians. In China, while having electoral democracy, we [the party] adopt deliberative democracy. That means, the citizens can discuss the subjects or candidates before voting and can evaluate the effects after voting" (Li Junru, 2006f). It is claimed that "in fact, some important public policies were initiated in the deliberative democracy in China in recent years" (Li Junru, 2006f). It is also argued that "the party, people's congresses and governments all attach importance to the proposals made by the CPPCC" and "the prospect of democracy in China is bright" (Li Junru, 2006f). According to the theorists, "perhaps they [the Americans] are despising our democracy [socialist democracy with Chinese characteristics] now, but when we accomplish building up our political system [the system combining electoral democracy and deliberative democracy], it will be superior to the American political system" (Li Junru, 2006a). The theorists also stated that "we [the Chinese people] must have confidence in our own political system and we can create a form of democracy which will contribute more [than western democracy] to human beings and we are actually doing it now" (Li Junru, 2006d).

Brief Comments of the Chinese "Deliberative Democracy" Theory

Democracy Cannot be "Under the Leadership" or "In Good Order"

First, it is difficult to understand how deliberative democracy or any other forms of democracy can be practised if it must be "under the leadership of an authoritarian political party." In fact, the party makes the final decision after the deliberation because it holds absolute power. Thus, the process and result of a deliberation seem not to be very important because the process has to be "in good order" and the leaders can choose to ignore the deliberation result when making a decision. Such a feature of Chinese "deliberative democracy" being "under the party's leadership" and "in good order" guarantees that such form of "democracy" will not have any impact on the party's authoritarian position.

The CPPCC System Is Not a Kind of Deliberative Democracy

Second, the system of the people's political consultative conference, a bigger "rubber stamp" than the people's congress system, has its members appointed or examined by the party.[4] The political consultative conference at various levels is made up of the "elites" from some social groups. Among them, some even "inherited" the title from their parents (Renminwang, 2008). The CPPCC is actually an elite organisation which relies on the party and is tightly controlled by the party. It is different from a deliberative democracy institution, which, according to western political scientists, should be a group of "equal individuals" who can "freely express their opinions."

A Genuine Voting System Is Much More Important Than "Deliberative Democracy" for Chinese Politics at the Current Stage

Even though Li Junru brushed over "perfecting" the voting system in some of his articles promoting "deliberative democracy" in China, he gave top priority to developing "deliberative democracy" in China. Li criticised the deficiencies of electoral democracy in western countries and boasted that the "democracy" created in China combines "deliberative democracy" with "electoral democracy" and is superior to western democracy. In fact, the party refuses to adopt a genuine voting system in every sphere of Chinese politics. It even intervenes in and controls the direct elections for people's congresses at the most primary level.[5] Although Li has theoretically confirmed that the voting system and "deliberative democracy" are compatible in China's politics, some party theorists even insist that "deliberative democracy" is the only route to China's democratisation. For example, in an article, it was stated that "with the establishment of the market economy, the society pluralized and interest groups came into being. The social and political foundation for non-competitive democracy[6] weakens while the foundation for competitive and deliberative democracy strengthened. The choice will have to be made between competitive democracy and deliberative democracy." According to the author, in order to maintain "the nature of the socialist system," "the party's leadership" and the "efficiency of democracy"[7] and to avoid "pluralism in China's politics," "deliberative democracy" is the best choice because it is less competitive than the voting system or so called electoral democracy (Lin Shangli, 2006:69–70). Another researcher Chen Shengyong criticised Chinese voters' "low capability" as the reason for not adopting "aggregative democracy" or "competitive elections" in China:

> China lacks any robust democratic tradition. The culture of abiding by the law, behaving oneself, and respecting authority and hierarchy has been ingrained through thousands of years of despotism and power worship. Furthermore, the state has had complete control of public policy. Consequently, the social public sphere and the citizenry's capacity for criticism has not been developed. Two results have ensued: first, there is a severe absence of the citizenry's sense of independence and political responsibility. Second, even where there are opportunities for active citizenship, there is a low degree of public participation in politics. Thus, the proportion of the citizenry voluntarily participating in national political affairs is quite low. Even one of the most important opportunities for a contemporary Chinese citizen's political participation—the villagers' political participation in the vast rural area of the mid-western provinces of

> China—is routinely subverted by a mobilization style of political participation, in which local government and local organs, through compulsion and material incentive, guarantee a villager's participation. Accordingly, the participation is often initiated—notwithstanding village elections—thoroughly by CCP and government officials and not by villagers' independent volition. Therefore, it remains true that there are few social, political, and psychological foundations that promote the nascent competitive electoral democracy in China. It is not surprising, then, that many remain suspicious of aggregative democracy (Chen Shengyong, 2006a:162–163).

In the Chinese-version of this article, Chen added the following:

> Competitive electoral democracy should not be established in China at the current stage because there is no political, social and psychological foundation for it. Otherwise, the vast range of political mobilization may quite possibly lead to the "tyranny of the majority." The "Cultural Revolution" and Taiwanese-style "populism" just give us a good lesson (Chen Shengyong, 2006b:81).

Denying the feasibility of electoral democracy in China, Chen claimed that "it is essential for China to implement some forms of deliberative democracy" (Chen Shengyong, 2006a:163).[8]

Also in this article, Chen Shengyong defined deliberative democracy as "a theory attempting to remedy the institutional limits of electoral politics" and stated that "it has emerged as a response to the limits of democracy advanced by representative democracy and proposes solutions for the legitimacy deficits produced by aggregative policies" (Chen Shengyong, 2006a:162). This definition and the above-mentioned conclusions in one academic paper (Chen Shengyong, 2006a) are logically contradictory. If genuine "electoral politics" or "representative democracy" has been abandoned in China just as the researcher suggested, there is no foundation for deliberative democracy. In China, when there is the sheer authoritarian politics but not the "institutional limits" or "legitimacy deficits" of electoral politics, can deliberative democracy still "remedy" or "solve" the problem? For China's politics, building up a genuine voting system, which is the most primary framework of a democratic polity, is much more important than conducting "deliberative democracy" at the current stage. To delay or deny it will make other forms of "democracy" ineffective and meaningless.

The Party's Intention

Why Prioritise "Deliberative Democracy"?

The party's intention of promoting "deliberative democracy" becomes suspicious when its theorists neglect or even underrate the competitive electoral institutions in China's politics. As a researcher pointed out, "Beijing has used deliberative institutions as a form of moderate democracy to avoid a radical and substantial political reform that would directly challenge the political power of the CCP. It is believed that deliberative institutions are peripheral and marginal, so they do not undermine the power of the CCP" (He, 2006b:178). In such a condition, the ultimate purpose of the "democratic reform" for the party is to strengthen its power and stabilise its rule. The party strongly promotes the theory of "deliberative democracy" while it tries to confuse the criteria of democracy and to ignore the most efficient method to achieve democratisation. Very probably, the party just utilises the "fashionable" theory of "deliberative democracy" and just creates an opportunity to conduct propaganda among the citizens about the party's "achievements in political reform."

He Baogang positively speculates about the party's motives. He believes that the party tries to "reduce social protest and strengthen the government's ruling capacities." According to He, the power holders conducted the political experiments of deliberative institutions because they discovered that deliberative democracy "has solved community-related problems, avoided major mistakes in public policymaking, and saved money, personnel, and time in governing local affairs, thereby reducing the number of the people's petitions and complaints" (He, 2006b:178).[9] The effects of "deliberative democracy" will be examined by case studies in the second and third part of this chapter to check if He's statement about the party's motives is correct.

Researcher's View about the Local Power Holders' Motives and the Demands of the Private Sector

In He Baogang's article, the local power holders pushed the development of deliberative institutions because "they aim to achieve a genuine consensus so as to gain legitimacy for certain policies, to reduce social conflicts, and even to win personal honour." Some local power holders "see deliberative institutions as an effective tool to bring about democratic management and monitoring." Some of them "are under great pressure to introduce these institutions to ease the tension between the cadres and the masses." According to He, "political achievement is also an important motivation for local leaders." When they were awarded some prizes or were promoted in their political career, "they continue to develop and improve the existing institutions." In contrast, some local power holders "pressured from above to introduce similar deliberative institutions felt they could not achieve anything new. They lacked strong incentives, and the deliberative institutions in place in those localities are only a formality." In addition, "private businessmen and interest groups desire to express their voices about public policies that affect their economic life. As a result, consultative meetings and other institutions are organised in response to the demand from the private sector" (He, 2006b:178–179). These statements on local power holders' motives will be examined with case studies in the following part.

The Central Party is Still Cautious Towards Western Theory

Interestingly, the central party still refuses to use the term *xieshang minzhu* [deliberative democracy] in its official documents, even when it tries to express its "reform strategies" which do not differ from the party theorists' "deliberative democracy." For example, Party General-Secretary Hu Jintao said in his report to the Party 17th National Congress, "improve the system of political consultation, democratic oversight, and participation in the deliberation and administration of state affairs. We will incorporate political consultation in decision-making procedures. . . . To ensure scientific and democratic decision-making, we will improve the information and intellectual support for it, increase its transparency and expand public participation in it. In principle, public hearings must be held for the formulation of laws, regulations and policies that bear closely on the interests of the public." (Hu Jintao, 2007). In two paragraphs of this report to the party's National Congress (perhaps the most important party document), Hu used "political consultation" or "public participation" rather than "deliberative democracy." The central party's reluctance to use the term probably indicates it is still allergic to any forms of democracy which originate from western political theories, even though such a form of "democracy" has been modified to meet the party's favour and has been proven not to have any impact on the party's authoritarian political power.[10]

Five Important Cases in Zhejiang Province[11]

This section examines five "deliberative democracy" experiments in Zhejiang Province, which are the most influential cases and are promoted by the party's top level media such as *The Study Times*, *Renminwang* and *Xinhuawang* (Deng Yuwen, 2006; He Baogang, Lang Youxing, 2008; Jiang Zhaohua, He Baogang, 2005; Zhang Xiaoshan, 2008).

Some detailed information about the time, localities, reform contents and instigators and designers can be seen from Table 5.1 (Zhang Xiaoshan, 2008):

Background of the Five Cases

The "deliberative democracy" experiments were carried out in Wenling City from 1999. At the initial stage, the deliberations were held at the most primary level units such as government departments, villages, and urban communities, in which specific groups of people discussed the issues which were related to their personal interests.[12] In 2004, the Wenling City government won "the local governance innovation award" for the experiments. It then furthered the reform by upgrading the level to the township and expanding the scope of discussing to public affairs. The "deliberative polling" experiments (cases 1 and 2) were held

Table 5.1 Five "Deliberative Democracy" Reform Cases in Wenling City

Experiment	Locality	Time	Contents	Principal Designer and Researcher[13]
Case 1	Zeguo Township, Wenling City, Zhejiang Province	March and April 2005	Deliberative polling on infrastructure projects	He Baogang
Case 2		March and April 2006		
Case 3		February 2008	Deliberation on the government's financial budget	He Baogang
Case 4	Xinhe Township, Wenling City, Zhejiang Province	March 2006	Deliberation within the township people's congress on the government's financial budget	Li Fan
Case 5		April 2007		

under such a background. They were instigated and organised by the party committee of Wenling City (mainly the party's publicity department) and Zeguo Township. He Baogang[14] and some other researchers from both Chinese and overseas academic institutes designed and technically supported the experiments. In 2006, perhaps taking the suggestions from the party's senior research institutes,[15] the local party committee and political researchers sought to transplant "deliberative democracy" into the local people's congress. Therefore, on the basis of the deliberative polling, the "participatory budgeting" experiments were largely conducted in the townships of Wenling City from 2006. There were two different types of participatory budgeting experiments which were held in the township people's congresses of Wenling City,[16] which were respectively case 3 and cases 4 and 5. Case 3 in Zeguo, was designed and technically supported by He Baogang. Cases 4 and 5 in Xinhe, were designed by Li Fan, the director of The World and China Institute (Zhang Xiaoshan, 2008). The details of each case are discussed in the next part.

Main Procedures of the Cases

Selecting participants

In cases 1, 2 and 3, the experiment organisers randomly selected the participants from the local residents.

The method of a lottery was adopted in cases 1 and 2. In case 1, the organisers assigned four seats to each village which had over 1,000 residents and two seats to each village which had less than 1,000 residents. The random selection was held in each village. First, each family was assigned a multi-digit code. All assigned codes contained the same number of digits. Second, there were several opaque boxes. The number of the boxes was same as the number of the digits in the assigned codes. Each opaque box contained ten balls numbered from digit 0 to 9. The organisers randomly picked up one ball from each of the opaque boxes, and then formed the digits on the randomly-picked balls into a code. Third, the family whose assigned code was same as the formed code could put forward an adult as a villagers' representative to participate in the deliberative polling. Fourth, the policy said if the formed code is odd, the participant from the family must be a male and vice versa (Fu Piyi, Yang Jinzhi, Cai Yugao, 2006). However, He Baogang denied the existence of the fourth step and stated in his book that "one departure from deliberative polling as it has been practised elsewhere is that while the Chinese randomly selected households, they allowed the households to select which adult member of the household would participate in the deliberative polling. This resulted in a significant under presentation of women—only 29.9 percent of the participant sample (Fishkin, et al., 2006). Two-hundred and seventy-five participants were finally selected to attend case 1. In case 2, the organisers decided that two representatives out of every 1,000 villagers should be selected from each village to participate in the deliberative polling. In the following procedural steps, the organisers used the same method as that in case 1 to randomly select 237 participants from all villages. Each village had at least one participant and up to five participants were selected from the two most populous villages. In addition to these participants from the villages, the organisers randomly selected twelve representatives from around 150,000 migrants and their families to attend the experiment (He Baogang, 2007).[17]

Case 3 included two parts. In the first session, 197 participants were selected randomly from the registered villager voters to attend a deliberation on the local government's annual budget. Rather than use the lottery method in cases 1 and 2, the experiment organisers used a computer program to select participants in case 3 (Lin Long, Hu Guoqiang, 2008).[18] In addition to them, 95 township congress members were required to attend the deliberation. In the second session, the budget plan was examined, discussed and voted on by the township people's congress members.

In cases 4 and 5, the key session was the deliberation and voting of the government's annual budget, which was held within the township people's congress. Before that session, the experiment organisers designed a deliberation which was attended by a wider range of people. In addition to the local people's congress members, the "representatives" from various social organisations, industries and some lay citizens participated in this deliberation.[19]

Subjects of the Polls or Deliberations

In cases 1 and 2, the local government organised deliberative polling to assess the importance of the planned infrastructural projects and to rank the priorities of the projects so that the most important ones would be carried out to fit the limited budget for the next year. In cases 3, 4 and 5, the deliberations were focused on the next year's budget of the local governments.

Procedure

In cases 1 and 2, several days before the deliberative polling was held, the organisers sent the participants the introduction materials for each planned project. Before the poll, in addition, each participant was asked to complete a questionnaire regarding the importance of the planned projects. On the polling day, the participants were randomly divided into sixteen groups for group discussion.[20] In each group, there was a moderator who was a local high school teacher who had already been trained for the role by the experiment designers. In the group discussion, the participants examined the planned projects,[21] discussed their merits and identified key questions that they wished to ask the experts in the following plenary meeting. The first plenary meeting was held after the first group discussion, in which the participants raised the questions that most concerned them and presented the agreed opinions from the group discussion. Then the group discussion and plenary meeting were held once again. In both plenary meetings, the experts in project management responded to the participants' enquiries with their professional knowledge. All local government cadres listened to the two plenary sessions. After the discussions, the participants did the same questionnaires again. This process provided a before and after comparison for the same sample. In case 1, the survey data from the questionnaires completed after the deliberation session were then put into a computer to be processed and the projects were priority-rated. The deliberation result was presented to the township people's congress meeting which was held afterwards. The people's congress members approved the twelve top-prioritised projects to be carried out in the year.[22] In the existing documents, the deliberation procedure in case 2 was similar to the one in case 1,[23] but such information as how the deliberation result was formed and whether and how it affected the final policy making cannot be obtained from the existing documents.[24]

In the first session of case 3, one-hundred and seventy-eight villager representatives were divided into thirteen groups to discuss the government's annual budget.[25] A plenary meeting was held for the participants to present the agreed opinions from the group discussion. Some township cadres answered the questions raised by the villager representatives and debated with them over some budgetary issues. "Many representatives were excited in the debate. They examined the numbers in the government's budget plan and threw some sharp questions to the cadres" (Lin Long, Hu Guoqiang, 2008). Sixty-five township congress members listened to this deliberation session.[26] The designer thought it provided a good opportunity for the congress members to understand public opinion and thus form their viewpoints to the budget plan in the following deliberation session held within the township people's congress. A congress member said, "both the keen awareness and the courage of the villager representatives impressed us greatly. We felt the pressure and we must try our best to fulfil our tasks [voice the voters' opinions] at the people's congress" (Lin Long, Hu Guoqiang, 2008). As in case 1, the villager representatives were asked to complete an identical questionnaire before and after the deliberation to provide data for the comparative studies of their changed attitudes. However, different from the cases 1 and 2 in which a clear deliberation result was obtained that all planned infrastructure projects were priority-rated, the survey data from the questionnaires in case 3 could only "be the basis of policy-making" (He Baogang, 2008a). The second session of case 3 was the examination and voting on the budget plan in the township congress, which was a decisive step in the whole procedure. Therefore, how the result of session 1 affected session 2 remains questionable. In an interview, when He Baogang was asked about it, he expressed that there were two ways the first session affected the second one. First, the sixty-five congress members listened to the deliberation in session 1 so they could understand better what the villagers thought of the budget plan.[27] Second, the result of deliberation was composed into a report which would be viewed and discussed by the congress members in session 2. The second session of case 3 was the deliberation held within the township people's congress. In a congress examination of the government's annual budget plan, according to a report which was held before, the congress members "normally remained silent or expressed supportive views because they lacked financial knowledge or got the plan just at the conference so had little time to read it." In that case, "it was the few township leaders that made the budget plan and all congress members could do nothing but raise their hands to agree it" (Lin Long, Hu Guoqiang, 2008). In the congress session of case 3, however, the congress had all congress members trained by two financial experts on how to fulfil a congress member's responsibility to examine government's budget plan. The budget plan was distributed to the congress members earlier than before and the congress members proposed more than thirty critical suggestions to the government regarding the plan. At the congress's budget examination conference, the congress members debated with the government cadres over the budget plan and the proposed suggestions (including those from the deliberation in session 1). The plan was then amended on the basis of some suggestions from congress members. In the voting process, 60 members voted for the budget plan, 28 voted against, and 5 abstained. The affirmative votes were only six more than the minimum votes needed for passing a proposal,[28] which "shivered the township cadres" because "never has such a case happened in China that the government's budget plan was rejected by a people's congress" (Lin Long, Hu Guoqiang, 2008).

The reform experiments in cases 4 and 5 happened mainly inside the People's Congress of Xinhe Township. In both cases 4 and 5, the organisers arranged a deliberation meeting prior to the congress session, which allowed the lay citizens to participate. The participants of this session, however, were still mainly made up of the township congress members. Even though there were some non-congress participants, they were obviously the social elites (note 19 shows the details). The participants were divided into three groups, representing respectively industry, agriculture and society, to discuss the budget of the related subjects. In case 4, the township government did not send officials to attend the discussion because "the government hoped the participants would feel free to express their opinions" (Li Fan, 2007). In case 5, some government officials attended the group discussions and responded to the participants' enquiries.[29] The organisers of the deliberation meeting then formed a report based on the deliberation results. For example, the meeting report in case 4 contained fifty-six suggested amendments from the meeting participants. The report was then submitted to the township congress. In cases 4 and 5, the examination of the budget inside the congress was a key session. There were five steps in this congress session. First, the congress members examined the budget plan, questioned the related government officials about "suspicious" items and the officials made explanations. The suggestions proposed by the congress members, combined with the suggestions from the previous "outside-congress deliberation meeting" were all sent to the township government. Second, a joint meeting was held, in which the township party committee, government and people's congress leaders discussed the suggestions and made amendments to the budget plan. Third, the congress members examined and discussed the amended budget plan and debated with government officials over these controversial items. Fourth, five congress members or more could jointly make proposed amendments. The congress presidium checked the proposals and "selected" the "eligible ones" to be voted at the congress (Jiang Yun, 2007; Li Fan, 2007).[30] The amended proposals supported by the majority of the congress members had to be carried out. Fifth, the final amended budget plan[31] was voted by the congress. In case 4, the congress members voted in steps 4 and 5 by raising their hands. All congress members raised hands supporting the two amended proposals in step 4 and the amended budget plan in step 5 (Li Fan, 2007:61). In case 5, the voters cast votes instead of raising hands. In step 4, 100 congress members voted for the amendment proposal, while one was against it. In step 5, there were 94 affirmative votes, 2 negative votes and 1 abstention (Jiang Yun, 2007; Sui Binbin, 2008a:30).

Result

The results of these "deliberative democracy" experiments perhaps could express people's will more than before. In case 1, out of the thirty planned infrastructural projects, the government had to carry out the twelve ones which were most highly prioritised in the deliberative polling. Such powers used to be grabbed by the local power holders and the whole decision-making process was normally in a black box. The polling result also reminded the government officials that their ability to "represent the people's will" was weak. In that case, none of the five street reconstruction projects, which the government used to believe the most desirable ones by the citizens, was able to come into the top ten. One environmental project, which the government thought would be lowly prioritised because it had no direct relationship with people's life and would not be in effect in a short time, was ranked the second most important (Jiang Zhaohua, He Baogang, 2005). Case 2 was worse than case 1 in carrying out the deliberation result but most top-prioritised projects were still done by government, as described in note 24. In case 3, some changes were made in the final budget plan according to the suggestions of the citizen representatives and congress members. Budgeted items such as the financial subsidy for the local police were cut back, while the allowance for widowed and childless aged people was increased. The funds for building a township square were transferred to a school playground project (Chan Kenneth Ka Lok, 2008). In case 4, some amendments to the budget plan made in the second step of the congress session (steps were described in the paragraph on p. 85) included transferring the funds for the environment protection bureau's new office building to a waste-yard project, increasing the budget of such projects as sewage disposal and old street construction, and reducing the budget for a tourism project construction (Hu Nianfei, 2006). In the fourth step, the budget plan was amended according to the two congress-approved proposals: transferring part of the "birth-control" budget to the villages' public security and reducing the budget reserve[32] to increase the budget for garbage collection (Hu Nianfei, 2006). Case 5 resulted in some amendments of the budget plan, which were made on the basis of the suggestions from the congress. The changes included increasing the social welfare budget and reducing the government administration cost (Sui Binbin, 2008a:30).

Analysis and Commentary Conclusion

There are some improvements in the process of these experiments.

In cases 1, 2, and 3, the method used for selecting participants (sampling) was the highlight of the procedure. Random sampling of the population is rare in political reform in China. The analysis indicates "there are not many statistically significant differences between the participants and the whole sample from which they were drawn" so it "implied a statistical equality for everyone in the community" and created "a diverse and representative microcosm" of the whole local community (Fishkin, et al., 2006: 233, 242). In addition, the random sampling delivered a message to the masses that the experiment would be fair and out of the government's control, which in fact promoted the experiment among the citizens (He Baogang, 2008b). In case 1, the organisers randomly selected households and allowed the households to select which adult member of the household to participate in the experiment, which resulted in the under-representation of women. In case 2, the organisers improved the method to the random selection of individual adults, which solved the problem that occurred in case 1. The participants in most "deliberative democracy" experiments (including cases 4 and 5) were appointed by local power holders. The representative level of the participants was questionable in these experiments. Most likely, the deliberation session of these experiments, which were attended by the participants appointed by the local power holders, were "party-manipulated" or at least dominated by political elites.

In cases 3, 4 and 5, the detailed budget plan was a step forward. In most situations, examining annual budget plans in people's congresses was purely a formality. Even though some people's congress members intend to do the budget examination work carefully, they cannot fulfil the task because the budget plan is too simple. A normal budget plan which government presents to the people's congress contains only a few very rough items of expenditure and the expenses. The items are not divided into sub-items, nor is information provided as to why this amount of money is needed and how it will be used. Therefore, the examination of budget plans in congress has to be "empty talk" (Chen Yimin, 2007:37).[33] The budget plan became somewhat detailed in cases 3, 4 and 5. In case 4, fifteen items in the budget plan were divided into 110 sub-items. Taking the item of "government administration" as an example, it was divided into seventeen sub-items and the total of around sixteen million *yuan* in this item was separated into each sub-item, which made it easier for the congress members to examine whether the expenses were necessary and reasonable (Chen Yimin, 2007:37). In case 5, the budget plan was made in a way similar to that of case 4. The plan included sixteen items, which were divided into 76 sub-items with the planned expense for each of them (Government of Xinhe Township, 2007:39–41). The budget plan, which was examined in the people's congress in case 3, seemed to have more details. It was a 48-page document explaining the items, sub-items and the expenses. Li Fan, who was a designer of cases 4 and 5, highly commended the plan as "the most detailed one so far" (He Baogang, 2008a). Even though the budget plans in cases 4 and 5 were much more detailed than the previous ones, they were still not as good as what the congress members expected. In case 5, some congress members complained after the congress meeting that "the sub-items were still too rough so we could not know how these hundreds of thousands or even millions of *yuan* expenses were calculated and how they would be spent" (Wang Na, 2008:73).

Five or more congress members can jointly propose an amendment to the government's budget plan and the amended proposal voted for by the majority of the congress members must be carried out. Designed as the fourth step of the congress session in cases 4 and 5, this is progress towards "procedural justice." However, there were still manipulations in this step which will be discussed in the following part.

The defects of these experiments were obvious and "fatal." With them, the experiments can hardly be deliberative democracy as described by western political science.

First, cases 1, 2 and 3 were highly praised because of their random sampling, fully-developed deliberation and questionnaire survey. However, the big problem in cases 2 and 3 was that the deliberation result was not guaranteed to become the government's final decision. In case 2, the government's final decision was not fully in accord with the deliberation result. Instead, the government added their preference into the decision (details in note 24). In case 3 when the congress role was "strengthened," the result of the deliberation, which was achieved by using such scientific methods as "random sampling," "fully-developed deliberation" and "opinion difference analysis," could be only "public opinions" to which the congress session might refer. Although deliberation sessions were designed in cases 4 and 5, they were less liberal than those in cases 1, 2 and 3. The deliberations in case 4 and 5 abandoned the above-mentioned "deliberative democracy" methods that were adopted in cases 1, 2 and 3. Therefore, cases 4 and 5 were probably not "deliberative democracy" experiments even though they were called so. They were more like a kind of reform inside the people's congress to strengthen their power of monitoring the local government.[34] The deliberation held before the congress session was in fact not important. The defects of the cases are clear now. The experiments designed by He Baogang (cases 1, 2 and 3) were most able to profile public opinion but they could not be transformed into public policies (as in cases 2 and 3) or such a transformation was not institutionalised (as in case 1). In contrast, the experiments designed by Li Fan (cases 4 and 5) were most able to influence the government's public policy with the strengthened congress power but the result of the deliberation held within the congress did not sufficiently reflect the people's will.

Each of the experiments contained a deliberation session (held before the congress session) and the congress session. As shown in Figure 5.1, in cases from 1 to 5, the function of the deliberation session was gradually weakened while the function of the congress session was strengthened.

Figure 5.1 Strength of the Deliberation Session and Congress Session in the Reform Cases

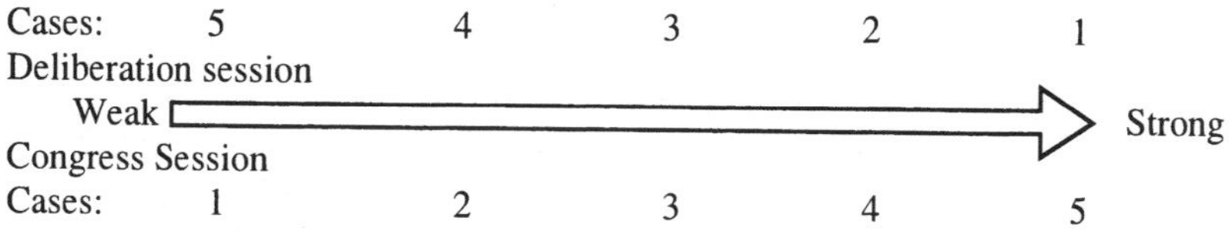

Such a trend could be explained by the party organisation's indication that "deliberative democracy" experiments should be integrated into the local people's congresses.[35] Although He Baogang explained in an interview that the party was to take this opportunity to "revive" the people's congress system, the party's other intention—trying to place political experiments of the masses within the institutionalised political system—is clear. In my opinion, to reform the congress system, the most effective method is to open the congress elections to the public.[36] Without genuine congress elections, the other kinds of people's congress reforms lack incentives. For example, to eliminate the elitism in his designed experiments which received criticism, Li Fan suggested that, besides attending the deliberation session (very weak in his designed experiments as shown in the above figure), the congress members should create opportunities by themselves to meet their voters, listen to their opinions and bring them back to the congress session (Zhang Xiaoshan, 2008). However, if the people's congress members are virtually appointed by the power holders, why would they bother to do that? Even in case 3 which had a deliberation session comparatively stronger than cases 4 and 5, the designer was not allowed to survey the influence of the deliberation session on the people's congress members (details in note 27). Without statistical evidence, it is difficult to examine how effective the party's strategy to "revive" the people's congress system by adopting "deliberative democracy" in and outside the people's congresses. A news report indicated that the local power holders preferred cases 4 and 5 to case 3 and the reform like cases 4 and 5 will be expanded to other townships of Wenling City (Zhang Xiaoshan, 2008). In the field research, several informants revealed to me that the party secretary of Wenling City went to the townships of Zeguo and Xinhe in 2009 to inspect the "deliberative democracy" experiments. It was the first time he did so in five years. After that, in August 2009, the Wenling City Party Committee wrote in its 2010 work plan that "the participatory budget reform, which should be in the form of the Xinhe experiments (cases 4 and 5), shall be carried out in the congress of other townships in the future."[37] He Baogang confirmed in an interview that most future budget reform experiments held in Wenling City (in townships other than Zeguo) would probably abandon those scientific methods such as random sampling, full deliberation and questionnaire survey in the deliberation session,[38] which would make the citizen deliberation session in these experiments become meaningless and the problem of party-control or elitism would remain unsolved in the following congress session.[39]

Second, the reform which was held in the congress session of cases 3, 4 and 5 has the following defects:

First, in step 4 of the congress session of cases 4 and 5, the congress presidium decided that most proposals were ineligible so they refused to have them voted in congress (details in note 30). The main reason to invalidate these proposals, according to the existing documents, was that the congress members failed to balance the budget and the expenses in their proposals (Zhang Xiaoshan, 2008).[40] It was understandable that the congress members had that problem in case 4 when they wrote such amendment proposals for the first time, but it was strange that the same problem arose in case 5, which was designed the same as case 4. In addition, according to an article in which Li Fan summarised the experience gained from case 4, the congress members would receive training on how to write amendment proposals before case 5 (Li Fan, 2007:61). Therefore, it remained questionable why the proportion of the eligible proposals in case 5 (1:16) was four times lower than in case 4 (2:8). The strange phenomenon may easily lead to a suspicion that there were manipulations in this step of experiments 4 and 5. In an interview, an informant confirmed the existence of such manipulation in this step. According to him, in cases 4, 5 and the similar experiments held in Xinhe Township in 2008 and 2009, the presidium of the township people's congress, which was actually the puppet of the township party committee, refused to put forward some of the eligible proposals to be voted on in the congress.[41] The informant revealed that the township party committee manipulated this step to meet their interest. They did not explain why they ignored these proposals or just made an empty promise that "they would consider these 'suggestions' in their future work." According to the informant, the local party secretaries were afraid of "too many" proposals and took measures to "eliminate" those they disliked, which resulted in decreasing the number of the proposals in

2008 and 2009. The informant thought that the experiments held in Xinhe Township in 2008 and 2009 were much worse than those in 2006 and 2007 (cases 4 and 5).[42] Some congress members were furious to know their proposals were "ineligible" and would not be voted on in the congress. In case 5, the congress members from an electorate chose to express their discontent by withdrawing from the congress conference. The township government and party committee leaders ran after the congress members to the outside of the conference venue before they could just manage to persuade the congress members to go back to the conference (Zhang Xiaoshan, 2008). As the informant expressed in an interview, "the biggest defect of the reform experiments in Xinhe Township (cases 4, 5 and the similar experiments held in 2008 and 2009) was that the township party committee refused to get all eligible proposals to be voted on in the people's congress."

Second, even though the power holders set the guidelines for the reform experiments in order to "revive" the people's congresses, they were afraid when they came into being. In an interview, He Baogang revealed that the local power holders felt very uneasy when the congress members showed their power in collective actions in congress, such as withdrawing from the conference in case 5 (details in the above paragraph) and casting negative votes in case 3 (details on p. 84). He Baogang told me in an interview that the local power holders readopted the "raising hand" method[43] in the congress voting in order to avoid too many negative votes in the experiment (in the form similar to case 3) held in Zeguo Township in 2009. A participant revealed in an interview that the power holders in case 5 changed the method from secret voting to "raising hands" immediately after some congress members threatened to withdraw from the conference and they kept using the "raising hands" method in the similar experiments held in Xinhe Township in the following years. He said the experiment organisers did not consult him about changing the method. An explanation from a local cadre for using the "raising hands" method was that "some people's congress members had too strong personal feelings when casting a vote. They could vote against the government's budget plan just because the local people's congress (actually the party, government) did not treat them to a good lunch" at the noon of the conference day. In an interview, the local cadre emphasised the importance of "controllability" in the "deliberative democracy" reform. He expressed that the local reformists tried to "depoliticise" the reform experiments to reduce the "political risk." Under such a guideline, the party actually met with every congress member before the voting. In the meetings, the party enquired about the congress members' voting intention, resolving the conflicts between the congress members from different interest groups, "persuading" (or perhaps luring or threatening) them to vote for the final budget plan, thus to achieve a rather unified and "harmonious" supportive voting result. Compared with the traditional "rubber stamp" people's congress system in which all congress members' opinions were largely ignored, it is obvious progress that the power holders in the reform had to listen to the congress members' views and had to do some work to "unify their minds." However, the party was still afraid of exposing the different views of the congress members in the final voting result so they manipulated the congress members' opinions before the voting and used the non-secret voting method to threaten some congress members not to vote against the power holders' interest. Considering the authoritarian party is still "all powerful" in the current Chinese political system, the deliberation and voting sessions in the reform experiments were still in a "black box." It remained unknown how much the true will of the people's congress members had been distorted in the black box.

Third, even such deliberation on township public affairs, like cases 1 and 2, is not to be held in the future and such budget reform, like case 3, is to be confined to only Zeguo Township (as described on p. 89), He Baogang introduced in an interview that deliberations like those in cases 1 and 2 are still to be held but at the lower levels such as villages or privately-owned enterprises and the deliberation subjects are to be directly related to the participants' interest.[44] However, even such deliberation meetings at the lowest levels are confined to such minor or "safe" topics by the local power holders. He revealed that the local government always refuses his suggestion to hold deliberation meetings between township government and villagers on village land problems, which are perhaps the issue of greatest concern to the villagers and the biggest reason of the conflicts between local government and villagers. He explained in an interview that the government is trying to guarantee the huge profit it gains from land transactions. The deliberation meeting would compel them to publish inside information or even to give up the profit, which is surely not what they want. Such an opinion of He that the "deliberative democracy" reform could hardly resolve the land problems was confirmed in the field research.[45] In May of 2009, a mass protest against the government's land policy happened in Zeguo Township on the site of land which the government was going to expropriate. The township officials and police suppressed the on-site protest with violence to start the building project on the land. Once the event was exposed on the internet,[46] the township government was severely criticised. The "deliberative democracy" and "harmonious society" in Zeguo Township, which were evaluated highly in lots of official propaganda articles, were then doubted by the villagers and outside observers. After the event, some local villagers and researchers in Beijing pointed out that "the experiments were just like a fraud for credit" (Ye Chuan, 2009). A conclusion can be drawn on this basis that the "deliberative democracy" experiments were not as effective as described in the party's propaganda in resolving the conflicts between the villagers and local governments.

Fourth, it remains questionable if "deliberative democracy" can be upgraded to higher levels or expanded to more localities. All the experiments in Zeguo or Xinhe were instigated and organised by the party committees at the city and township levels. The publicity department of the Wenling City's party committee played an important role in every part of these experiments.[47] An important intention of these local party and government cadres to do the reform was to win more credit for their future promotion. In that case, the first reason might be as Li Fan stated in a news report, "it has been a principle that no local party secretaries or government executives want to copy a reform from other local governments, no matter how good it is, [because it will not win them credit if their reform is just a copy of someone else]" (Hong Qihua, 2008:90). Therefore, the local cadres who want to take credit by carrying out reform are perhaps not willing to do the same "deliberative democracy" experiments.[48] Things might be different if the central party holds positive attitudes towards the reform. However, the central party's attitudes to the experiments have never been clear, which has hindered the reform from being promoted to the higher-levels (Zhang Xiaoshan, 2008). This becomes the second obstacle to the further development of "deliberative democracy."[49] The third reason is such a reform must restrain the power of the local party and government cadres who are surely not willing to give up their power. Officials from other provinces visited Wenling City to study the reform but they all felt pessimistic about adopting the same reform in their places because "no cadres in their townships like to be restrained in their power" (Hong Qihua, 2008:89). It took Li Fan great efforts to persuade the Xinhe Township government to publish their over one-million *yuan* annual "hospitality expense" in the budget plan (Hong Qihua, 2008:89). This will be harder or even impossible in other places. He Baogang explained in an interview that an incentive for such a reform may come from the local cadres who hope to find a way to reduce the social conflicts in their localities in order to stabilise their official positions or to be promoted in the future. However, as discussed in the previous paragraph, the reform usually stops before it really touches the power holders' interest. Based on all these points, the reform may not be quickly expanded or upgraded if there is still no obvious supportive attitude from the central party. The few experiments in the future are likely to be conducted only in the same places where they have already been held and to be restricted to the township or lower levels.

Other Forms of "Deliberative Democracy" in China

There are three other "deliberative institutions" in China, namely *tingzhenghui* [consultative meetings], *gongmin pingyihui* [citizen evaluation meetings] and *jumin huo cunmin daibiaohui* [residential or village representative assemblies], which are all thought by researchers to be forms of "deliberative democracy" (He, 2006b:186). Among these three deliberative institutions, the residential or village representative assemblies are non-governmental activities so they are not in the context of the "deliberative democracy" discussed in this chapter.[50] The citizen evaluation meetings aim at local cadres' work achievements, which the local power holders are inclined to resent and resist. As a result, the experiments are getting fewer and can be held in only certain localities (mainly in Zhejiang Province). Considering this, I will not discuss these experiments in this part. This part of the chapter focuses on the third kind of "deliberative institutions," the consultative meetings, which aim to gather citizens' opinions on important public affairs for policy making. These meetings are widely held at the levels of city or below and have been institutionalised by a state council law (The State Council of PRC, 2008).[51] However, these most "popular" and "party-supported" "deliberative democracy" experiments have obvious defects in every procedural step and receive more criticism compared with the other "deliberative democracy" reform experiments.

First, the selection of the citizen representatives is manipulated. Although lay citizens are allowed to apply to attend the meetings in many cases, the selection step is normally manipulated in the "black box." In some cases, the organisers refused to publish the backgrounds and contacts of the selected participants (Xinjingbao, 2007). The organisers appointed the elites as "citizen representatives"[52] or the organisers purposely selected the participants who were not related to the deliberation subject to avoid opposition.[53]

Second, the deliberation session was just a formality. In most cases, the participants could "express their opinions" but could not vote on the subject (He, 2006b:187). Even when there was voting in some cases, the result was only a "reference" for the government officials to make policies. In some consultative meetings regarding the prices of electric power, water, heating or taxi fares, the government departments colluded with the state-owned monopoly enterprises producing false excuses for increasing the prices. The citizen representatives knew little about the hidden truth so they were normally weak in opposing a government's decision which was actually made before the meeting.[54] In some cases, the organisers prohibited the participants from disclosing the meeting materials, agenda and deliberation contents to the outside, or even prohibited them from being interviewed by journalists (Xinjingbao, 2007).[55] In some cases, before the meeting was held, the organisers prepared and sent to the press media the unified news materials which contained "their expected results" (Liu Binglu, 2004).

Third, the results of these consultative meetings were surely far away from the people's real interest. According to a news article, all twenty "citizen representatives" agreed to increase the electricity power price in Beijing at a consultative meeting. The plan, however, was opposed by over eighty percent of people in an online survey (Tang Hao, 2006). The proposal of increasing the ticket price of the tourist attractions in Beijing (described in note 53), which was supported by all twenty-one participants of the consultative meeting, was opposed by over ninety-five percent of surveyed netizens (Yu Ping, 2004). In Changsha City, Hunan Province, a proposal unanimously agreed by twenty-three participants at a consultative meeting was opposed by ninety-three percent of surveyed citizens. More ridiculous, at some consultative meetings, all participants abandoned the proposals of slightly increasing the price and chose to support the one with the most substantial price increase, which was said to have astounded even the government officials (Tang Hao, 2006). A news report revealed that the organisers bribed the meeting participants to gain their support for the proposal (Li Changhong, 2006). Some reports sarcastically called these meetings "press conferences" because they were held for nothing but "publishing the decisions" which had already been made long before (Jiang Xiaowei, 2005; Liu Shixin, 2004b). Some reports summarised that such meetings were "unexceptionally the prelude of the increasing-price policy." Some reports criticised such consultative meetings as the good example of *jia minzhu* [fake democracy] (Cheng Chunrong, 2006; She Jiao, 2004; Xi Xuchu, 2006). In some reports, the consultative meetings are exposed as under control of the interest groups (Shao Daosheng, 2006). The citizens are gradually losing their interest in such activities, which will probably lead to the crisis of the people's confidence in government (Legal Daily, 2006; Yang Xiaohong, 2004).

A Brief Conclusion to the Chapter

Most of the reform experiments in China, which are called "deliberative institutions," do not fully meet the criteria for deliberative democracy. Some of them are in fact the people's congress reform or the reform in public administration, which have a common feature that they will have no impact on the one-party polity in China. Some experiments, like cases 1 to 5 discussed in this chapter, may liberalise some policy-making process at the local levels, but this kind of reform is not democratic nor can it lead to China's democratisation in the future. Even knowing that, the party is still cautiously watching these "risky" experiments and it will probably take immediate measures to suppress the grassroots power or even the local elites who utilise the power obtained from the reform to challenge the party's authoritarian rule. The consultative meetings, a kind of "deliberative institution" which has been approved by the party and has been institutionalised as a method of governance, are manipulated at every step of the procedure. As analysed in the chapter, they are actually "democracy" designed to deceive the masses. In conclusion, none of the "deliberative democracy" experiments, which are examined in this chapter, will possibly lead China to political democratisation.

Notes

1. "Deliberative democracy," a term originated from some rather new western political theories but widely used by the Chinese Communist Party in its propaganda and by some party theorists in their research papers, has been purposely misinterpreted by the party in the Chinese political context. In contrast to the deliberative democracy in western political science, the effect of Chinese "deliberative democracy" is exaggerated, its feature of "non-competitiveness" is over-emphasised, and its essential condition that a sophisticated voting system or genuine representative democracy must have been established as the basis is largely ignored. Even though I know that the "deliberative democracy" in the party's propaganda and these government reform experiments do not conform to the deliberative democracy theory in western political science, I still call them "deliberative democracy" in this chapter because the label is widely used in the Chinese press media and in western academic research. However, I apply a quotation mark on the "deliberative democracy" in China in order to distinguish it from what western political scientists discuss.

2. Party theorists wrote many articles promoting such points of view. Among others, some important articles written by Li Junru, the vice president of the Central Party's School, are (Li Junru, 2005, 2006a, 2006b, 2008), and an article by Chen Jiagang, a theorist from the party's Central Compilation and Translation Bureau who first translated deliberative democracy as xieshang minzhu (Chen Jiagang, 2007).

3. In some articles, while highly evaluating deliberative democracy, Li did not deny the importance of electoral democracy in China. In more articles, however, Li tried to emphasise the defects of electoral democracy in the western countries. These problems actually do not arise in current Chinese political system because the system still lacks a genuine voting system. Li's warning seems too early and unnecessary but it indicates that the party is afraid of genuine electoral democracy because it will finally ruin its authoritarian rule in China.

4. The specific method of nominating the CPPCC members is at http://news.xinhuanet.com/ziliao/2003-03/10/content_768951.htm.

5. This will be discussed in chapter 6 of the book.

6. The term "non-competitive democracy" coined by Lin Shangli actually refers to traditionally authoritarian politics in China.

7. This is a term coined by Lin too. I guess the author is trying to express that the current authoritarian government in China is highly efficient as there are no opposition political powers.

8. In addition to these party theorists, a local cadre in Zhejiang Province, who instigated and organised the most important Chinese "deliberative democracy" experiments, admitted in an interview that he started the "deliberative democracy" reform because reforms in other aspects, especially in elections, were prohibited by the central party. That is to say, the Chinese "deliberative democracy" reform was carried out under an authoritarian political system, in which there were no genuine elections.

9. He also realised that "at the same time, the Chinese government takes action to suppress dissident groups, control intellectual activities, and close down some internet discussion forums."

10. When the local reformists in Zhejiang Province first used the term "deliberative democracy" to describe the experiments they organised, the Press and Publications Administration of Zhejiang Province criticised the cadres for defining a Chinese local reform with a western political theory. The crisis ended and the reform was resumed only when the senior party theorists such as Li Junru published articles to support such a definition.

11. The information about the five cases was obtained from field research which I conducted at the two experimental localities (the townships of Zeguo and Xinhe) in November of 2009. I interviewed fourteen people there, including the local cadres who instigated, designed or organised the experiments, the citizens who participated in the experiments and the local party theorists who closely watched the experiments. To comply with Monash University's human research ethics and to protect the safety of the interviewees, this part does not disclose the names of interviewees while using the materials they provided. In addition to the field research at the experimental localities, I also interviewed two researchers respectively in Melbourne and Beijing, who were thought to be the principal promoters and designers of the five cases. Apart from the information obtained from the field research, this part also includes some data from collected documents. These data have all been checked and confirmed during the field research.

12. It was known from the field research that the most important instigator of the "deliberative democracy" reform in Wenling City was Chen Yimin, a cadre of the Wenling City's party committee's publicity department. He set up an annual award for the township secretaries who conducted some kinds of "deliberative democracy" reform experiments and the awardees could win extra credits in the annual examination of their work. To win the award was perhaps a direct and important instigation for the local cadres' to do the reform experiments. In addition, Chen instructed and coordinated with the township secretaries in all five cases discussed in this section.

13. The information is obtained from field research and the article by Zhang Xiaoshan (Zhang Xiaoshan, 2008). Some other researchers who were involved in the experiments are not listed in this column.

14. He is a political researcher from Deakin University in Melbourne, Australia.

15. In 2004, the government of Wenling City won "the local governance innovation award." The awarders, the party's Central Compilation and Translation Bureau and the Central Party School, clearly suggested that the Wenling City government should integrate "deliberative democracy" into the local people's congress (China Innovations, 2004).

16. The people's congress system in China has been known as a "rubber stamp." Both the congress and the government are the integrated part of the party-dominated political system. The congresses do not genuinely elect the government leaders nor can they monitor government activities. The power of a people's congress to examine and approve the government's budget plan has actually been a formality, even though it has been written in Article 9 of the organisation law (NPC, 2004a). The reform experiments in cases 3, 4 and 5 targeted the problem that the people's congresses are unable to carry out their function of examining and approving the budget plan. The effect of the reform will be discussed in the latter part of this chapter.

17. This is an improvement but the seats for migrants were obviously too few.

18. He Baogang stated in the interview that using computer software in the selection was his suggestion but it was not carried out in the experiment. According to him, the organisers still used the lottery method in case 3.

19. In case 4, apart from the nominated "representatives," the citizens of Xinhe Township were allowed to participate freely in this deliberation session, which was held before the people's congress session (Chen Yimin, 2007:36). In case 5, such information cannot be found from the existing documents. Most probably, there should be no obvious innovation in the method of selecting representatives in cases 4 and 5. Generally, the lay citizens were not interested in the deliberation even though they were allowed to attend it or perhaps they were not informed news before the deliberation. Thus, these participants (the "representatives" called by the government) were more likely the "social elites" who were preferred and nominated by the local power holders to attend the deliberation. According to a report, these participants were party congress members, entrepreneurs, village heads, industry association heads etc (Li Fan, 2007:58). The information obtained from the interviews was that such a policy was carried out in only case 4. In case 5 and the same experiments held in Xinhe Township in 2008 and 2009, the organisers did not publish a notice calling for lay citizens to participate in the deliberation prior to the people's congress session. In these cases, nearly all participants in the deliberation session were people's congress members. One interviewee expressed that the deliberation in these cases was actually a formality or a "political show" and "it had no impacts on the people's congress session."

20. Out of the 275 selected representatives, 259 participated in case 1 (Jiang Zhaohua, He Baogang, 2005). Out of the 237 selected representatives, 198 participated in case 2 (Deng Yuwen, 2006).

21. There were thirty planned projects discussed in case 1 and thirty-eight in case 2 (He Baogang, 2007; Jiang Zhaohua, He Baogang, 2005).

22. The result of the congress voting was 84 affirmative votes, 7 negative votes and 1 abstention (Jiang Zhaohua, He Baogang, 2005).

23. Compared with case 1, some minor changes were made in the procedure of case 2, such as, put 5% to 10% of the total infrastructure budget as a special fund for the projects not listed but strongly desired by the masses, reduce the number of the "project management experts," who were actually local officials, ask congress members to monitor the

process, decrease the cost of the case from 80,000 *yuan* to 47,000 *yuan* (Fei Wenting, 2006).

24. Although the information regarding how the deliberation result affected policy-making in case 2 cannot be found from the existing documents, He Baogang, in an interview, proved that most of the top-prioritised projects (eight out of nearly a dozen most highly-prioritised projects) were finally carried out by the government. Some top-prioritised projects were taken off from the list because the projects were jointly funded and had problems with the external financial sources. In addition, some projects were added in the list as requested by the higher-level government. He Baogang's explanation was confirmed in the field research.

25. Out of the 197 people who were randomly selected, 178 attended this session (Lin Long, Hu Guoqiang, 2008).

26. All 95 congress members were required to attend this session but 65 of them were present. Another paper says only 63 congress members turned up (He Baogang, 2008a).

27. As in cases 1, 2 and 3 He and his fellow researchers did questionnaire surveys before and after the deliberations to examine how the villager representatives' opinions changed. I then asked He Baogang if he once thought of doing an identical survey among the congress members in case 3 to discover if and how their opinions were changed after listening to the deliberation held as the first session of case 3. The survey result could provide statistical evidence of the influence which the deliberation session (session 1) had on the congress session (session 2). He Baogang told me he once suggested such a survey to the local power holders but they rejected it with the excuse that such a survey was probably against the organisation law.

28. To be approved by a congress, a proposal must be supported by at least more than a half of all the congress members. There were 107 members in Zeguo Township People's Congress (14 members were absent from the conference) so the supportive votes had to be 54 or more to get the budget plan passed.

29. For example, the deputy township executive attended the discussion in the industry group (Sui Binbin, 2008a:23).

30. In case 4, two out of eight submitted amendment proposals were thought "eligible" to be voted on. In case 5, one out of sixteen submitted proposals was voted on (Jiang Yun, 2007; Li Fan, 2007:59). This step will be analysed and commented on in the conclusion.

31. This plan might be different from the one after step 3 because it was amended again according to the proposals passed in the fourth step.

32. The budget reserve, a fund included in the whole budget package, is used for urgent projects or for projects that have to be stopped because they have run out of funds.

33. This critical comment, made by Chen Yimin who was the officer of the party's publicity department at Wenling City, confirmed the weak role of the people's congress in fulfilling its responsibility of monitoring the government. The same problem also exists at the national level. Chen Shu, a national people's congress member criticised at the NPC's conference in 2007 that the national budget plan made by the ministry of finance was too simple so that the NPC members could never examine it. According to him, the examination of budget plans by the national people's congress is just a meaningless formality (Zhongguowang, 2007). Sharper criticism came from Lew Mon-Hung, a Chinese People's Political Consultative Conference member from Hong Kong. In January 2009, he questioned the leaders of the NPC's standing committee and the Ministry of Finance at a conference: "should the 4,000 billion *yuan* financial rescue program be discussed and approved by the NPC before being published by Premier Wen Jiabao?" and "why the annual expenses for government officials' travel, entertainment and car purchase and mainte-

nance reached 900 billion *yuan*, which was nearly 321 times more than the 2.9 billion *yuan* budget published by the finance ministry" (Ji Shuoming, 2009).

34. A researcher, who greatly contributed to Xinhe experiments, admitted that the participants of case 4 and 5 (mostly congress members) were local elites and the defect of the case was its elitism. In other words, the people's congress members could hardly represent the township voters' interest in the experiments.

35. Such an intention of the party was described in note 15 and He Baogang confirmed this intention of the party in an interview.

36. In an interview, a local official, who was the chief organiser and designer of the "deliberative democracy" experiments in Wenling City, firmly denied the possibility to have "free elections" for people's congress members in the townships. According to him, the people's congress reform can only start from the "participatory budgeting" reform. An important reform participant admitted in an interview that the people's congress system would keep being a "rubber stamp" if no free elections for the people's congress members were allowed to be held. In his opinion, it was very difficult to change this status of the people's congress system because the CCP took all measures to repress the liberal tendency in congress elections. In such a case, according to him, the reform experiments such as the "participatory budgeting" are perhaps the only thing that can be done at the current stage to improve the people's congress system. It at least enabled the "rubber stamp" to do something to monitor the local governments. In addition, the participant, who greatly contributed to Xinhe experiments, insisted that the "participatory budgeting" experiments (including cases 4, 5 and the similar experiments in Xinhe Township in 2008 and 2009) were actually a reform on the local people's congress system. He denied that the Xinhe reform was related to "deliberative democracy" and he suggested the local reformers not define the Xinhe reform as a kind of "deliberative democracy." In his opinion, electoral reform, rather than "deliberative democracy" reform, was more suitable for Chinese politics at the current stage.

37. The document of the party committee's 2010 work plan cannot be obtained, but four cadres and scholars confirmed this information in the interviews.

38. In my opinion, there were probably two reasons the power holders in Wenling City decided to abandon He Baogang's methods in future experiments. First, the local power holders were afraid of the grassroots power which was established by "random sampling" and their participation in the policy-making processes. Even though the local cadres and the party theorists refused to admit this was a reason in the interviews, one reformist cadre accidentally revealed to me that many local party and government cadres once questioned if it is legal that the randomly-selected representatives could participate in making a policy. To defend the reform experiments, the reformist had to explain to them that "it was still the local party committees or governments who made the final decision, the deliberation was only one step in a policy-making process, which enabled the party committees or governments to know more about the people's opinions." Knowing this, we might be able to understand that in no circumstances did the power holders like to see the formation of grassroots power, not to mention to grant them some political power. Second, most local power holders and party theorists in the interviews believed that many randomly-selected people's representatives were not capable of carrying out their duties in the deliberations. One theorist contemptuously said that by using the method of random sampling the organisers could choose only "illiterate people" for the experiments. Another theorist said these "selected women or old people" knew nothing about public affairs. One theorist thought that too many grassroots villagers were selected to attend the experiments. He believed that these villagers were generally narrow-minded and selfish so they always considered their own interests when making a decision. This theorist and a cadre suggested that there should be more entrepreneurs in the deliberations because they were

wealthy and then more powerful in every social sphere. Another cadre stated that the random sampling was not suitable for China because the political quality of the Chinese people was much lower than that of people in western countries. Several informants told me in the interviews that there would still be "deliberative democracy" experiments held in Zeguo Township in the future but the method of "random sampling" would be altered. According to them, people will be firstly divided into groups according to their jobs, such as cadres, entrepreneurs and business owners, professionals (medical and legal practitioners, accountants, etc.), workers, villagers or according to their ages, such as 18 to 30, 31 to 45, 46 to 60, above 61. The organisers assigned seats for each group and then randomly selected representatives from each group. In their opinion, such a method may guarantee a bigger proportion of those representatives who are from the groups of "influential people" or from the groups of younger people who have more knowledge about public affairs.

39. Here I do not mean the case 3, as the local people's congress's reform, is generally better than cases 4 and 5 and is able to solve the problems of the current people's congresses. The best solution to these problems, as I described in the early part of this paragraph, is to hold democratic elections for people's congress members. Cases 1 and 2 had too weak a congress session so these two deliberative polling experiments were actually not related to the congress reform.

40. According to the Xinhe Township government (Government of Xinhe Township, 2007:71), if members of the people's congress wish to increase a budget item, they had to decrease the total budget by the same amount. Similarly, if they wish to decrease the budget, they had to increase other items by the same amount. In other words, the people's congress could not change the overall size of the budget.

41. In the two experiments held in 2008 and 2009, two out of four eligible proposals were decided not to be voted on according to an informant.

42. Several informants revealed that the base of the participatory budgeting experiment would be changed from Xinhe Township to another township in Wenling City in 2010 because the Xinhe Township party secretary held a negative attitude towards the reform and thus was reluctant to carry it out. Details are in note 48.

43. In case 3 held in 2008, congress members wrote and cast ballots instead of raising hands, which guaranteed the secrecy of the congress members' votes.

44. Some famous cases include: the deliberation meeting in Bianyu Village on such village affairs as environment, public security and public facilities, and the deliberation meeting in Longbiao Factory on such issues as workplace safety, HR management, salary and allowance. All these experiments were held outside China's government system so the research subject of this chapter does not include these experiments.

45. A local cadre revealed in an interview that local governments gain huge profits by selling land. For example, in a township in Wenling, they bought land from villages at the price of 80,000 *yuan* per *mu* (around 677 square metres) but sold them to the land developers or entrepreneurs at 900,000 *yuan* per *mu*. According to the officer, even if there were deliberation meetings organised by a village over the land issues, the villagers could not talk about whether they agreed to sell the land or if the selling price (such as 80,000 *yuan* per *mu*) was reasonable. The meetings aimed to solve the problem of how to distribute the money the village gained by selling the land. At the meetings the villagers could try to struggle for a larger part of that money for themselves and perhaps could discuss how the village would spend the rest of that money. However, powerful village heads tended to decide all these things in a black box without organising such meetings. The officer in the interview admitted that it was normally extremely difficult to persuade the power holders, no matter at what levels, to organise a deliberation meeting on the land issues.

46. Some photos of the event can be viewed from http://www.tianya.cn/techforum/content/665/41730.shtml.

47. Some evidence can be found in research papers and news reports such as (He Baogang, Lang Youxing, 2008) and (Wang Kongrui, 2008:81–82). This point was also confirmed by my field research in the experimental localities.

48. The reform in the townships of Wenling City has not been institutionalised. In other words, it has not been fixed as a part of the governmental or people's congress system. Some facts known from the field research can provide factual evidence for this conclusion. First, as described in note 12, to win the annual award set up by the Wenling City's party committee's publicity department and thus to gain extra credits in the annual examination of their work became the most important motivation of a township party secretary to start a reform in his locality. However, the policy of awards was cancelled after the party secretary of Wenling City was moved to another position and a new secretary took his place. Accordingly, many township party secretaries lost their interest in the reform because of the cancellation of the award system. Obviously, an accidental change of a local cadre greatly affected the progress of the reform. Second, according to a local cadre who was the initiator of most reform experiments in Wenling City, he could go to discuss with only the township party secretaries who were his friends about the possibility of conducting a reform experiment in their localities. For example, in 2005, the participatory budgeting reform experiment was designed in February but it could not be carried out in the chosen township because the township party secretary (the friend of the reform initiator) had received an order to move to another position. The reform experiment was then postponed to May when the reform initiator found Xinhe Township as the new experimental locality. The experiments in Xinhe Township were successful in the years of 2005, 2006 and the township secretary won credits for the experiments. In 2007, however, when a new party secretary took the position, he was unwilling to continue his predecessor's reform, thus the reform was nearly stopped in the year. Under the pressure from the People's Congress of Wenling City, he had to agree to continue the participatory budgeting reform in Xinhe Township but his reform experiments were much worse than those of his predecessor. Several informants revealed to me that the base of the participatory budgeting reform may be moved to another township in Wenling City in 2010 if the Xinhe Township party secretary still remains reluctant to carry out the reform. Such a thing happened in Zeguo Township too. In 2007 when the Zeguo Township party secretary, who was an enthusiastic reformist, was moved to the Wenling City's deputy-mayor position, the deliberative polling experiment was not conducted in the township in that year. In my opinion, a reform that relies on the interpersonal relationship and a cadre's personal desire rather than a political or legal system has poor prospects.

49. He Baogang provided some evidence to prove the central party's ambiguous attitudes to the reform. According to He, when Xi Jinping (the possible CCP's next General-Secretary after Hu Jintao) inspected the government's work in Zhejiang Province, some local cadres from Wenling City made a long report to him on the "deliberative democracy" achievements, but Xi did not make any comments on the report.

50. Like the cases described in note 44, these experiments were called non-governmental activities because they are held at the level below the lowest government level. However, it does not mean the party or government do not exert their power to influence the activities.

51. The relevant part is in article 8 of the document.

52. In a deliberative meeting which was held in Guangdong Province on increasing the water price, the five citizen participants were all party secretaries of residential communities. The other seventeen participants were all government officials (Xinjingbao, 2006).

53. For deliberative meeting held in Beijing regarding increasing the ticket price of tourist attractions, all citizen participants were selected from local residents in Beijing who accounted for less than ten percent of the tourists visiting these tourist attractions (Wang Xuejiang, 2009).

54. Some news reporters providing facts for this statement include Guo Xiaojun (Guo Xiaojun, 2006), Liu Binglu (Liu Binglu, 2004) and Liu Shixin (Liu Shixin, 2004a). A news article criticises the collusion of the government and the monopoly enterprises (Mao Fei, 2004).

55. A CPPCC member then presented a proposal to the CPPCC conference that all information regarding deliberative meetings should be published in the future (Zhao Lei, Tang Huimei, 2006).

Chapter 6

Independent Candidates in China's Local People's Congress Elections*

Introduction

As discussed in the previous chapters, reform experiments have been conducted in the governmental and party system in some localities. In the people's congress system, however, no reform experiments have been made on an extensive basis. The "participatory budgeting" reform described in chapter 5, which was actually a kind local people's congress reform, is still confined to one township and is defined by the local power holders as a form of "deliberative democracy." In the Chinese political system, according to the constitution and laws, a primary-level people's congress (township and county people's congresses in rural areas and district people's congresses in urban areas) is the only institution which is "directly elected" by the voters.[1] Based on "direct election," the people's congress theoretically should be the most "democratic section" in the entire political system where the grassroots voters can participate in politics by directly electing their local member. On this basis, any political reform which could lead to China's democratisation might be located in the primary-level people's congresses. The real situation, however, is different. The party actually dominates the whole people's congress system. In particular, it tightly controls the "direct

---

* The author thanks the *Journal of Chinese Political Science* for permission to republish the material previously published: "Independent Candidates in China's Local People's Congress Elections," *Journal of Chinese Political Science*, vol. 16, no. 4, 2011.

elections" for people's congress members and takes every repressive measure in the elections to prevent grassroots power from entering even the primary-level people's congresses. There has indeed been no officially-organised political reform in the people's congress system. In recent years, however, grassroots power has kept struggling for its legal rights in the direct elections held in a few localities, to which the party committees of various levels had to react. This can be thought of as a special "reform" initiated by grassroots power.

Focused on grassroots power in local people's congress elections in 2003 and 2006–2007, this chapter studies the background of independent candidates, their motivations and behaviour in elections. Furthermore, in order to stop grassroots power from entering the local people's congresses, the party took all possible measures, which seemed very unnecessary in these traditionally "non-competitive" elections. In this chapter, the research on the party's suppression in these elections is important because it exposes the true nature of the people's congress elections and helps readers to understand the party's authoritarianism in Chinese politics. In addition, this chapter tries to analyse whether the "rebellious electoral activities" of the independent candidates, which I define as a kind of "special political reform experiment," will have impacts on China's political structure. To fulfil the three tasks, some first-hand information obtained from three months of field research in China will be used.[2] Some archival and online research will be also used in the chapter. In the first part of this chapter, some important terms relevant to the candidates and local congress elections are defined. The second part includes general information regarding the independent candidates such as their number and distribution. This part also tries to summarise some features of these candidates by analysing their backgrounds and motivations. The third part researches the behaviour of independent candidates and the party's suppressive methods in each stage of the election. The fourth part of the chapter studies the results of these elections, the response of the independent candidates to the results, their feelings towards the local elections and the people's congress system, and their plans for future elections. In the last part, based on the previous analysis, a conclusion is drawn that the participation of the independent candidates in local people's congress elections was firmly suppressed by the party. It will be very difficult for this "reform," instigated from outside the party by grassroots voters, to lead China towards political democratisation in the near future.

Terms and Definitions

Some terms which appear in the context of this chapter are applicable only to China's elections. In English, they make no sense or have different meanings, so they must be clearly defined. The terms are independent candidates, organisation-nominated candidates, organisation-preferred candidates, additional candidates, voter-nominated candidates, self-nominated candidates, formal candidates and informal candidates.

In *The Electoral Law of the National People's Congress and Local People's Congresses of the People's Republic of China*, article 29 refers to the candidate nomination method:

> Political parties and people's organisations may either jointly or separately recommend candidates for deputies. A joint group of at least ten voters or deputies may also recommend candidates. Those who submit recommendations shall inform the election committee or the presidium of the congress of their candidates' backgrounds (NPC, 2004c).

According to the Electoral Law, article 29, the voter-nominated candidates refer to the candidates who are nominated by a group of at least ten voters.

Article 37 of the Electoral Law states:

> a voter may vote for or against a candidate for deputy and may vote instead for any other voter or abstain (NPC, 2004c).

According to the Electoral Law, article 37, voters have the right to vote for any other voter whose name is not listed on the ballot. They can do so just by writing down the name of their preferred "candidate," who must be a qualified voter, under "Voting for someone else." Self-nominated candidates are candidates who do not go through the formal nomination procedure. Instead, they contact voters privately before the voting day, hoping the voters can use the "voting for others" right to vote for them.

The term "independent candidates" includes both voter-nominated candidates and self-nominated candidates. Opposed to this conception are the "organisation-nominated candidates,"[3] who are nominated by the higher-level party committee, government, people's congress, other political parties or some *renmin tuanti* [people's organisations].[4] In fact, the Chinese Communist Party (CCP) holds absolute power to decide who should be nominated by these organisations. Included in the organisation-nominated candidates, organisation-preferred candidates are those whom the party really expects to win the elections. According to the Electoral Law, there must be more candidates than available congress seats in local congress elections.[5] In order to comply with the law, the organisation normally nominates some "additional candidates" who are obviously weak and expect to be "defeated" by the organisation-preferred candidates in the election.

The difference between "formal candidates" and "informal candidates" is whether the candidates have gone through the formal nomination procedure. Thus, the formal candidates include the organisation-nominated candidates and the voter-nominated candidates, while the informal candidates are the self-nominated candidates.

History and Development, Population and Distribution

In the 1980s and 1990s

Independent candidates initially appeared in some local congress elections in the early 1980s when the party started to carry out its "reform and opening to the outside" policy and citizens, especially intellectuals, showed great enthusiasm for political democratisation. A new Electoral Law enacted in 1979 allowed direct elections for people's congress members to be extended up to the county in rural areas and the district level in urban areas. Thus intellectuals, who were mainly urban residents, had the right for the first time to vote and stand for the congress elections. The independent candidates in 1980 were few in number and most were university students or teachers. The campaign activities they organised in the elections such as delivering public speeches and distributing self-promotion letters were more advanced than the campaign methods that candidates today can use.[6] A document indicates that the earliest independent candidates appeared in the district congress elections in the cities of Chongqing, Changsha, Chengdu and Beijing in 1980. At least seven independent candidates, who were all university teachers and students, won in a district congress election in Chongqing city. The cases of independent candidates winning elections were also reported in three other cities (Luo Liwei, 2003). In Beijing, eighteen students of Beijing University[7] competed in the district people's congress elections and they made high-powered election campaigns for the election. One of them won the election (Qian Liqun, 2008). Students from other universities in Beijing also participated in the district people's congress elections as independent candidates (Hu Ping, Wang Juntao, 1990). In addition to the four above-mentioned cities, in Shanghai, Jinan and Guiyang, there were university students and teachers who participated in the district people's congress elections as independent candidates. In Shanghai, Beijing and the provinces of Guangdong, Guizhou and Hebei, some non-university independent candidates also competed in the elections (Qian Liqun, 2008). In the following years in the 1980s and 1990s, there were still a very few cases where independent candidates competed and won in local elections. Some famous cases included independent candidate Zeng Jianyu[8] who won district congress elections in Luzhou city of Sichuan Province in 1992 and 1997, and the famous independent candidate Yao Lifa,[9] who won a congress election in Qianjiang City of Hubei Province in 1998. Also in that year, two independent candidates won elections in Sichuan Province. Influenced by Yao Lifa, three independent candidates won elections in Qianjiang City in 1999 (Zhou Hucheng, 2003).

Elections Held in 2003 and 2006–2007

In 2003, more than one hundred independent candidates competed in the local congress elections, mainly in Shenzhen, Beijing and some cities in Hubei province.[10] The sudden burst of Chinese citizen enthusiasm for local elections drew attention from Chinese journalists who wrote media reports on this topic.[11] Researchers in Shenzhen University studied some important cases and published their research results in two books.[12] Considering the strict censorship in China, the publication of these journalistic reports and academic papers seemed to indicate the positive attitudes of the central party. In addition, the National People's Congress (NPC) amended the Electoral Law in 2004 in response to the complaints made by some independent candidates that they were treated unequally in previous elections.[13] Also in 2004, the Chinese constitution was amended and tenure of the local people's congresses was changed from three to five years. To ensure that future local elections would be organised in a unified time, the NPC ordered that all Chinese townships, counties and districts should hold direct elections in the eighteen-month period between 1 July 2006 and 31 September 2007 for their new people's congresses.[14] All the factors, including the seemingly positive attitude from the party, the publication of independent candidates' personal information and their electoral activities in the public media, and the NPC's arrangement to unify the time of all future local people's elections, enabled those independent candidates who were unrelated or only loosely-related in the previous elections to establish connections and coordinate their efforts in their future activities. However, the independent candidates and democracy advocates were soon disillusioned. According to an informant, the director of the Media Press Bureau of the NPC Standing Committee General Office, Kan Ke, gave a warning at a closed-door meeting in 2006 that journalists and scholars should stop writing media reports and academic research papers on the issues regarding independent candidates. This warning, however, was largely ignored by the press and academia. Then the Publicity Department of the CCP Central Committee soon secretly confirmed the order to the press and academia through the party's mechanisms. Since then, independent candidates became a forbidden subject for all Chinese press and academia.[15] Media reports and research papers on the independent candidates in the elections held in 2006 and 2007 are rare.[16] Such basic important data as the candidate number and distribution can hardly be obtained by archival research. Information including some data and the experience of some candidates in this chapter were mostly obtained from interviews with non-government researchers and some independent candidates themselves. A researcher estimated that in China there were possibly more than ten thousand independent candidates in 2006 and 2007 but there is no accurate statistical data.[17] According to the researcher, compared with 2003, there were fewer independent candidates in Shenzhen in 2006. Another informant said there were only around five independent candidates in Shenzhen in 2006. The researcher also said there were no independent candidates in Wuhan and Shanghai in 2003, while dozens of independent candidates appeared in Wuhan and a few in Shanghai in 2006. According to him, due to the local power holder's seemingly "lenient" policy at the initial stages of the elections, there were ten thousand independent candidates in Beijing in 2006.[18] In addition to the above mentioned places, in 2006 and 2007, independent candidates also appeared in Chongqing Municipality and in some cities in the provinces of Hebei, Henan, Shandong, Shanxi, Sichuan, Hubei, Jiangxi, Jiangsu, Zhejiang, Hunan, Gansu, Guangdong and the Inner Mongolia Autonomous Region.[19]

Who Are They and What Do They Want?

It is not easy to summarise the common points in the backgrounds and motivations of the independent candidates. As a researcher once told me, the independent candidates were grassroots heroes with various backgrounds and they participated in the elections for different reasons. There were no typical cases which had common features or can represent all the other cases. In other words, each case had its unique characteristics and all cases had equal value in research. Another researcher agreed with this point, but he was trying to summarise a principal feature of all Chinese independent candidates on the basis of viewing the various cases as a whole. According to this researcher, a person's belief in the CCP (perhaps not his/her real belief but he/she at least pretends to have such a belief) decides how much political power he/she is assigned. In addition, the more political power one obtains will definitely bring more financial benefits. In such a mode of distributing power and wealth, these independent candidates were obviously at a disadvantage. They normally obtained little political power and were thus disadvantaged in the competition for wealth. These people, however, had some elite qualities and the strong desire to be promoted but they were denied access to the bureaucratic system or they refused to associate themselves with the system because of their different political beliefs. Blocked in the traditional channels, they were trying to seek political advantage by standing for direct elections for the local people's congress seats, which was generally believed the most "democratic" section in the current Chinese polity and was theoretically feasible under Chinese laws.

Although some researchers insist on the unique value of each individual case and argue that summarising features of the independent candidates in research possibly leads to an incomplete conclusion, we can still categorise the independent candidates according to their backgrounds and try to find and analyse the common motivations of these candidates.[20] I divide the independent candidates whom I studied into four categories.

The independent candidates in the first category were lawyers. The lawyer independent candidates, as far as I know, appeared mainly in Beijing and in the provinces of Guangdong, Henan, Hebei, Hubei and Hunan. As legal practitioners, they had a strong belief in laws and had a strong desire to maintain social justice and to protect a citizen's political rights. However, most lawyers felt distressed that their opponents were often power holders or rich people with substantial power. All three lawyer independent candidates I interviewed told me that they often met difficulties in their work, which were deliberatively created by the power holders or rich people. One lawyer specified that it mostly happened when he tried to interview the relevant people, to view the official documents in the government departments or to make investigation of power holders or rich people. These lawyers had a strong belief in the current legal system but were often disillusioned when they were unable to practise the rights that the laws guaranteed them. In such a situation, some of the lawyers sought more political power by standing for elections. Their initial and direct motivation was that the political power obtained by winning a local congress seat could strengthen their role as a lawyer.[21] Some of the lawyer independent candidates had an additional consideration. Knowing that a large number of successful statesmen in western countries used to work as lawyers, they were proud of their career and had a strong sense of mission to improve China's politics.

The second category of independent candidates included urban citizens and villagers who were normally disadvantaged in economic affairs and thus sought to strengthen their power by winning local congress seats. The most distinctive feature of the independent candidates in this category was that they had most probably been the victims in conflicts with power holders or the rich and had suffered some financial loss. For example, some independent candidates in Shenzhen were the representatives of the property owners in their communities, struggling against the alliance between the government-controlled community offices and the real estate management firms.[22] One candidate explained his motivation to the researcher, "I gradually found our rival, the head of a real estate management firm, won more and more political titles including member of the people's congress. They were trading in political power to strengthen their role in business, which made it more difficult for us to maintain our rights. Then an idea became clear in my mind: being supported by a large number of property owners, I should compete in the election for a congress seat. It must be more effective if I, as a congress member, write the property owners' opinions into the motions and submit them to the congress" (Zou Shubin, 2003:74). Similar things happened in villages. In order to struggle against the local officers, the land developers and the village heads who allied with them to embezzle public funds and resources, the villagers who genuinely represent the interest of the majority of the villagers, were seeking more political power by competing in the elections for village committees. Some of them took the further step of standing for local congress elections. In addition, there were some entrepreneurs who stood for the local congress elections as independent candidates in Zhejiang province in 2007. Different from the above mentioned property owners and villagers, they were not so disadvantaged but I believe they wanted more political power to improve their capability in business. Some of these people won the elections, something very rare for independent candidates in 2006 and 2007. According to an informant, both the entrepreneurs and the local government refused to reveal any information to the outside. Therefore, it remains a mystery why they stood for the elections and how they won. I categorise these entrepreneur independent candidates in this group even though their motivation remains unclear.

The independent candidates in the third category were "idealistic" intellectuals (mainly teachers and students) and social activists. Some of these candidates told me in interviews that they stood for the elections mainly because they would like to practise the political rights written in laws, even if such "disturbance" of the party-controlled elections would bring them punishment. They said such "disturbing behaviours" made them feel proud and could expose to people what the so-called "democratic" elections were really like. I cannot simply conclude that the activities of the candidates in this category were purely in the public interest. It is possible that an individual candidate in the category might have his own consideration rather than for the public interest. However, their desires for personal interest were less obvious or less material compared with the desires of the candidates in the second category. Thus, most intellectuals and activists are categorised into the third group.

The independent candidates in the fourth category were political dissenters. They could be individuals or members of secret political organisations. The independent candidates of this category were featured by their publicised anti-CCP ideology. These dissenters had the clear intention that they should win the congress seats in the elections and would then become more politically powerful in their struggles against the CCP's rule. The Union of Chinese Nationalists[23] is a dissenting organisation of such a kind. In September 2006, the union convenor encouraged the union members to stand for local people's congress elections.[24] In answer to the convenor's call, more than one hundred union members[25] competed in the congress elections in their localities (Boxun, 2006). Compared with other independent candidates, the electoral activities of these dissenting party members were more organised and they kept closer connections with each other.[26] In addition, they had further and more specific political intentions and carried out their plans in a more strategic way.[27] Among the independent candidates of the four categories, these political dissenters who stood for the elections suffered the severest persecution. Among the existing cases, some dissenting independent candidates lost their jobs, some were bashed in their activities, some were frequently detained for investigation, some went missing, some were kept in custody for some days and some were even found guilty and sentenced to jail.[28]

Even though I try to categorise the independent candidates according to some features which a group of candidates commonly have, the boundaries between each category are still not definite. In other words, the motivations and backgrounds of the independent candidates in different categories may have great similarities in some circumstances. For example, many lawyers in the first category were "the lawyers for public welfare," who devoted a large part of their time and energy to the non-profit legal cases for maintaining the public interest or protecting the interest of the disadvantaged. They probably have been in close connection with the independent candidates of the second category in "maintaining rights" activities and such connections were possibly kept in the elections. Besides the major motivation of the lawyers to obtain more political power to maintain their own rights in their work, all lawyer independent candidates I interviewed expressed that they would like to use the professional knowledge a legal practitioner has to test how lawful the elections were. At this point, these lawyers were not different from the candidates of the third category who wanted to seek the answer from their own experience about the true nature of the "democratic elections." It is also difficult to distinguish the dissenters in the fourth category from the social activists in the third category. They were the same in all aspects except the dissenters have clarified their dissenting political views against the party's rule. Under the party's iron-handed repression, however, some social activists might think it unwise or unnecessary to publish their genuine political views. They were also political dissenters who remained "invisible." Some social activists of the third category had been actively involved in the "maintaining rights" movements, which even became their major work.[29] These people had surely associated themselves with some independent candidates of the second category. Some dissenters of the fourth category were also emphasising their work of helping the disadvantaged people to maintain their rights.[30] According to a report, the Union of the Chinese Nationalists was heavily involved in a series of such maintaining rights activities in various localities (Jiang Xun, 2008). In that case, some dissenters might be in contact with the independent candidates of the second category. Thus, we know that the independent candidates of different categories may have many similarities as well. Therefore, viewing the independent candidates in an integrated way is necessary in the research. Although some connections between them may be purposely concealed by them for safety concerns, I found in my research that some of them might interact with each other in their activities either consciously or unconsciously.

The Behaviour and Sufferings of the Independent Candidates during the Electoral Process

Among all the independent candidates since 1980, only a very few won election.[31] Research shows that the independent candidates were deliberately obstructed by the election organisers throughout the whole process and they failed because of the organisers' devious interference or flagrant violence. By analysing the evidentiary facts extracted from certain procedural steps of the collected cases, this part of the chapter exposes the illegal methods the power holders used to suppress the independent candidates in the elections. This part is organised in the sequence of procedural steps in an election.

Zoning of Electoral Districts

In the Electoral Law, article 24 refers to the zoning of electoral districts.

> The zoning of electoral districts may be decided according to the voters' residence or on the basis of production units, institutions and work units. The zoning of electoral districts shall be decided on the basis of one to three deputies to be elected from each electoral district (NPC, 2004c).

The power holders' strategies in this step to obstruct the independent candidates were hidden but effective. Knowing the existence of potential independent candidates in the elections, the election organisers normally separated them and their supporters into different electorates. The election organisers also sometimes arranged the independent candidates into an electorate which included some huge government departments or state-run firms. The heads of these departments and firms would normally be the organisation-preferred candidates in the electorate and their staffs were highly organised and mobilised to vote for them.[32] In that case, the independent candidates could hardly win the elections even if they had a group of supporters. For example, in an election held in Handan, Hebei Province in 2006, the election organisers abruptly redivided the electorate and put the competitive independent candidate Tian Qizhuang in an electorate which included the Party School of Handan and another big government bureau.[33] In the election, the voters from these two firms accounted for ninety percent of all voters in the electorate. In the second case, the village in which an independent candidate lived was put into an electorate containing a populous village where a hostile clan resided, although the two villages were far from each other and there might be problems in setting up a voting station. In addition, the head of the hostile village was an organisation-preferred candidate in the election. Such an arrangement greatly reduced the possibility of the independent candidate winning the election.[34] In an election held in Chongqing in 2006, a conventional electorate of a high school, in which the independent candidate was working, was separated and then combined into other electorates. In contrast, other school electorates, which had no independent candidates standing for election, remained unchanged. In an election held in Wuhan in 2006 and 2007, two adjoining villages were separated into two electorates. One of the villages was combined into an electorate with the villages at least five kilometres away. In addition, this happened after the voters' registration. The illegal operation was to stop an independent candidate in the village. In the election held in Qianjiang in 2003, the election organisers added some very far village schools into the independent candidate Yao Lifa's electorate which previously included only urban schools. Yao had been actively campaigning for the election in these urban schools for a long time, but he had never done so in the village schools so it certainly gave Yao more difficulties in the election. In 2006, the election organisers abolished Yao's electorate and separately registered the voters into other different electorates. In 2007, knowing the independent candidate Zhou Changqing was going to stand for an election in Jinan, Shandong province, the election organisers changed the zoning method which had already been published and redivided the adjoining villages, which were united in protest movements, into separate electorates. In an election held in Beijing in 2006, the competitive independent candidate, Shu Kexin, was put into an electorate in which there was a more competitive candidate, the speaker of the urban district people's congress. Perhaps the most ridiculous case occurred in an election held in Shanghai in 2006. The election organisers combined a resident community with a very far electorate just in order to guarantee the organisation-preferred candidates could be at the top of the candidate list (the candidates should be listed in order by the number of strokes in their surnames). An independent candidate Liu Shengmin was standing for election in that electorate.

A researcher pointed out that it was common for the election organisers to divide the electorates very shortly before the election started. In some cases they changed their decisions and redivided the electorates to hinder the independent candidates from winning the elections. In several cases, they redivided electorates even after voter registration was completed. The organisers normally kept unpublished how they would divide electorates so that the independent candidates had no targets in their campaign activities. In order to obstruct independent candidate Du Quanbing's electoral campaign in Wu'an, Hebei Province, the election organisers divided the electorates thirteen days *after* the publication of the voters' list.[35] Even worse, they did not publish the method for another few days. In the election held in Zhijiang, Hubei province in 2006, it was not until a few days before the voting day that the independent candidate Lu Banglie knew how the electorates were divided. Lu was an incumbent people's congress member at the time.

Voter Registration

In *The Electoral Law of the National People's Congress and Local People's Congresses of the People's Republic of China*, Article 3 guarantees a Chinese citizen the right to vote and stand for election (NPC, 2004c). However, according to Articles 26, 27 and 28 of the law, in order to be able to practise the right in an election, a citizen must register in his electorate to become an eligible voter. Article 4 of the Electoral Law emphasises, "Each voter shall have the right to vote only once in an election." Explaining this article, the State Council Law Office wrote, "a voter can vote in only one electorate" (The State Council Law Office, 2008: 7). Following this logic, a citizen should finish his/her voter registration in an electorate before he/she has the right to vote in the electorate and stand for election(s) in this or other electorate(s).[36] To stop the competitive independent candidates from winning elections, barriers were also set in voter registration.

Jiang Shan, a famous social activist in Shenzhen who intended to stand for the congress election in 2006, was refused voter registration by the election organisers in the electorate where he resided. Their excuse was that the official document, which was issued by the election officer in Jiang's hometown (where his *hukou*[37] was) to certify that Jiang had not registered as a voter in his hometown, did not meet the requirement.[38] Based on article 28 of the Electoral Law,[39] Jiang sued the election organisers in the local law court for his voter qualification. Before the law court started judging the case, the election organisers changed their decision and approved Jiang's voter qualification. But the candidate nomination had been closed and it was too late for Jiang to organise an effective electoral campaign if he wanted to compete in the election as an informal and self-nominated candidate. Zou Tao, another social activist in Shenzhen who had the intention of standing for the election in 2006, was also stopped at the voter registration stage. Zou had his *hukou* in Shenzhen so his registration should have been a very simple thing. Before the election, Zou went to ask the election organiser in his electorate when and how to do his voter registration. The organisers explained to him that the electorate had not been divided so the registration work had not been started. The election organisers told Zou that they would call to notify him about the registration time and place. However, Zou received no such information from the election organisers until he was finally told that the registration had been closed. Zou missed the chance to register as an eligible voter and had to give up his plan of standing for election.

In contrast to these obstacles, the power holders provided great convenience for their preferred candidates. In an election held in Shenzhen in 2003, an election winner named Chen Caiqiong was exposed as not having done her voter registration before the election. The election organisers in her electorate later explained that they called the local authority of Chen's hometown and it was confirmed in the phone call that Chen did not register at her hometown. Chen's voter qualification was registered after the election.

Some cases show other manipulations of the power holders in the voter registration step which aims to obstruct the independent candidates from winning elections. According to article 41 of the Chinese Electoral Law, "in a direct election of deputies to the people's congresses, the election shall be valid, if more than half of all the voters in an electoral district cast their votes." Thus, in order to obtain a valid voting result, the election organisers must guarantee more than half of the registered voters come to vote in the election. Yet, the law does not specify the legal voter registration rate, so some election organisers deliberately neglect the "uncontrollable" citizens in the voter registration, which results in very low voter registration rates for the local people's congress elections. One informant from Shenzhen revealed that there were around 1,300 families (roughly 4,000 people and more than 2,500 of them eligible for voter qualification) living in his resident community but there were only twenty-six registered voters from this resident community in both the election for the community committee in 2005 and the election for people's congress members in 2006. The one percent voter registration rate looks ridiculous, but this is not a single extreme case. A researcher stated in interview that the party-manipulated elections had disillusioned the Chinese people. He also asserted that the "biggest success" of the party is that they extinguish the people's passion for any political activities, which temporarily stabilises the party's rule.[40] Having only "obedient" voters in the elections, the power holders ensured the success of their preferred candidates. However, when finding the popularly-supported independent candidates standing in elections, the power holders had to instigate more people who work in government departments or state-run firms to register as voters and then vote in the election for the organisation-preferred candidate. An election in Shenzhen in 2006 is a good example. In this case, when Ma Jianhua, a competitive independent candidate decided to stand for election, the election organisers illegally registered a large number of "controllable" voters after the closure of registration, even though the closing date had already been announced in the published official documents. In an election held in Shenzhen in 2003, the independent candidate Ye Yuanbai met the same difficulty.

While motivating those who were easily controlled to register as voters, the power holders sometimes may hinder the potential supporters of the independent candidates from voter registration. In the election held in 2003 in Qianjiang, Hubei Province, the election organisers illegally deprived the voting rights of more than 1,000 tertiary students who were from other places (they had non-Qianjiang *hukou*) but were studying in Qianjiang. These student voters were an important source of support for the independent candidate Yao Lifa, who won election in 1998.

In some cases, the election organisers purposely registered uninterested voters and persuaded them to entrust the election officers or some party-controlled voters with proxy votes, but the election organisers did not ask about their voting intentions in advance. According to existing documents, the independent candidates Wu Haining and Xie Xiaoying exposed such misconduct in the elections where they stood in Shenzhen in 2003. Both of them reported that an election officer or party-controlled voter illegally voted proxies for more than three persons on the voting day.[41] In the election where Wu stood, the collected ballots even exceeded the number of distributed ballots.[42] In the election where Xie stood, she saw some aged voters stand proxy for more than three voters and receive gifts from the election organisers at a place near the voting site. Also in the election held in Qianjiang in 2003, while depriving the students of their voting rights, the election organisers did voter registration for the teachers who had retired and moved to live in other places. These voters were obviously unable to vote at the voting site and their proxy votes were all for the organisation-preferred candidates.

There were other tricks the power holders played in the registration step. To sabotage the campaign activities among the voters, the election organisers refused to provide the voters' list to the lawyer and independent candidate Du Peng in an election held in Luoyang, Henan Province in 2006. Such a situation was common for the independent candidates in the elections.

Nominating Candidates

Even though the independent candidates include both voter-nominated candidates and self-nominated candidates, nearly all self-nominated candidates first attempted to become voter-nominated candidates, but their attempts were mostly in vain because of the power holders' interference.

The initial hindrance lies in the distribution of the nomination forms. According to the Electoral Law, a group of at least ten voters or deputies may nominate candidates. According to a researcher, there were no officially standard nomination forms in the elections held in the 1990s. To complete the nomination process at that time, the independent candidates just needed to compose a nomination letter and have it signed by ten or more voters. In the elections held in 2003 and 2006–2007 when more independent candidates appeared, the election officers at different localities made the nomination forms in their own formats and kept independent candidates from obtaining them. In 2003 and 2006, the election organisers refused to give the independent candidate Yao Lifa a nomination form which resulted in his failure to gain voter-nomination. In an election held in Shenzhen in 2006, a group of voters wanted to nominate an independent candidate for the election, but the election officers found excuses not to give them the form until after the nominations had closed. In the elections held in Wuhan in 2006, the election officers delayed giving the forms to most of the independent candidates. Some of them got the form only two days before the nominations closed (Li Fan, 2008:25). In 2006, Yan Yuxiang, an independent candidate in Wuhan, was given a form at 4 pm one day and was ordered to submit the signed form on the next day at 8:20 am. Luo Qiulin the independent candidate in Hengnan, Hunan Province, got the form at 3 pm one day and was asked to submit the signed form at 10 am the next day. In 2006 in Shanghai, independent candidate Liu Shengmin got the form in the late afternoon before the closing day so he had to collect the nominations in his resident community during the night. Even worse, the election organisers denied him the list of the registered voters. In an election held in Luoyang in 2006, the election organisers refused to give a nomination form to the independent candidate Du Peng and explained to him that the official forms were only prepared for organisation-nominated candidates. Using a form obtained from another electorate, Du made a form by himself and got it jointly signed by the voters but the election officers refused to accept it. The independent candidate Xie Xiaoying had the same problem in the election held in Shenzhen in 2003. In that case, the election officers directly told Xie that they could not accept Xie as a voter-nominated candidate because Xie was an unemployed pensioner with inferior health. The officer confirmed to Xie that it was an order from the higher-level election organisers that such a person like Xie could not be nominated. In an election held in Luoyang in 2006, the election officer told the independent candidate Lu Jin that he had only one copy of the form and had not been allocated any funds to duplicate the form. He insisted that Lu should ask for the form from the election organisers at the higher-level. In an election held in Jinan, Shandong Province, an election officer refused to accept the nomination form which the independent candidate Sun Wenguang made by himself. When Sun requested an official form, the officer told him that they had sent out all nomination forms and asked him to come and get it in a few days. When Sun followed his instructions, the officer told Sun the nominations had closed. Even worse, the independent candidates in some cases were not allowed to use the original forms which they obtained through non-official channels. In some cases, the election organisers did not allow the independent candidates to take away the form. Instead, they asked the independent candidates to gather at least ten nominators to sign the form at the election office. In fact, it was not easy to gather the nominators on any working day when the office was open. In an election held in Zhijiang in 2006, the independent candidate Lu Banglie met the above difficulty. In an election held in Shenzhen in 2003, the election officers organised a nomination meeting, requiring all nominators to gather and sign the nomination forms at the meeting site. However, they did not inform the independent candidate Xie Xiaoying about the meeting. Even worse, they deliberately arranged the meeting on the Chinese tomb-sweeping day when Xie's nominators were most likely to be absent.

The problem also lies in the step of collecting forms. For example, in an election held in Luoyang in 2006, the independent candidate Lu Jin was told that the nominations were closed when he went to lodge the completed form at the time the officer had told him. An official document clarified the procedure and the timetable, but the election officer locked it into his filing cabinet and never released it.

After accepting the nomination form, the election organisers normally check with the nominators to confirm their intention. It was very common that the election organisers took advantage of this to intimidate the nominators and destroy their unity. In 2006 in Luoyang, the election officers, accompanied by policemen, went to the nominators' homes to "confirm" their intention of nominating the independent candidate Du Peng. Also in Luoyang in 2006, the nominators of the independent candidate Lu Jin were disturbed by the election organisers too. In an election held in Wuhan, the election organisers intimidated the independent candidate Yan Yuxiang's nominators at their homes. In an election held in Shenzhen in 2006, the nominators of the independent candidate Hu Guojian were called to the election office to receive inquiries one by one. Ironically, in 2006 the election organisers in Qianjiang "originally" and "considerately" made out "The Declaration Form of Withdrawing a Nomination" and persuaded the nominators to sign it. Such dissuasion was in vain in most cases as the independent candidates could anticipate it and had got the nominators prepared for it. In some cases, however, the election organisers successfully destroyed the unity of the nominators and their nomination. According to a researcher, in an election held in Wuhan in 2006, the election officers successfully invalidated a nomination by forcing some of an independent candidate's thirteen nominators to withdraw their nomination. One noticeable thing is that in most existing cases, the election organisers managed the confirmation process without allowing the independent candidates or a third party to watch it. Some independent candidates used to think they could submit the nomination just before the nomination process closed so that the election organisers would have no time to destroy their nominators' unity. However, a serious problem might arise that the submission would quite possibly be late and rejected if the election officers happened not to be in their offices or deliberately stayed away when the independent candidates went to submit the nomination form.[43]

Deciding Full Candidate Lists

Article 31 of the Electoral Law regarding the determination of the full candidate list states:

> The election committee shall, 15 days prior to the date of election, collect and publish the list of nominees and submit it to voter groups in the respective electoral districts for discussion and consultation to determine the list of full candidates. If the number of nominated candidates exceeds the maximum percentage for competitive election as specified in Article 30, the election committee shall submit the list of candidates to voter groups for discussion and consultation, and the list of full candidates shall be determined according to the opinions of the

> majority of voters; if a relative consensus cannot be reached on full candidates for deputies, a preliminary election shall be conducted and the list of full candidates shall be determined by the order of the number of votes that the nominees have obtained in the preliminary election (NPC, 2004c).

This step is possibly the biggest black box in the whole procedure in which the election organisers can drop independent candidates. Focusing on this article, Yao Lifa told the BBC that China's current Electoral Law was "evil" because it created great obstacles to independent candidates by using ambiguous expressions such as "[decide the formal list of candidates] in accordance with the opinion of the majority of voters." The law, however, does not specify the operational methods, thus it enables the local power holders to suppress independent candidates in a "black box." [44] Referring to article 31, a researcher in an interview pointed out that "the purpose of the Chinese Electoral Law is to disallow true elections."

In fact, most of the independent candidates who survived the nomination step were dropped out of the election by the election organisers in this step. In an election held in Shenzhen in 2003, the independent candidate Ye Yuanbai, who was jointly nominated by more than ninety voters, was removed from the full candidate list. The election organisers explained to him that the higher-level had decided that the congress member elected from the electorate should be a female.[45] After the "discussion and consultation" there were two full candidates on the list, including an organisation-preferred candidate and an additional candidate. Most ironically, the additional candidate gained only nine votes in the election, which was even less than the least nomination votes one must have to become a formal candidate. Also in Shenzhen in 2003, the candidate Xu Bo, who was nominated by a "democratic party," was taken off from the full candidate list without "discussion and consultation." Xu was irritated by such illegal conduct and decided to stand for the election as an informal/voter-nominated candidate. In an election held in Shenzhen in 2003, the election officers organised a "discussion and consultation" meeting and appointed sixty-five "representatives" out of nearly 3,000 voters to attend the meeting. As a result, the independent candidate Xie Xiaoying was dropped from the full candidate list.

In an election held in Chongqing in 2003, the independent candidate Yao Shaofan was taken off from the full candidate list as the higher-level had decided the congress member elected from the electorate must be a female. In 2006, the election officers of Yao Shaofan's electorate "discussed and consulted" with some individual voters about the full candidate list in tea houses or restaurants. Among all five candidates, they "discussed" only two independent candidates. As a result, Yao Shaofan was dropped out from the full candidate list even though he was jointly nominated by more than 300 voters.[46]

In an election held in Luoyang in 2006, the local power holders instructed the city government's justice bureau to meet with the lawyer and independent candidate Du Peng three times, threatening him that they would close down the law office where he was working if he insisted on his candidature. They later took off Du from the candidate list without informing him how the "discussion and consultation" was conducted.

In an election held in Shenzhen in 2006, the "discussion and consultation" was conducted among only seven "voter representatives" who were all appointed by the election organisers. All independent candidates who were on the initial candidate list, including the lawyer Hu Guojian, were dropped out from the full candidate list. In an election held in Shanghai in 2006, the "discussion" was conducted between the election organisers and the initial candidates. In the discussion, the election organisers clarified to the initial candidates, who were not the organisation-preferred or additional candidates (independent candidate Liu Shengmin was one of them), that the local party committee had arranged the winners for the upcoming election and they should give up their candidatures.

In the "discussion" step in an election held in Handan in 2006, a township deputy party secretary tried to persuade the independent candidate Du Quanbing to give up his candidature. In an election held in Shanghai in 2006, independent candidate Liu Shengmin, who himself was a party member, was informed by the secretary of his party's branch that he could not enter the full candidate list. They even warned him that the unconditional acceptance of the result was a party member's responsibility. In an election held in Luoyang in 2006, according to an independent candidate, the election officers appointed some unemployed people as the "voter representatives" in the "discussion" step. They bribed these people with some gifts or with the promise to offer them some casual work.

In the elections held in Qianjiang in the 1980s and 1990s, according to an independent candidate, the thirty "voter representatives" appointed by the election organisers decided the full candidate list. The independent candidate also stated that more than ninety-nine percent of the full candidate lists were illegally made by the power holders in the 151 electorates in Qianjiang city for the elections held in 2003 and 2006. In an election held in Handan in 2006, according to an independent candidate, the two organisation-preferred villager candidates did not know they were nominated by the party and they were even feeling annoyed when they discovered that the party had put them into the full candidate list. They refused to go to vote on the voting day.

Article 30 of the Electoral Law says, "The number of candidates for deputies to be directly elected by the voters shall be from one third to 100 percent greater than the number of deputies to be elected." In some elections, however, the power holders held the "discussion and consultation" just in order to drop out the independent candidates even when this procedural step was unnecessary according to the law. In an election held in Shenzhen in 2006, five formal candidates could be legally competing for three congress seats which were assigned to the electorate. The election organisers, however, still ran the "discussion and consultation" process to form the full candidate list which included four candidates. The independent candidate Xie Xiaoying was deprived of her candidature in this illegally-held procedural step. The same thing happened in an election in Wuhan in 2006 where the election organisers illegally ran the "discussion and consultation" process in order to reduce the candidature number from four to three in an electorate with two congress seats. In the "discussion and consultation," the independent candidate Yan Yuxiang was taken off from the list.

In some elections, in order to legalise this "discussion and consultation" step, the power holders took such measures as reducing the assigned congress seats or adding more candidates. In an election held in Chongqing, the power holders added one candidate after they published the initial candidate list. In the following "discussion and consultation" step, the independent candidate Yao Shaofan lost his candidature. In an election held in Wuhan in 2006, three candidates including one independent candidate were competing for the two congress seats assigned to a university electorate. The election organisers, however, decreased the seat number to one in order to legalise the "discussion and consultation." In that step, the competitive independent candidate Chi Haiping was deprived of his candidature.

In contrast to the above cases, the power holders might refuse to reopen the nomination when it was necessary. In an election held in Shenzhen in 2003, when another candidate voluntarily gave up his candidature, there was only one candidate (the independent candidate Wu Haining) who was jointly nominated by 151 voters in the election for the one congress seat assigned to the electorate. In that case, the election organisers should have reopened the nomination process. Instead, the power holders simply cancelled the election.[47]

Receiving a lot of complaints about the "discussion and consultation" step in the elections held in 2003, the standing committee of the 10th National People's Congress amended the Electoral Law in 2004. The following content was added to article 31:

> If a relative consensus cannot be reached on full candidates for deputies, a preliminary election shall be conducted and the list of full candidates shall be determined by the order of the number of votes that the nominees have obtained in the preliminary election (NPC, 2004c).

Most independent candidates expressed positive attitudes towards the preliminary election. They thought a preliminary election would be more open compared with the "discussion and consultation" black box and it would provide them with an extra opportunity to conduct election campaigns and to mobilise the voters. Some researchers, however, were pessimistic because they thought "there are still many excuses [such as lacking funds, balancing the congress members' proportion in age, gender or background] for the local power holders not to hold preliminary elections" (Zhao Xiaoli, 2004). In reality, in the elections held in 2006 and 2007 when the new Electoral Law article was valid, there were very few cases of preliminary elections. The only collected case happened in Wuhan in 2006, in which a competitive independent candidate Fan Jianmin was given an opportunity to compete with other candidates in a preliminary election for a place on the full candidate list. As for that preliminary election, a social activist said that the local power holders had no choice because Fan was too powerfully supported by a huge number of villager voters in his electorate, but such a situation would never become popular. Even in this single case of a preliminary election, according to the activist, the local power holders tried to control the process by taking such measures as "starting the voting abruptly," "using only mobile ballot boxes" and "distributing and collecting ballots at the voters' home." In most other localities, where the local power holders ruled with an iron-hand and where the voters had neither collective intention nor action, preliminary elections were impossible. In an election held in Beijing in 2006, some voter representatives insisted on a place in the full candidate list for the independent candidate Shu Kexin in the "discussion and consultation" step. On the condition that "a relative consensus cannot be reached," the power holders refused to hold a preliminary election. Some similar cases were found in Shenzhen elections in that year (Li Fan, 2008:26). A social activist thought that the National People's Congress added the preliminary election into the law under pressure but they did not expect it would be widely carried out in the local elections. In addition, the amended law does not specify the meaning of "relative consensus" and this imprecision is used to deny voters the opportunity to vote in a preliminary election. The activist also stated that none of the provincial people's congresses had made laws regarding the preliminary election method, which also indicates that the party's real interest lies in not having preliminary elections.

Election Campaigns

As stated in note 6, the Chinese Electoral Law was becoming worse in its content regarding "candidate promotion" when the law was amended in 1982. In fact, the organisation-preferred candidates were normally very quiet if there were no independent candidates in the elections. For them, promotion was meaningless and unnecessary because the power holders had already arranged their success in the non-competitive elections. Such promotion, however, is crucial for independent candidates, especially the informal/self-nominated candidates, to win the elections. Deleting from the Electoral Law 1982 these words "all political parties, people's organisations and voters can use any method to promote candidates" actually ruined the legal basis of the independent candidates' election campaigns.

In most cases, the independent candidates met obstacles when conducting their election campaigns. Some independent candidates in the elections held in Shenzhen in 2003 including Xiao Youmei, Wu Haining, Zou Jiajian, Ye Yuanbai, Xu Bo and Xie Xiaoying had difficulties when trying to distribute their campaign letters or put up posters (Tang Juan, Zou Shubin, 2003: 13, 32, 78, 92, 112, 171). In the elections held in Hengnan and Ji'nan, the local governments interfered in campaign activities of the independent candidates Luo Qiulin and Sun Wenguang. In another election held in a village electorate in Ji'nan, the township executive drank with the independent candidate Zhou Changqing for nearly seven hours the day before the voting day in order to spoil his campaign plan.

The local power holders suppressed the independent candidates more severely in the elections held in some other places, especially in Hubei province. In the elections held in Qianjiang in the 1980s, the local power holders marked the independent candidate Yao Lifa's campaign activities as "bourgeois liberalisation" and judged that Yao was "politically guilty." In the election held in 1998, Yao "sneaked into" the resident communities in his electorate to campaign and had to "climb over the walls to get in late at night" when the prohibition was getting stricter in the election of 2003 (Zhu Ling, 2006).[48] In 2006, the prohibition was upgraded to "red terror" when the local power holders sent the police force to suppress Yao's campaign activities. In the election, the police dispersed Yao's campaign meetings, detained Yao's supporters who helped to print or distribute campaign posters and letters, followed and watched Yao day and night, monitored the phones of Yao and all his contacts and, even worse, they frequently threw Yao into a "black jail" at every crucial moment in the election campaign. Suffering severe suppression, Yao and his supporters were unable to organise an effective election campaign in 2006 (Sui Binbin, 2008b: 119–120). In the election held in Zhijiang in 2006, the police searched the home of the independent candidate Lu Banglie and took away his campaign materials and even his diary. They even tried to take away the campaign materials that Lu had already distributed to the voters. Lu was also under surveillance and he was detained at the police stations or government buildings several times at critical times in the election campaign. In addition, the power holders sent "working teams," which were made up of cadres of the government and party departments of the city, county and township levels, stationed in every village preventing Lu from entering the villages and campaigning among the voters. Ironically, while suffering such suppression, Lu was an incumbent congress member (Sui Binbin, 2007: 203–205). Yan Yuxiang and Wang Guoqiang, the independent candidates in the elections held in Wuhan in 2006, were detained and investigated by the police overnight after they distributed their campaign letters in their electorates (Ding Xiao, 2006a; Yan Yuxiang, 2008: 148–149). A businessman in Wuhan happened to see an independent candidate's newsletter and he felt that it was good. He then made 2,000 copies and distributed the letters. He was therefore detained and investigated by the police even though he did not know the independent candidate at all. The terror atmosphere which the local power holders created frightened and held back some independent candidates. According to a researcher, knowing that police activities aimed at some other independent candidates, the independent candidate Xiao Shuixiang in Wuhan was terrified. He burnt his campaign materials and took cash with him, getting ready to escape at any moment. In an election held in Handan, Hebei province in 2006, the police knew all the campaign plans of the independent candidate Tian Qizhuang by secretly monitoring his phone calls. The political commissar of a police station then threatened Tian and the business firms who produced Tian's campaign materials. In 2006, the election organisers in Shenzhen illegally refused to organise a meeting for the independent candidate Ma Jianhua and the voters. In addition, they warned Ma that any such meetings she organised by herself were against the law and would bring her severe punishment. According to a researcher, in another electorate in Shenzhen in 2006, the election organisers deprived an independent candidate of his candidature just because of his campaign activities (Li Fan, 2008: 26).[49]

The situation seemed better in Shanghai and Beijing. Though disturbed several times by the *chengguan* (the urban management officers) in his campaign activities in Shanghai in 2006, independent candidate Liu Shengmin, said that the power holders in Shanghai were more "civilised" than those in other places (Liu Shengmin, 2008: 226). In the election campaign in 2006, Liu set up a 24 hour hotline and published his home address for the voters. He even promised that the voters could closely watch his work and even life if they felt like it. In Beijing, there were no existing cases of suppression in the independent candidates' campaign activities. In an election in Beijing in 2003, the independent candidate Shu Kexin even established his election campaign office and his electioneering team which was made up of some professionals in public relations and law. According to the available materials, they managed the office scientifically and conducted the campaign strategically (Hu Kui, Wu Peishuang, Zhang Lan, 2003). Shu confirmed that "they did not meet obvious obstacles in their campaign activities . . . perhaps because they were in Beijing" (Huang Xiaomei 2008).[50] However, as a researcher pointed out, the soft attitude towards the nominations and election campaigns does not mean the power holders in Beijing were more tolerant of the independent candidates. This researcher revealed that there were more than ten thousand jointly nominated independent candidates on the initial candidate lists[51] in Beijing in 2006 but very few of them could finally win congress seats. Analysing this phenomenon, the researcher believed that the election organisers in Beijing, unlike the iron-handed power holders in some other places, eliminated the independent candidates furtively but ruthlessly in the "discussion" and "voting" stages.

In some places where the tension between the independent candidates and the local power holders kept increasing, the election organisers neglected their duty to mobilise voters and promote elections. Some independent candidates themselves promoted the elections. This made the election organisers nervous and they even tried to stop the independent candidates from promoting the elections even in a neutral way. In 2002, the independent candidate Yao Lifa compiled into a brochure some important national and local Electoral Law articles and made some copies of the brochures for the voters in his electorate. The power holders in Qianjiang took them away from Yao and penalized him 8,000 *yuan* for making "illegal publications." In 2006, funded by some researchers in Beijing, the independent candidate (and incumbent people's congress member) Lu Banglie in Zhijiang composed some booklets which were mainly made up of law articles and official documents. The police searched his house and took away these booklets. In Shenzhen in 2006, the election organisers did not put up official promotion banners in the independent candidate Jiang Shan's electorate.[52] Jiang selected four slogans out of the eighteen which had been officially approved by the higher-level election organisers, made them as banners and hung them up in his electorate. The security soon came to take them down. Considering the serious legal consequence of taking down the election banners, Jiang believed it must be the local power holders who encouraged the security to do it. Jiang wrote an accusation letter to the police but there was no response.

Voting

The illegal operations at the voting stage varied from case to case. However, the most obvious and massive offences against the law were in elections held in the two urban districts of Wuchang and Hongshan, Wuhan in 2006. When the local power holders felt they were having difficulties controlling the election result, they just organised the voting one day[53] ahead of the published schedule without giving notice in advance.[54] On that day, instead of establishing voting stations, the election officers took mobile ballot boxes to the voters' homes for voting. The whole process including ballot distribution, collection and counting was not witnessed by scrutineers. According to the Electoral Law of Hubei Province, which was in effect for these elections, the voting date can be changed and only postponed due to irresistible natural disasters and the mobile ballot boxes can be used only for voters who have difficulty casting a vote at the voting station because of age or handicap (People's Congress of Hubei Province, 2006). As a result of the illegal operation, none of the nearly twenty popularly-supported lawyers, intellectuals and social activists who were standing for the elections as independent candidates in these two urban districts could win a congress seat. A researcher commented that in Wuhan in 2006 "the power holders would rather break the laws than let independent candidates win the elections."

Another big black box was the process of counting ballots. In an election in Handan in 2006, a competitive independent candidate Tian Qizhuang had gone through the steps of nomination, "discussion" to be a formal candidate and he had met with the voters three times at officially organised campaign meetings. However, he was stopped from winning the election by the power holders at the last step. On the voting day, when the voting was ended, the election officers transferred the ballot boxes from the voting site to an isolated building, where only the election officers were allowed to enter and count the ballots. Tian's lawyer wrote an accusatory letter to the higher-level people's congress, but the government's justice bureau soon forced him to withdraw the letter. A similar thing happened in an election in Shanghai in 2006. When the voting process finished, the election organisers took away the ballot boxes. The independent candidate Liu Shengmin and other voters in the electorate were never informed of the election result. In an election held in a university electorate in Ji'nan in 2006, it was not until four days after the voting day that the election result was published. The independent candidate Sun Wenguang criticised the election organisers for delaying the publishing of the result just because they wished to dissipate the passion of the student voters (Sun Wenguang, 2007). In an election in Shenzhen in 2006, the lawyer independent candidate Hu Guojian was detained by the police during the whole voting process. Immediately after he was set free, he took his supporters to the voting station, hoping to watch the process of counting ballots. However, they were held back by the police at a place thirty metres away from the ballot counting site, where the ballot boxes were entirely surrounded by numerous election officers. Most ironically, in the election held in Zhijiang in 2006, an election officer shouted at a low ranking staff member, who was reporting to the voters the current voting result, "I will sack you immediately if you mention Lu Banglie's (the independent candidate) name again."

The election organisers also tried to control the scrutineers to guarantee the election organisers' cheating in the process of counting votes. In the election held in 2006 in Shenzhen when the independent candidate Jiang Shan stood, the election officers organised a vote to elect the scrutineers in the very early morning of the voting day. However, nearly none of the registered voters (only registered voters were eligible to vote for scrutineers) were present because of the time. The people who voted in that election for scrutineers were only the community security staffs who were controlled by the power holders, but they were not registered voters and thus were actually not qualified to vote to elect the scrutineers.

In some cases, the local governments or police detained and threatened the independent candidates on the eve of the voting day or on the voting day itself. The available cases include independent candidates Lu Banglie in Zhijiang in 2006 (Yu Meisui, 2006), Yao Lifa in Qianjiang in 2006 (Yao Lifa, 2008: 136), Hu Guojian in Shenzhen in 2006, and Yan Yuxiang and Wang Guoqiang in Wuhan in 2006. A report exposed that detention and threats to the independent candidates were common in the elections held in Wuhan in 2006 (Ding Xiao, 2006a). There were also cases of violence against independent candidates. For example, on the voting day, the independent candidate Wang Guoqiang (a police inspector and CCP member in Wuhan) was violently attacked by three policemen in a police station (Ding Xiao, 2006b). The independent candidate Wen Yan, who was a member of the Union of Chinese Nationalists, was also violently attacked on a street in Wuhan by four unidentified men days before the voting day. Wen's mother was also injured in the attack (Li Jianjun, 2006).

According to a researcher, it is common for the election organisers to fail to establish a booth at the voting stations for voters to complete their ballots secretly (Qiu Jiajun, 2008: 52).[55] The available cases included an election in Handan in 2006 (reported by independent candidate Tian Qizhuang) (Tian Qizhuang, Wang Weixing, 2007), elections in Shenzhen in 2003 where independent candidate Wu Haining, Zou Jiajian and Xie Xiaoying stood (Tang Juan, Zou Shubin, 2003: 37, 79, 181), an election in Handan in 2006 where Du Quanbing stood (Peng Lanhong, 2008: 285), an election in Ji'nan in 2006 where Sun Wenguang stood (Sun Wenguang, 2007), and elections in Qianjiang in the 1990s, 2003 and 2006 where Yao Lifa stood (Yao Lifa, 2008; Zhu Ling, 2006). There were other various kinds of special tricks that the local power holders played in the voting process aimed at independent candidates. In an election held in a university electorate in Wuhan in 2006, the *fudaoyuan* [political advisors] and student cadres repeatedly checked the ballots of student voters to ensure they were not for an independent candidate (Yao Lifa, 2006). In an election held in Zhijiang in 2006, the government officials and local police watched the voters completing their ballots. They even followed the voters who wanted to fill in their ballots somewhere else and persuaded them not to vote for the independent candidate Lu Banglie (Sui Binbin, 2007). Since 1998, the election officers in Qianjiang have watched the voters completing their ballots in every election. In a voting station established in a high school in Qianjiang in 2003, every group of four voters was arranged to complete their ballots at one desk with a cadre voter appointed to each group. In some voting stations in Qianjiang in 2003, the election organisers required the voters to stay in their seats after completing their votes. They then went to collect the completed ballots from every seat without carrying a ballot box with them. In the elections held since 1998, the election organisers gave a hint to the voters in some voting stations that the voters should unfold their ballots when casting them into boxes. Some "progressive" voters did show their loyalty to the power holders. The election officers tended to be more attentive to those voters who ignored the hint and those who spent a longer time in completing their votes because it normally took more time to write down an independent candidate's name in the "voting for others" item on a ballot than just crossing out the names of the formal candidates. To make full use of the administrative power to control the voters, the election organisers established twenty-three voting stations in Yao's electorate.[56] As the voting stations established in the very small units of the schools (for example a teaching group for a grade), the head of the small unit would not escape from punishment if Yao was successful in the ballot box set in his/her unit.[57] In the elections held in Qianjiang in 2006, the election officers continuously shouted to the voters in many electorates "do not vote for Yao Lifa." In the election held in Shenzhen in 2003, to stop the independent candidate Xie Xiaoying, the election organisers warned some voters at the voting station that "completing the part of 'voting for others' will definitely invalidate your vote" (Tang Juan, Zou Shubin, 2003: 181).

There was other misconduct of the election organisers in the voting process. For example, they negligently or deliberately accepted proxy votes without checking the proxy certificates.[58] They distributed ballots without carefully checking the voters' certifications. One such case was during an election held in Qianjiang in 1998 where the independent candidate Yao Lifa stood (Zhu Ling, 2006).

Other Problems in and after the Electoral Process

Threatening and Luring

In some cases, the local power holders created political tension among the voters by spreading rumours about the independent candidates and threatening the voters. The organisers of an election held in Shenzhen in 2003 created and spread the rumour that the independent candidate Xie Xiaoying was in a gang with someone who was monitored and investigated by the secret police. In an election held in a university electorate in Ji'nan in 2006, the party committee announced at a meeting that the independent candidate Sun Wenguang was funded by an enemy alien power. At the meeting, the party published an order prohibiting the voters from viewing Sun's campaign posters. The party also warned that they would ask the police to check the handwriting on the ballots to find out who voted for Sun and then punish them accordingly. The warning that the police would "check handwriting" to identify those who voted for independent candidate Yao Lifa was widely spread in Qianjiang during the election periods in 2003 and 2006. Some other rumours included that Yao had connections with foreign agencies and had been wanted by the police, and that the central party had already prohibited Yao from being elected. Normally, the rumours started from the local party or government meetings and then quickly spread to the grassroots voters. Such rumours were usually very effective in threatening the voters not to vote for the independent candidates, especially after the voters saw with their own eyes that the independent candidates and their supporters were frequently detained and investigated by the police. Regarding the effect of such propaganda campaigns against the independent candidates, a social activist commented that "after suffering cruel political movements, a Chinese person tends to choose keeping silent when sensing any political insecurity." An extreme case happened in Rongcheng, Hebei Province in 2006. An incumbent county congress member felt sympathy for an independent candidate who was unjustly treated in an election and he spoke for the independent candidate. He was then criticised by the county party leaders and insulted by local policemen. The congressman felt so distressed that he committed suicide by hanging himself.

On the other hand, in order to separate and soften voters who supported the independent candidates, the power holders promised or offered some tangible benefits. In the election held in Zhijiang in 2006, in order to reduce the hostile emotions among the villager voters who supported the independent candidate Lu Banglie, the local government promised the voters some infrastructure projects in the villages. Just before the election, they assigned to each poverty-stricken family a sum of money, which was directly sent to the villagers to avoid being skimped by any level of cadres. They also sent out some doctors to visit and treat the poor villagers in the electorate before the election. The government was trying to weaken Lu's reputation. Lu had found some outside families who would like to adopt orphans in the villages. Knowing that, the local government immediately sent the orphans to a government orphanage and established a fund for these children, which aborted Lu's adoption project. In an election held in Ji'nan in 2006, in order to soften the independent candidate's Zhou Changqing's supporters, the local government promised some infrastructure projects in the villages and they even displayed to the voters the budget plan they had made for the projects. In an election held in Qianjiang in 2006, during the time of the independent candidate Yao Lifa's election campaigns, the power holders organised dinner parties for the voters in the electorate and sent some gifts of business suits to them.[59] Also in that election, the local government created a temporary highly-paid work position for an important campaign worker of Yao Lifa. The work required the person to live at the working site and to be on call day and night, which made him unable to assist Yao in his campaign activities. The position was cancelled soon after the election. Another case happened in Shenzhen in 2003 after the election. When the voters who supported the independent candidate Wu Haining proposed a motion to recall the newly elected congress member Chen Huibin, she took quick measures to soften the voters by proposing to the local people's congress to improve the infrastructure such as bus stations, drainage system and primary schools in the locality. In addition, she held a meeting with the voters after coming back from the congress conferences and reported the conference situation to them at the meeting. Chen's actions had rarely been seen before in Shenzhen or even in the whole of China.

Election Organisers Standing for Elections plus the Legal System Having no Judicial Power

The Chinese electoral laws do not prohibit election organisers from standing for the elections that they are organising. The leaders of the party committees, governments and people's congresses of various levels are often the organisation-preferred candidates who must be guaranteed a win in the people's congress elections. In fact, this phenomenon is common in Chinese elections. There were some obvious cases. For example, in Beijing in 2006, independent candidate Shu Kexin competed with an incumbent district people's congress speaker in the election held in this district. In Shenzhen in 2003, independent candidate Wu Haining competed with a party secretary of urban community. The community formed the electorate and the party secretary was appointed chief election officer of this electorate. In Shenzhen in 2003, independent candidate Xie Xiaoying had a rival, who was the party secretary of Xie's urban community and the chief election officer in her electorate. Undoubtedly these independent candidates were very disadvantaged when competing against a rival who was also the "referee of the game."[60]

Even worse, judicial remedies were not available when there was a breach of the legal rights of the independent candidates in the congress elections. Article 28 of the Chinese Electoral Law states that the People's Law Courts deal with suits raised by voters against the decisions of election organisers on their voter qualifications.[61] The Electoral Law contains no other information about the law courts' judicial power on any other election affairs. Having no judicial power, the law courts actually never accept nor hear a case regarding election conflicts other than voter qualifications.[62] In a case, the independent candidate Xie Xiaoying tried to bring a law suit to a law court in Shenzhen for the illegal treatment she received in the election, but the law court told her that they would not accept nor hear her case. Instead, the independent candidates were told to appeal to the higher-level people's congress for their grievance, but normally there is no result from such appeals. A researcher said in an interview that "the party thoroughly dominated the people's congress system and in most cases the local party committee secretary has carefully examined backgrounds of the organisation-preferred candidates and selected those who would enter the people's congress before the election was held." Knowing that, we can easily understand that any appeal through the channels inside the organisation would be futile. Still holding the belief in the Chinese legal system, some lawyers and researchers loudly argued for the availability of judicial remedies for the conflicts in the elections (Huang Xiaomei, 2008: 70). The party-controlled law makers, however, seem not to have reacted to their appeal. During the field research, a researcher revealed that the local power holders in most cases destroyed the original documents shortly after the elections. The files kept in the archives were created afterwards to match the election results. If what the researcher said was the truth, the law courts would have great difficulties in the investigation of the past elections.

Retaliation, Long Term Surveillance and the Black List

In some cases, the persecution of the independent candidates did not stop until long after the election was over. For example, according to an informant, a special office was permanently established in Qianjiang aimed at the independent candidate Yao Lifa, which was made up of cadres from the government, the party, the police and the firm that employed Yao. The office coordinated the above-mentioned departments to monitor Yao's daily life and suppress all his political activities. Another persecution, according to the informant, was a prohibition order made by the central party's publicity department in 2005 that Yao's name would never appear in any media in China, which was an obvious breach of Yao's basic human rights. In Wuhan, to avenge the independent candidate Yan Yuxiang for his participation in an election in 2006, the local power holders forced the property owner to terminate a rental contract with Yan. After Yan moved to another place to live, they tried to find his new address, perhaps to enable the election organisers in that electorate to take pre-cautionary measures. In Luoyang, the foreign media interviewed independent candidate Du Peng by telephone after the election. The local power holders soon began to investigate this. It was generally believed that Du's phone was monitored so that the power holders could know this matter so quickly. In Shenzhen, the independent candidate Hu Guojian was detained several times at the airport when he was to fly to other cities for business. The airport security had to wait for permission from the police before they would allow Hu to board the plane. Obviously Hu was on a black list which was distributed by the power holders or the police to the security departments of all traffic terminals.

Strategies and Impacts

Strategies

It was known from the field research that a rather large number of independent candidates were connected during and after the elections. Some of them not only stood for the elections held in their localities but also mobilised the independent candidates and provided them with training and assistance in adjoining places or even in other provinces.[63] These independent candidates could view the elections from a more comprehensive perspective and summarise some strategic counter measures against the power holders' suppression on the basis of the lessons drawn from various cases.

Some of these independent candidates revealed that they had been making preparations for the next elections. They said they would make full use of the five-year period between elections to mobilise and train independent candidates, to do various campaign activities among voters and to organise charity and rights movements to win them a greater reputation. They hoped such long and persistent preparation work would weaken or make ineffective the power holders' threatening or luring of voters and their other interference in the independent candidates' election campaigns. When more independent candidates were mobilised to participate in the elections in more electorates, the tricks that the power holders played in dividing electorates would become less effective. In the past elections, the local power holders devoted a huge amount of human and financial resources to suppress the individual independent candidates. Taking the Zhijiang election as an example, the power holders sent out "work teams," which were made up of cadres from government and party departments at three levels, to the eight villages in Lu Banglie's electorate. In addition, according to an informant, the power holders at Lu's locality spent more than one million *yuan* in preventing him from winning the election. In contrast, Lu's campaigning fund was only six thousand *yuan*, donated by some university teachers in Beijing. According to the strategies of these independent candidates, if the number of independent candidates keeps increasing and they are widely spread in more electorates, the power holders will lack human and material power to aim at each of these candidates. Then, some independent candidates will possibly take advantage of the loosened control to win congress seats.

Some independent candidates attached great importance to the elections for village and urban resident community heads. The value of these elections has long been underrated because villages in rural areas and resident communities in urban areas are all below even the lowest level in China's political system. In an independent candidate's opinion, however, to democratise the elections at this level may help to improve the local congress elections. The independent candidate gave two reasons. First, the village and resident community heads are normally assigned some specific and important tasks in the local people's congress elections such as voter registration, distributing ballots, checking voter qualifications and counting ballots. The term of a village committee or a resident community is three years while the term of a local people's congress is five years. In that case, the villager or resident community heads, who have been democratically elected in the lowest level elections and genuinely represent the villagers' or urban residents' interest, can hardly be controlled by the power holders when carrying out those basic and important tasks in the people's congress elections. The quality of the people's congress elections may be improved on that basis and the independent candidates may have greater chances to win in the people's congress elections. Second, the genuinely democratic elections for village and resident community heads may become good examples for the future people's congress elections. Through participating in these primary-level elections, villagers and urban residents will learn that they can voice their opinions by casting votes. With such experience, they will naturally resist the party-manipulated elections. According to some researchers, that the party keeps strengthening its control on the village and resident community elections in the recent years is partly because of the above mentioned reasons. In reality, a group of independent candidates including both urban residents and villagers have been actively involved in the village elections held in some localities.

An independent candidate also called attention to the student voters and lawyer independent candidates. This independent candidate pointed out that the student voters were an active power in the elections. They were passionate, courageous, critical, and interacted with each other. Since the year 2003, the independent candidate started his plan to campaign at the schools in his locality and mobilised student independent candidates in other places. He had established good relations with many university and high school teachers, who he said had strongly supported his campaign and mobilisation activities on campuses. Besides the university students, the independent candidate highly evaluated the role of high school students in the elections. He believed that providing training to them was important because these year-12 students, some of whom have attained the legal age to be eligible voters, would soon study in universities and play a vital role in the voting held in university electorates. In addition, according to some researchers, the role of the lawyer independent candidates should be emphasised and their work in the legal cases of "public interest litigation" and "maintaining rights for the disadvantaged" should be financially funded. In their opinion, these legal cases would greatly help these lawyers to establish their reputation among voters. Since such cases were normally financially unprofitable, obtaining financial aid for these lawyers would enable them to devote more time and energy to such kinds of legal cases, which would help to maintain social justice and help the disadvantaged. More importantly, the legal cases in which the lawyers had actively participated could provide vivid examples to the voters how these lawyers would represent their interest after they were elected as people's congress members. The participation of the lawyers in these legal cases would actually become a kind of election campaign that was more effective than the campaign activities organised shortly before the voting day.

Another strategy was to encourage the self-nominated/informal independent candidates to compete for congress seats in more electorates which included but was not restricted to the electorates where they were registered as voters. The Chinese national and local electoral laws rule that a voter can be nominated and become a formal candidate in only one electorate, which can be the same as or different from the electorate where he or she has his or her voter registration (The State Council Law Office, 2008: 33), but the laws do not prohibit that a candidate can win an election in an electorate while he or she is registered as a voter in another electorate. On that basis, different from a formal candidate who can stand for the election in only one electorate (his/her electorate or another electorate), a self-nominated/informal candidate can freely choose to campaign and stand for elections in many various electorates.[64] In reality, during the break period between two elections, some social activists and lawyers got actively involved in the work of helping the disadvantaged people in some different localities to maintain their rights. In the elections, these activists and lawyers who have been well coordinated and organised in their actions can assign members to stand for the elections in the electorates where they have established good relations with the voters. The cases where independent candidates stood for the elections in other electorates were not rare in 2006. In addition, there were the cases in the elections that some independent candidates won votes in dozens of electorates in a locality and the adjoining localities. A researcher commented that "this phenomenon seems able to provide a reference for the possible direct elections for local government executives in the future."[65] Furthermore, if such coordination of these independent candidates and their unified planning keeps improving in future elections, their "organisation" may possibly become the prototype for an opposition political party in China.[66]

Some Existing Impacts

The independent candidates' participation has had some positive effects on their elections. On one hand, it reignited voters' passion for the local congress elections in some localities. An independent candidate described the change of voters' attitudes in his electorate. According to him, the voters had been indifferent to electoral affairs for many years because they felt it made no difference whoever was elected in the controlled elections. The participation of the independent candidate seemed to awaken the voters and they began to realise they could use their votes to support a grassroots candidate in an election, who would genuinely represent their interest. Even better, some independent candidates such as Yao Lifa, Lu Banglie, Zeng Jianyu and Yao Shaofan were successfully elected and they did excellent work for their voters when they were congress members, which further convinced the voters that the local people's congress elections were an available and perhaps the easiest channel through which they could play their own role in improving the politics in their localities.

While in nearly all the elections the power holders suppressed the independent candidates, there was a single case that the "open-minded" election organisers did not interfere with the independent candidate. Instead, they campaigned for the organisation-preferred candidates. According to the independent candidate who stood for the election, the power holders in his locality had never made election campaigns for the organisation-preferred candidates in the previous elections because such campaigns were "unnecessary" and meaningless when winners were decided in advance. In this election, however, imitating the independent candidate, the organisation-preferred candidates distributed campaign letters and made public speeches to the voters. With the participation of independent candidate, this election became more liberal than the previous ones. However, the case happened in 1993 when independent candidates were very few and the party had not determined to suppress them with an iron hand. In my research, I have not found any other similar cases. Such a liberal election is very unlikely to be allowed by the party in the future.

Future Population

Around three quarters of the interviewed independent candidates said that they would not participate in future congress elections if there were no obvious improvements in the elections and the laws.[67] A researcher who had long been engaged in field research on this subject optimistically speculated that the population of independent candidates in the congress elections held in 2011 and 2012 would reach hundreds of thousands or even up to more than one million. Considering the power holders' suppression, I had to agree with another researcher's opinion that there would be a "moderate increase" rather than a "big boost" in the independent candidate population in future elections.

A Brief Conclusion

Value of the "Reform" Experiments

An increasing number of independent candidates, some of whom were connected and interacted with each other in their activities, stood for the local people's congress elections according to the rights allowed by the Chinese Constitution and electoral laws. In order to prevent the independent candidates from being elected as people's congress members, the party committees at various levels, especially the primary-level party committees, reacted to the independent candidates' electoral actions during the elections and even before and after the elections. In most cases the party suppressed the independent candidates with obvious or furtive illegal methods. In a few cases they used the governmental resources to increase the competitiveness of the organisation-preferred candidates. The independent candidates' electoral activities and the party's reactions brought some changes to the people's congress elections in these localities, which, in my opinion, formed a kind of local people's congress "reform" experiment. Different from the reform described in other chapters, this "reform" was instigated from outside the party system, but it will have impacts on China's political structure if it continues to develop. On the other hand, as a researcher who for a long time has closely watched Chinese political changes said in an interview, "the authoritarian party will not automatically reform the current Chinese political system unless it yields to the growing opposing power. It is like a face-to-face struggle. Only when the people yearning for democracy move one step forward, the party moves a step backward. Political democratisation will be finally achieved in China when enough reforms accumulate and fundamental change takes place." Political reform experiments which were instigated outside the party organisation and were started from the grassroots level, such as those described in this chapter, have much more value than the experiments that the party organised mainly for propaganda purposes.

Prospects

At the current stage, as can be seen, power holders tend to severely suppress the legal electoral activities of independent candidates in the local people's congress elections. As a result, electoral victories for independent candidates were very rare.[68] It is difficult to anticipate the prospect of the "reform" because there are many uncertain factors in future elections such as the central party's attitude, the local power holders' reaction, the level of the voters' support, the population of independent candidates, their strategies and resolution etc. These factors are linked. One fact is clear that the continuous cruel suppression of the "people's political expression through legal channels" may make the people thoroughly disillusioned with the constitution and laws, which will lead to social instability or even a violent revolution.

In summary, the future expansion and further development of such "reform" on the local people's congress elections, which are started and pushed by the independent candidates, may perhaps become a breakthrough to China's eventual democratisation. The prospect of the reform is uncertain and which deserves more observation and research in the future. At the current stage, however, it is highly unlikely that the participation of the grassroots power in Chinese local elections can lead China to political democratisation.

Notes

1. According to Article 2 of *The Electoral Law of the National People's Congress and Local People's Congress of the People's Republic of China*, "Deputies to the people's congresses of cities not divided into districts, municipal districts, counties, autonomous counties, townships, nationality townships, and towns shall be elected directly by their constituencies"(NPC, 2004c).

2. The names and other identifying characteristics of all informants interviewed in the field research are not disclosed in the chapter because of concerns for their safety.

3. Some candidates in this category might be nominated by other *minzhu dangpai* [puppet political parties] rather than the CCP or some *renmin tuanti* [people's organizations]. Here, organization refers to a bureaucratic system in a range wider than the CCP but the CCP holds the absolute power in the system.

4. In an interview, an independent candidate revealed to me that in his locality many organisation-preferred candidates became "voter-nominated candidates" after the party's manipulations. As he described, only the district party's organisation department could nominate candidates. There were a large number of organisation-preferred people but the department could nominate only some of them. In that case, after the party's manipulation, the rest of the organisation-preferred people all became candidates with "voters' nominations." To define the categories of candidates, we need to pay special attention to this trick, even though it is not known if such a thing commonly happens in the elections in other localities.

5. According to Article 30 of *The Electoral Law of the National People's Congress and Local People's Congresses of the People's Republic of China* (2004), "The number of candidates for deputies to the national and local people's congresses shall be greater than the number of deputies to be elected. The number of candidates for deputies to be directly elected by the voters shall be from one third to 100 percent greater than the number of deputies to be elected . . ." (NPC, 2004c).

6. In the electoral law enacted in 1979, article 30 states "all political parties, people's organisations and voters can take any method to promote candidates." This article provided a legal basis for the independent candidates who campaigned and won the local congress elections in 1980. However, when the electoral law was amended in 1982, the relevant content was changed to "the election committee shall brief voters on the candidates for deputies. Political parties, people's organisations, voters and deputies that have nominated candidates for deputies may brief voters on those candidates at group meetings

of voters or deputies." In 2004 when the law was again amended, some new content was added into article 33 that "the election committee may arrange for the candidates to meet with voters and to answer their questions. However, such briefings must stop on the day of election." In the electoral law amended in 2010, article 33 was "election committees shall, upon request of voters, arrange meetings between deputy candidates and voters to allow deputy candidates to introduce themselves and answer voters' questions." Article 33 regarding election campaigns in this latest-edition of the electoral law is worse than article 30 of the electoral law of 1979. In fact, emphasising the election committee's function in the campaign activities becomes a good excuse for prohibiting the self-organised campaigns of independent candidates, a huge obstacle to winning the elections. This point will be further discussed on p. 121.

7. A few of them later became famous democratic activists.

8. Zeng Jianyu, according to an informant, is a reputable grassroots hero, influential independent candidate and brave social activist. The power holders resented him and were afraid of his activities of "protecting rights." They then created the crime of "fraud" for him and put him in prison from 2001 to 2002 and from 2006 to now.

9. Yao Lifa has now become the most well-known social activist in China struggling for freedom in local elections. Although he has not been arrested and put into prison, he continuously suffers the authority's persecution, such as being monitored 24 hours a day, being frequently subjected to house searches and having possessions confiscated, and being frequently detained or house arrested. On March 18, 2010 when this book was nearly completed, VOA revealed the news that Yao's environment was worsening and he had been out of contact with his friends for some time. See http://www1.voanews.com/chinese/news/china/CHINA-HUBEI-20100318-88392757.html.

10. Qianjiang, a small county-level city in Hubei Province became a focus in the 2003 elections. Motivated and guided by the famous independent candidate Yao Lifa, forty-one people competed in the elections for congress seats as independent candidates (BBC, 2008).

11. The article by Gou Ye (Gou Ye, 2003) published in *Nanfangdushibao* on 22 April 2003 was believed the first one of the massive media reports on the independent candidates in the elections of 2003. According to an informant, the reporter got the hint for his article from a press conference organised by a district people's congress in Shenzhen, in which the congress officers introduced an independent candidate's campaign activity in his electorate and highly commended it as evidence of the citizens' enthusiasm for elections. Making such positive comments, the congress officers perhaps did not expect that the grassroots power would grow so rapidly and would possibly threaten the party's control over the elections.

12. The two books *The Memoir of the Elections in Shenzhen in 2003* (Tang Juan, Zou Shubin, 2003) and *The Memoir of the District and County People's Congress Elections in Beijing in 2003* (Zou Shubin, 2004) constitute nearly all research on independent candidates Chinese researchers have conducted up to now. The researchers cautiously avoided using the word "independent candidate" in both book names and contents to reduce the sensitivity of the books.

13. The preliminary election was added into the electoral procedure as a selective step since 2004. This will be further discussed in the following part.

14. More information is at http://politics.people.com.cn/GB/4514649.html.

15. A researcher pointed out that many independent candidates at various localities got to know each other from the relevant media reports and research papers. They inquired from the journalists and researchers about the contact details of each other and then they could become closely connected during and after elections. According to the researcher, this was probably one of the reasons why the party prohibited news reports and

academic research on this subject. On the other hand, when the party felt the potential threat the independent candidates made to their authoritarian rule, they had to control the influence of these people and had to prevent more people from following their path.

16. Another informant confirmed the existence of the party's furtive manipulation and he estimated that the party's prohibitive order was made and transmitted in the middle of 2006. He made this estimation because the last journalistic report in mainstream media on this subject (Zhang Jun, A Ji, 2006) appeared in late March 2006 and there were almost no such reports thereafter. Neither of these two informants, however, could provide direct evidence for the party's prohibition. Some words in an official propaganda article might be able to suggest the party's real attitudes, "[the media should] fully understand the spirit of the notice from the central party [referring to the central CCP's No.12 document of 2006, which is a party's internal document regarding the organisation work of the local people's congress elections in 2006 and 2007] . . . absolutely control the guiding opinion of journalism . . . ensure that all reports will have no negative effects ..." (Huang Shunxiang, 2007). In addition, an expert in Chinese media studies told me that the central party's publicity department often transmits through the party's mechanisms these orders that the press media should be quiet on certain topics. The party and governmental publicity departments at various levels and the party mechanisms established inside the public media units will take immediate actions to carry out the order. The media researcher also said such orders are normally not written into any official documents in order to avoid being leaked and being used as evidence of the party's control over the mass media. This information is in agreement with the above statement that the party could secretly and suddenly keep all media and academia quiet on independent candidate issues.

Shenzhen University used to be an important base for these researchers studying independent candidates and they published two influential books in this area (see note 12 for details). However, according to an informant, after receiving the prohibition order from the central party, the party leaders of Shenzhen City instructed the party leaders of the Shenzhen University to stop the researchers' work on the subject. Since then, the researchers in Shenzhen University dared not research the subject. In addition, they refused to attend conferences or to be interviewed on the subject.

17. In my opinion, there are two possible reasons for the unavailability of the statistics of independent candidates in China. First, a survey was prohibited by the party. Second, as a researcher said in an interview, independent candidates, especially self-nominated/informal candidates, could emerge or disappear during any procedural step in an election. This makes calculating their total numbers very difficult.

18. This estimated figure seems much higher than expected, so it remains questionable.

19. I have collected the cases in these provinces except for Sichuan, Gansu and Inner Mongolia. The information that there were independent candidates in these three places was obtained from some researchers but they could not or would not provide the candidate names and other details.

20. The cases I collected and studied were only a very small part of all cases in the 2003 and 2006–2007 elections and they can certainly not represent the whole. However, by categorising the independent candidates from the collected cases and summarising some common features of each category, I hope this part of the chapter can help readers to understand the independent candidates and their motivations more easily.

21. A mass protest movement may reflect the lawyers' dissatisfaction with authority. In order to maintain their legal rights, on 26 August 2008 three lawyers in Beijing published a letter appealing for a direct election for the chiefs of the Beijing lawyer's association, which were actually organised and controlled by a government department, the Justice Bureau of Beijing (Tang Jitian, Cheng Hai, Zhang Lihui, 2008). Very soon thirty-five

other lawyers expressed their support by signing the letter and more than seventy lawyers and perhaps eighty-two lawyers signed the letter by October (Wang Youjin, 2009; Xu Zhiyong, 2009). The party-controlled lawyer's association over-reacted to the letter. On 5 September 2008, they published a statement which was in the "red terror" style, criticising these lawyers as "negating the current political system" (The Beijing Lawyer's Association, 2008). The party took drastic measures to dissuade the lawyers from supporting the appeal. Some lawyers were summoned to the justice bureau to make explanations (Wang Youjin, 2009). The justice department of a district government forced the nineteen lawyers in that district who had signed the document to write reports about their "intentions." Three lawyers had their work contracts terminated because of signing the document (Xu Zhiyong, 2009).

22. In the field research on the elections for property owner's committees, some property owner representatives and their lawyers provided me with some detailed information about the conflicts between the property owners and the real estate management firms. Briefly, some huge profits (tens of millions of *yuan* for a medium size resident community) are generated from the property management fee paid by the property owners and from leasing the public spaces as business premises, parking spaces etc. The elected property owner's committee, fully on behalf of all owners in the community, has the right to audit how the money is used. However, the government-controlled community offices, allied with the estate management firms, make every effort to invalidate or control the election results. Without any effective inspection from the property owner's committee, the real estate management firms are quite free when using the money. They can easily bribe the officers for their previous and future support.

23. The Union of Chinese Nationalists is a political dissenting organisation which was active in the local congress elections in 2006 and 2007. The organisation was established in 2004 by a group of Kuomintang (KMT) supporters in mainland China. The organisation regards the Three People's Principles as their ideological guideline and it advocates political democratisation in China and the reunification of Mainland China and Taiwan. Even though the union members think they are the "spiritual party members" of the KMT according to the KMT's party constitution, the KMT negates any relations it has with the union and states it is not responsible for the activities of the union (BBC, 2007). The CCP announced the union's illegal status in April of 2007 (Zhang Yuke, Zhang Haiyan, 2007). The communication between the union members is mainly on the internet. The union is actively involved in the activities of maintaining villagers' rights and competing in the local congress elections.

24. The activities of political organisations (except for the "legal" puppet parties) are strictly prohibited in China. The open activities of political organisations in elections will definitely bring severe punishment to the participants. In order to avoid being persecuted, the convenor asked the organisation members to stand for the elections as non-political individuals (Boxun, 2006) and the union would not fund their electoral activities (Xu Xing, 2006: 44).

25. The union declared on its website that 112 union members would stand for the elections in 2006 and 2007 but only twenty of them were on a published list (Xu Xing, 2006: 44). The detailed information of the twenty union member independent candidates is available in an article in the magazine *Beijng Spring* (Zhao Xin, 2006: 12).

26. A union member expressed in his article that "his comrades could understand, respect each other. They could also support, cooperate with and keep watch for each other in their electoral activities" (Zhao Xin, 2006: 12).

27. A union member clearly stated in his passage their intention and strategies in the elections (Lao Gu, 2006). Another member briefed the intentions and strategies in a passage (Zhao Xin, 2006: 12).

28. Since the union members who suffered these persecutions may have been actively involved in other political activities apart from the congress elections, their participation in elections perhaps was not the only reason for their persecution but it was at least an important one.

29. Two independent candidates I interviewed, who could be defined as social activists in the third category, were actively engaged in the work of helping the property owners in cities and the villagers in rural areas (possibly the independent candidates of the second category) to maintain their rights.

30. According to a researcher, some dissenters searched for the news of "rights-infringement" cases and then contacted the victims. They tried to help the victims to maintain their rights through all possible legal ways but normally their efforts were in vain. By that time, the dissenters would clarify to the victims that the main problem was in the nation's political system. They would try to persuade the victims to be a member of their organisation or at least a supporter of them. The researcher said that it had become an efficient method of these dissenters to strengthen their power or expand their influence, which also explained why the dissenters were interested in maintaining rights activities. The party might have secretly tightened the control over the mass movements of maintaining rights after knowing the dissenters' intention but there is no published evidence for the party's attitude and measures except for two reports in China Review News (China Review News, 2009) and Takungpao (Takungpao, 2009).

31. No exact number of the successful cases can be obtained from both archival and field research. According to some researchers and social activists, the total number of successful independent candidates in the elections of 2003 and 2006–2007 was less than ten.

32. Article 24 of the electoral law gives the election organisers great freedom of dividing the electorates. A researcher calculated and concluded in his paper that the law allowed the election organisers twenty-one possible options if they freely match the four types of units (voters' residence, production units, institutions and work units) and the three possible candidate numbers (Qiu Jiajun, 2008: 44).

33. Tian was working in a business firm. It was neither in the same system with the party school and the government bureau (institutions) nor was it near the two firms. The power holders had the clear intention to obstruct Tian from winning the election.

34. The interviewed researcher did not reveal detailed information about the names of the independent candidate and the villages.

35. According to the Electoral Law, "zoning of electoral districts," the topic of Articles 24 and 25, is a procedural step before "registration of voters" which is discussed in Articles 26, 27 and 28. Also, Article 26 states that "the registration of voters shall be conducted on the basis of electoral districts," which confirms this order.

36. The relation between voter registration and standing for elections is further discussed on p. 131.

37. *Hukou* is one's registered residence in the official record.

38. According to the Chinese electoral law, a voter can register and vote in only one electorate. In that case, a migrant who wants to register and vote in the electorate in which he/she is currently residing needs to submit the official documents that he/she is not registered as a voter in his/her *hukou* locality.

39. The law article says, "Anyone who has an objection to the roll of voters may appeal to the election committee. The election committee shall make a decision on the appeal within three days. If the appellant is not satisfied with the decision, he may bring a suit in the people's court at least five days prior to the date of election, and the people's court shall make a judgment before the date of election. The judgment of the people's court shall be final" (NPC, 2004c).

40. More political researchers and social activists, when interviewed, expressed that the people lacking interest in any kind of elections was actually a dangerous signal. Such a wide-spread feeling of disappointment and disbelief among the Chinese people for the state's polity might become the root of political instability in the future.

41. Article 38 of the electoral law says "A voter shall not stand proxy for more than three persons" (NPC, 2004c).

42. According to Article 40 of the electoral law, "An election shall be null and void if the number of votes cast is greater than the number of people who voted...." In Wu's case, the illegal proxy votes that the election organisers created to guarantee the success of the organisation-preferred candidate finally invalidated the election result. In another case, however, the election organisers were trying to make use of this law article to fail a competitive independent candidate in the election. In Handan, Hebei province in 2007, the election organisers anticipated that the independent candidate Li Haishun would win but they could not stop him in the steps prior to the voting. When the voting was nearly ended, the election organisers deliberately cast many proxy votes into the ballot box in order to invalidate the result.

43. In fact, the election officers created such difficulty in the step of collecting the nomination forms. The case of Lu Jin on p. 117 proves that.

44. See http://news.bbc.co.uk/chinese/simp/hi/newsid_7260000/newsid_7267600/7267601.stm.

45. It is common that the power holders interfere in the elections by presetting some criteria for the winners of the elections. For example, in this case, the election organisers illegally dropped out Ye because of his gender. In another case in Shenzhen in 2003, the organisation-preferred candidate Chen Caiqiong (her case was also used on p. 114) was arranged to be successful because of her "migrant worker" status. However, the criteria can be changed easily when power holders find it necessary. In an election held in Shenzhen in 2003, when the power holders needed a "reliable" and "competitive" candidate to compete with the independent candidate Wu Haining, they just deleted the previous "non-party person" criterion for the candidature and appointed a party secretary as a candidate.

46. Some social activists advised that the independent candidates should try to win possibly more nominating votes so that the election organisers could not easily drop them out in the "discussion and consultation" step. However, based on the analysis of the existing cases, the effect of the suggested solution was limited.

47. Later, the power holders reopened the election because of the protest of the independent candidate and his supporters. The party nominated a party cadre to compete with the independent candidate in the election. The party-nominated cadre won.

48. Since the book *I Oppose: The Legend of a People's Congress Delegate* (Zhu Ling, 2006) was forbidden in Mainland China shortly after it was published, I cannot obtain a copy. The book's contents, to which this chapter refers, were obtained from the internet so the exact page numbers are not known. The book can be viewed from http://www.nchr.bookfm.com/book/bookdetail.html?bid=103288.

49. In the article, the researcher did not disclose the name of the candidate nor did he specify in which electorate this event happened.

50. In my opinion, there was less obvious suppression in the elections held in Beijing because many foreign embassies, news agencies and NGOs were stationed there and watched the elections so the authorities had to suppress the independent candidates with more furtive methods.

51. As discussed in note 18, this number seems higher than expected and remains questionable.

52. Before an election, the organisers normally put up some banners in the electorate to mobilise the masses to attend the election.

53. In some electorates, the voting was conducted four or seven days ahead of the schedule (Yao Lifa, 2006).

54. According to some independent candidates, the election organisers did not notify the voters that they would organise the voting one day ahead of the schedule. However, it was revealed from an online article that the election organisers notified the voters by posters one day before the voting was conducted (Yao Lifa, 2006).

55. Although the Electoral Law 2004 does not specify that election organisers should establish a booth at the voting stations for voters to complete their ballots secretly, Article 36 states that "the election of deputies to the national and local people's congresses shall be by secret ballot" (NPC, 2004c). In addition, explaining how to use mobile ballot boxes, the State Council Law Office wrote, "[at voters' home], the election organisers should stay away from the voters [when they fill out ballots], and they should not watch the voters filling out their ballots, and should let the voters insert the completed ballots into the box by themselves in order to ensure secrecy of the ballots ..." (The State Council Law Office, 2008:36). According to the Xinhua News Agency, "Establishing a booth at the voting stations for voters to complete their ballots secretly" was in the list of the proposed amendments to the Electoral Law, which was presented to the National People's Congress for approval on March 8, 2010 (Zhou Tingyu, Hou Lijun, 2010). On March 14, the amendment was approved by the NPC (Xinhua, 2010). In the amended Electoral Law which was enacted on March 14, 2010, Article 38 requires that "confidential voting booth should be set up in an election" (NPC, 2010).

56. There were six voting stations in Yao's electorate in 1993, sixteen in 1998, twenty-one in 2003 and twenty-three in 2006.

57. The normal method requires the election officers to count votes only after mixing the ballots colleted from all voting stations established in an electorate. In Yao's electorate, the votes from various voting stations were separately counted to achieve the goal of using administrative power to control voters.

58. Some cases are listed on p. 115.

59. All the dinner parties and other such activities were organised on public holidays. According to a social activist, rather than luring the voters, another purpose of organising these activities was to eliminate any opportunity for Yao to gather the voters for his campaign plan.

60. In the amended Electoral Law enacted on March 14, 2010, Article 9 states that "an electoral committee member should resign his/her position in the committee before he/she can become a candidate" (NPC, 2010). In the future, according to this Article, it will become unlawful for the election organisers to stand for the elections that they organise. This improvement of the Electoral Law, however, is unlikely to reduce the party's manipulations of the people's congress elections.

61. For example, the case described on p. 113 regarding Jiang Shan's voter qualification.

62. As far as I know, Jiang Shan's case in Shenzhen is the only available case of the law court accepting a voter's appeal for his voter qualification.

63. These independent candidates are basically in the third category which is described on pp. 109–110 as "public intellectuals and social activists." Their names and the exact cases of their activities in the places other than their hometowns are not disclosed in this chapter for their safety.

64. To fail the independent candidates who stood for elections in other electorates, it was very common that the local power holders misled the voters by publicly announcing

at the voting station that any votes for the candidates registered in other electorates would be invalid.

65. In my opinion, the researcher was obviously over-optimistic when making this comment. The party-controlled "direct elections" for township executives, such as those discussed in chapter 2, were prohibited by the central party. Free direct elections, in which the grassroots power can participate and win, can be only a fantasy in current Chinese political situation.

66. This is only a hypothesis at the current stage and perhaps will be very difficult to become a reality considering the CCP's control and suppression.

67. This information obtained from interviews may not be very reliable as some independent candidates might think their plans for future elections were something sensitive which should not be revealed to an outsider.

68. During a field trip I happened to access some data regarding a local people's congress election which was held in Shanghai in 2009. Due to a special reason, the combination of two districts and their people's congresses, this was perhaps the only local people's congress election held in China between the last election year (2006–2007) and the next election year (2011–2012) and very luckily there was an independent candidate in the election. Therefore, the case was very valuable for the research of any new developments in this area. The analysis of the data leads to a conclusion that the party tightened its control of the election and strengthened the suppression of independent candidates. The data show that the party took more drastic measures to stop the independent candidate in nearly all procedural steps discussed in this chapter. Viewing this case, I feel pessimistic about the prospect of this reform.

Chapter 7

Conclusion

Nature and Efficacy

Although the five categories of political experiments are very different in nature, their efficacies are comparable. In the following section, the five categories of reform experiments are listed in an order from the low to high level of liberalism and some brief comments are made on them.

The local party congress reform in chapter 4, called a form of "inner-party democracy," was the least liberal among the five categories. In the party's propaganda, this reform is to strengthen the function of local party congresses while decentralising the power of the local party committees. However, the party committees are guaranteed authoritarian power by the party constitution and laws. In practice, the conventional operating system of the party powerfully disables these naively-designed reform measures that target only some small and individual parts of the party's giant and wholly authoritarian mechanism. As for the reform, the party might not have expected effects other than "propaganda achievements." Therefore, this particular reform, in no way improves China's democratic prospects and does little to promote "inner-party democracy."

The reform of "directly electing" township party secretaries in chapter 3, another form of "inner-party democracy," was the second least liberal one among the five. In the reformed elections, some steps were open to grassroots party members. In nearly all cases, however, the party committees (more possibly the party secretary) still dominated the electoral procedure and result. The reformed elections were neither fully competitive nor direct. The reform involved limited liberalisation of part of the electoral procedure but it has not led to any fundamental change in the elections, which are actually dominated by a very few local party leaders. In addition, we have to consider the possibility that the democratisation of the ruling party in an undemocratic country may revitalise the party and extend the single-party authoritarian rule (Linz, 1999:8). If a negative correlation between a nation's democratisation and its ruling party's democratisation does exist, these two "inner-party democracy" reforms have negative value in the context of China's political democratisation. In reality, the emergence of a mighty party secretary (even if he is elected by party members) or a strengthened party congress is not good for the evolution of politics at the locality.

The "deliberative democracy" reform in chapter 5 was more liberal compared with the two inner-party reforms. The "deliberative democracy" reform was held in spheres formally outside the party system.[1] In some of the experiments grassroots villagers were allowed to participate in governmental policy-making process and in some other experiments the local people's congress members were allowed to genuinely carry out their task of examining and revising the government's annual budget. Interestingly, the reform was instigated by the city party (immediate higher-level) publicity department and was organised by the township party committees. In all cases, however, the local party committees controlled the entire experiments and they interfered in some parts. As a result, the local party leaders could change the outcomes of the experiments in the interests of their local party organisations or even for their private interests. One thing that must greatly assure the power holders is that this kind of reform, even though it allows grassroots villagers or people's congress members more political participation, will definitely have no impacts on the single-party system because it has nothing to do with the elections. Based on all these considerations, I rank this reform the third lowest in liberality.

The reform of "direct elections" for township executives in chapter 2 was the second most liberal reform among the five categories. Compared with the inner-party reforms, both the "deliberative democracy" reform and the reform of "direct elections" for township executives were more important because they were aimed at systems outside the party. Comparing the "deliberative democracy" reform and the reform of "direct elections" for township executives, I think the latter is more important. Unlike the "deliberative democracy" reform which was designed "safe" enough not to affect the electoral system, the reform of "direct elections" for township executives was focused on the elections. Elections are perhaps the most important political activity that decides the source of the power and forms the foundation of a political system. Thus, the reform in this area was more important than the three reforms discussed in the above paragraphs. Nevertheless, the reform was still controlled by the party and not completely liberal. In the reformed elections, only one procedural step was open to grassroots voters while "black boxes" existed in all other steps. The case studies show that the local party committees instigated, carried out the reform and manipulated its procedures and results. The elections were not actually "direct" and were not fully competitive. Viewing the reform, I find it had potential to be the most important reform of all five categories of reforms, but unfortunately it failed because of the party's manipulations throughout the procedure of all reform cases.

The participation of independent candidates in local people's congress elections in chapter 6, a reform instigated by the grassroots power, is potentially the most valuable and most liberal reform among the five categories. In this reform, the grassroots powers challenged the party's domination of the elections and enabled a few independent candidates to become competitive. More importantly, some reform experiments demonstrated to the masses how to participate in politics under the constitutional and legal system. However, the reform has two problems. First, there are very few reform cases. Second, the independent candidates receive more and more severe suppression. In fact, instead of enhancing the capability of the party-preferred candidates to compete with the independent candidates, in most cases the party used illegal methods, both obvious and furtive, in the elections to hinder the independent candidates from winning congress seats. The effectiveness of the reform was very low due to these factors.

The Party's Attitudes

It is interesting to find a negative correlation between a reform's liberal level and the party's attitude to the reform. That is to say, the party held the most positive attitudes to the comparatively least liberal reform. If we analyse the five factors of the party's attitude to a reform (three positive ones and two negative ones), the party's overall attitude to each reform is clear. Table 7.1 on p. 146 shows the details.

The assessment of the party's attitudes in Table 7.1 shows a negative correlation between a reform's liberal level and the party's attitude to the reform.

In addition to such a comprehensive assessment as the above, the amount of the media reports about a reform which have been published in Mainland China might be an indicator of the party's preference for the reform in consideration of the strict censorship carried out by the party's mechanisms in Mainland China. To be specific, under the strict news censorship, a reform having been reported by more news articles is more preferred by the party, and vice versa. On March 8, 2010 at 5 pm, using WiseNews, a powerful Hong Kong-based search engine for media articles in Chinese language, I calculated the numbers of media articles[2] regarding each of the reforms. The result can be seen from Table 7.2 on p. 147.

As can be seen from Table 7.2, the result of this survey, using the method of journalistic studies, is generally in agreement with the result shown in Table 7.1. Thus, this survey confirms the negative correlation between a reform's liberal level and the party's attitude.

With this conclusion, we are able to answer the principal question for this book: is liberal democracy compatible with the single-party authoritarian political system? The answer is obviously negative. The party prohibits and suppresses reform having liberal characteristics, whereas it praises a "reform" that fully dominates for propaganda purposes. Understanding this fact, we know that the party actually disallows any reforms that might possibly lead to China's political democratisation. The party is unwilling to accept and it represses anything

Table 7.1 Party's Attitude to the Reforms

Reforms listed from least to most liberal (left to right)	Local Party Congress Reform	Reform of "Direct Elections" for Township Party Secretaries	"Deliberative Democracy" Reform	Reform of "Direct Elections" for Township Executives	Participation of the Independent Candidates in Local People's Congress Elections
Support of the Party's Propaganda	+	+	+		
Support from the Central Party	+	+	Refer to note 3[3]		
Instigated and Organised by the Local Party Committees	+	+	+	+	
Prohibited by the Central Party				–	–
Suppressed by the Party					–
Overall	+3	+3	+2	0	-2

Table 7.2 The Numbers of Media Articles Regarding the Reforms

The numbers of media articles	**Reforms listed from least to most liberal (up to down)**
881	Local Party Congress Reform
352	Reform of "Direct Elections" for Township Party Secretaries
Roughly 212 or less	"Deliberative Democracy" Reform
55	Reform of "Direct Elections" for Township Executives
91	Participation of the Independent Candidates in Local People's Congress Elections

Notes for Table 7.2:

1. "Deliberative democracy" reform in the table specifically refers to the "deliberative democracy" reform experiments held in the townships of Wenling City, Zhejiang Province. There were 432 articles discussing Chinese "deliberative democracy" but 220 of them were focused on the CPPCC system. Therefore, there were roughly 212 or less articles talking about the reform experiments in the townships of Wenling City, Zhejiang Province.
2. Regarding "direct elections" for township executives, I found 55 articles. Unlike other reforms which all happened after the year 2000, some major reform experiments of "direct elections" for township executives occurred between 1998 and 2000. Considering the possibility that the database established in 2000 might exclude the news reports about these experiments, the existing news reports about the reform of "direct election for township executives" might be more than those in the search result.

truly democratic in China even if it happens at local levels. The party's authoritarian regime in China has the nature of being anti-democratic. Of course, "socialist democracy with Chinese characteristics" is not democratic.

Prospects for China's Democracy

Among the five categories of political reforms in China, the two "inner-party democracy" reforms are deceptive and have no impact on China's politics. The "direct elections for township executives" was a more liberal reform but it failed because it was still party-manipulated and because the central party eventually prohibited it. The "deliberative democracy" reform[4] allowed grassroots citizens and people's congress members more political participation in local governance but its impacts were limited because the local party committees tightly controlled the whole procedure and results. Furthermore, the "deliberative democracy" reform lacked motivation because the central party never showed any affirmative support of the reform. In fact, the central party will immediately prohibit the "deliberative democracy" reform once it finds the local party committees have loosened their controls. Thus, the "deliberative democracy" reform has actually failed if we understand that it cannot politically reform anything.

Unlike all other party-instigated and party-manipulated reforms, the participation of independent candidates in local people's congress elections, which is thought in this book as a "reform" instigated from outside the bureaucratic system by some grassroots voters, has the most democratic value compared with other reforms. However, nearly all independent candidates failed in their elections because of suppression and persecution by the whole party system from the central to local. The prospects for this reform are also not optimistic considering the current low number of independent candidates and the brutality of the party when suppressing the grassroots power in elections.

With all the factual evidence and analysis in the book, we are able to understand that it is impossible that China's political democratisation will begin from the party-instigated and party-controlled reforms. The authoritarian ruling party will never willingly transfer even the smallest part of its power to the people. China's political democratisation might be a time-consuming process, in which the opposing power keeps growing stronger and the minor reforms accumulate until fundamental change takes place. It might possibly be a quick process, in which there is social turmoil or even a violent revolution. No matter how political democratisation is to be achieved in China, one thing is certain that it is not the Chinese Communist Party but the people yearning for political democracy who will finally bring down the authoritarian single-party system. Any political reform, if it genuinely pushes the nation ahead to democracy, must be a reform which is motivated at the request of the people, widely joined in by the people and passionately supported by the people. The reforms instigated and controlled by the party are deceptive, meaningless and doomed to failure.

In summary, at present, none of the existing reforms can lead to China's democratisation. Compared with other reforms, the independent candidates' participation in local people's congress elections is still theoretically "promising." In the future, if grassroots power keeps growing in the elections and the party has to soften its policy to avoid social instability, this "reform" may possibly become a breakthrough to China's political democratisation. However, as can be seen, the current situation of the "reform" is bad, and its development in the future will probably become harder and harder.

Notes

1. This means the target of the "deliberative democracy" reform was non-party political institutions. The reform, however, was instigated, organised and absolutely controlled by the local party committees.

2. Here the media articles included only those published in Mainland China since the year 2000 when the database was established.

3. Normally a reform which is a focus of the party's propaganda must have won the central party's support, such as the local party congress reform and the reform of "direct elections" for township party secretaries shown in Table 7.1. As for the "deliberative democracy" reform in Table 7.1, which specifically refers to the "deliberative democracy" reform experiments held in the townships of Wenling City, Zhejiang Province, the situation is quite special. On one hand, the party highly promoted "deliberative democracy" in its propaganda. However, most of the propaganda articles focus on the application of the "deliberative democracy" theory in the CPPCC system or the integration of "deliberative democracy" into "socialist democracy with Chinese characteristics." In contrast, the articles promoting the Wenling experiments are fewer. On the other hand, the central party has never shown any positive attitude to the "deliberative democracy" reform experiments held in Wenling City. It even uses the term "political consultation" rather than "deliberative democracy" in its official documents to avoid sending out any affirmative signals about the reform experiments. Thus, as seen in Table 7.1, the "deliberative democracy" reform, which is highly praised in the party's propaganda articles, does not actually win support from the central party.

4. Here the reform refers to the political experiments made in Wenling City, Zhejiang Province, but not the "consultative and deliberative meetings" as described on pp. 92–94 or the CPPCC system in the party's propaganda.

Bibliography

Acemoglu, Daron, & Robinson, James A. (2006). *Economic Origins of Dictatorship and Democracy*. Cambridge: Cambridge University Press.

Bao Yajun (2007). Pingchangxian jiceng minzhu zhengzhi jianshe de shehui diaocha [A survey on the local political democratization in Pingchang County]. In Wang Changjiang, Zhou Hongyun, Wang Yongbing (Ed.), *Dangnei Minzhu Zhidu Chuangxin [The Breakthrough to Inner-party democracy]*(pp. 126–143). Beijing: Central Compilation and Translation Press.

BBC (2007, May 25). Guomindang xiugai dangzhang, tuxian taiwan bentu jiazhi [The KMT amended its constitution to strengthen its value to Taiwan]. Retrieved April 18, 2009, from http://news.bbc.co.uk/chinese/simp/hi/newsid_6690000/newsid_6690600/6690621.stm.

BBC (2008, February 27). Zhongguo duli houruanren he zhongguo xuanjufa [Chinese independent candidates and electoral law]. Retrieved March 15, 2009, from http://news.bbc.co.uk/chinese/trad/hi/newsid_7260000/newsid_7267600/7267601.stm.

Bell, Daniel A. (2006). Deliberative democracy with Chinese characteristics: a comment on Baogang He's research. In Ethan J. Leib & Baogang He (Eds.), *The Search for Deliberative Democracy in China* (pp. 149–160). New York: Palgrave MacMillan.

Boxun (2006, September 26). Fanlan jinqi huodong zongjie yu shoudu chengyuan zhanshi guoqi dangqi tupian [The recent activities of the Union of Chinese Nationalists and the photos of the union members in the capital area displaying the national and the party flags]. Retrieved April 18, 2009, from http://www.peacehall.com/news/gb/party/2006/09/200609260531.shtml.

Cai Dingjian (2003). Gongmin suzhi yu xuanju gaige diaocha [Survey on citizens' quality and election reform]. *Strategy and Management* (2).

Cai Xia (2008). Dangnei minzhu: tansuo yu wenti [Inner-party democracy: research and questions]. Retrieved March 18, 2008, from http://www.chinaelections.com/NewsInfo.asp?NewsID=123743.

CCP (1956). *Zhongguo Gongchandang Dibaci Quanguo Daibiao Dahui: Zhongguo Gongchandang Zhangcheng [The 8th CCP's National Congress: The Party Constitution]*. Retrieved May 2, 2008, from http://ww http://www. chinapilot.net/Politics/01/01/article/8_2.htm.

CCP (1980). Zhongguo gongchandang di shiyijie zhongyangweiyuanhui diwuci quanti huiyi: guanyu dangnei zhengzhi shenghuo de ruogan zhunze [The 5th plenary meeting of the 11th central committee of the CCP: Several regulations about the inner-party political activities]. Retrieved August 10, 2007, from http://www.china.com.cn/policy/zhuanti/hxsh/txt/2006-11/09/content_7338276.htm.

CCP (1990). Zhonggong zhongyang: zhongguo gongchandang jiceng zuzhi xuanju gongzuo zanxing tiaoli [The Central CCP: The provisional ordinance of the CCP's organizational and electoral work at the primary level]. In *Dang De Difang He Jiceng Zuzhi Xuanju Gongzuo Liucheng [The procedure of the Party's local and primary organizational and electoral work]* (pp. 202–208). Beijing: The CCP's History Publishing House.

CCP (1994). Zhongguo gongchandang: zhongguo gongchandang difang zuzhi xuanju gongzuo tiaoli [The CCP: The Ordinance of the CCP's Local Organizational and Electoral Work]. In *Dang De Difang He Jiceng Zuzhi Xuanju Gongzuo Liucheng [The procedure of the Party's local and primary organizational and electoral work]* (pp. 193–202). Beijing: The CCP's History Publishing House.

CCP (2002a). *Dangzheng Lingdaoganbu Xuanba Renyong Gongzuo Tiaoli [The Ordinance for Electing or Appointing Party and Government Cadres]*. Retrieved November 26, 2007, from http://news.xinhuanet.com/ziliao/2003-01/18/content_695422_1.htm.

CCP (2002b). *Zhongguo Gongchandang Dishiliuci Quanguo Daibiao Dahui: Zhongguo Gongchandang Zhangcheng [The 16th CCP's National Congress: The Party Constitution]*. Retrieved April 19, 2007, from http://cpc.people.com.cn/GB/104019/104101/6434553.html.

CCP (2004a). *Dang De Difang Weiyuanhui Quanti Huiyi Dui Xiayiji Dangwei,Zhengfu Lingdaobanzi Zhengzhi Niren Renxuan He Tuijian Renxuan Biaojue Banfa [The Method of the Party's Local Committee Voting on the Candidates of the Chief Heads of Its Direct Subordinate Party committee or Government]*. Retrieved November 25, 2007, from http://www.jc-dj.gov.cn/Article/ShowArticle.asp?ArticleID=95.

CCP (2004b). *Gongkai Xuanba Dangzheng Lingdao Ganbu Gongzuo Zanxing Guiding [The Provisional Regulations for the Open Selection of Party and Government Cadres]*. Retrieved December 10, 2007, from http://news.china.com/zh_cn/domestic/945/20060516/13322063_1.html.

CCP (2004c). *Zhonguo Gongchandang Dangyuan Quanli BaoZhang Tiaoli [The regulations for protecting the CCP members' rights].* Retrieved April30, 2008,fromhttp://news.xinhuanet.com/newscenter/2005-01/16/content_2467830.htm.

Chan Kenneth Ka Lok (2008). Zhejiang Zeguozhen de minzhukentan zhi [Democratic deliberation in Zeguo Township, Zhejiang Province]. Retrieved June 3, 2009, from http://www.civicparty.hk/cp/pages/posts/E6809DE6BDAE—E6B599E6B19FE6BEA4E59C8BE98EAEE79A84E6B091E4B8BBE68787E8AB87E588B62728.php?g=9.

Chen Jiagang (2007). Xieshangminzhu: hexieshehui de yizhong zhili jizhi [Deliberative democracy: a model of governance for a harmonious society]. Retrieved July 24, 2009, from http://theory.people.com.cn/GB/49154/49156/5318184.html.

Chen Shengyong (2006a). The native resources of deliberative politics in China. In He Baogang (Ed.), *Search for Deliberative Democracy in China* (pp. 161–173). New York: Palgrave Macmillan.

Chen Shengyong (2006b). Zhongguo de xieshangzhengzhi chuantong yu difang minzhu de fazhan [The tradition of political consultation in China and the evolution of local democracy]. In Cheng Shengyong, He Baogang (Ed.), *Xieshang Minzhu De Fazhan [The Development of Deliberative Democracy]* (pp. 79–91). Beijing: China Social Sciences Press.

Chen Xuelian (2007). Minzhu yu xinren—jiedu Pingchangxian gongtui zhixuan xiangzhen dangwei banzi [Democracy and trust: Interpreting the open recommendation and direct election of the township party committee members in Pingchang County, Sichuan Province]. In Wang Changjiang, Zhou Hongyun, Wang Yongbing (Ed.), *Dangnei Minzhu Zhidu Chuangxin [The Breakthrough to Inner-Party Democracy]* (pp. 51–64). Beijing: Central Compilation and Translation Press.

Chen Yimin (2007). Yusuan minzhu: xiangzhen canyu shi gonggong yusuan de tansuo [Democracy in budget planning: the participatory budgeting at the township level]. In Li Fan (Ed.), *Zhongguo Jiceng Minzhu Fazhan Baogao 2006–2007 [Grassroots Democracy in China 2006–2007]* (pp. 34–40). Beijing: Zhishichanquan chubanshe.

Cheng Chunrong (2006). Tingzhengzhidu buying shi minzhujuece de huangzi [Hearing system should not be made into fake democracy]. Retrieved July 26, 2009, from http://www.chinaelections.com/NewsInfo.asp?NewsID=86947.

China Innovations (2004). Zhejingsheng Wenlingshi minzhu kentan [Deliberative polling in Wenling City, Zhejiang Province].Retrieved July 26,2009 from http://www.chinainnovations.org/showNews.html?id=94.

China Innovations (2003). Sichuansheng Suiningshi Shizhongqu gongtui gongxuan xiangzhen dangweishuji he xiangzhenzhang [Self-nomination and test in the elections for township party and government heads in Shizhong District, Suining City, Sichuan Province]. Retrieved October 11, 2006, from http://www.chinainnovations.org/showNews.html?id=80.

China Review News (2009, February 18). Quanzong daguimo yuan nongmingong, yanfang diduishili shentou poguai [All China Federation of Trade Unions strongly supports the migrant workers in order to guard against the enemy power's infiltration and disturbance]. Retrieved April 13, 2009, from http://gb.chinareviewnews.com/doc/1008/8/9/7/100889773.html?coluid=7&kindid=0&docid=100889773&mdate=0218092059.

Chou, Helen (2005). Lost in translations: a report on an aborted village election. *Chinascope*(5), 41.

Chung, Jae Ho (2004). *Social challenges to governance in China: Mapping the major trends.* Paper presented at the International Conference on Grassroots democracy and local governance in China, at Center for China Studies of National Chengchi University, Taiwan.

Clem, Will (2009, December 23). Top think tank expels outspoken academic. *South China Morning Post.*

Deng Xiaoping (1956). Guanyu xiugai dangzhang de baogao [The report on the revision of the Party Constitution]. Retrieved April 29, 2008, from http://news.xinhuanet.com/ziliao/2004-12/29/content_2392051.htm.

Deng Yuwen (2006). Dang minzhu chengwei shenghuo de xiguan [When democracy becomes a life style]. Retrieved July 2, 2009, from http://theory.people.com.cn/GB/49150/49152/4333930.html.

Ding Xiao (2006a). Wuhan gong'an toupiaori qian kouya duli houxuanren [The Police in Wuhan detained independent candidates before the voting day]. Retrieved March 12,2008, from http://crd-net.org/Article/Class55/200609/20060921061605_2198.html.

Ding Xiao (2006b). Wuhan jingdu duli canxuan renda daibiao bei ouda [A police inspector was violently attacked in Wuhan for being an independent candidate in the people's congress election]. Retrieved March 17, 2009, from http://crd-net.org/Article/Class55/200610/20061015011317_2390.html.

Dittmer, Lowell, & Liu, Guoli (Eds.). (2006). *China's Deep Reform:Domestic Politics in Transition.* New York: Rowman & Littlefield Publishers.

Dryzek, John S. (2006). Deliberative democracy in different places. In Ethan J. Leib & Baogang He (Eds.), *The Search for Deliberative Democracy* (pp. 23–36). New York: Palgrave MacMillan.

Fei Wenting (2006). Dui xieshang minzhu kentanhui jiben qingkuang de jieshao ji sikao [The introduction and some thoughts regarding the deliberative polling]. Retrieved May 10, 2009, from http://www.shanghailaw.gov.cn/fzbChinese/page/researchreport/legalwordbrief/legalwordbrief2092.htm.

Fishkin, James S, He, Baogang, & Siu, Alice (2006). Public consultation through deliberation in China: the first Chinese deliberative poll. In Baogang He (Ed.), *Search for Deliberative Democracy in China* (pp. 229–244). New York: Palgrave Macmillan.

Fu Piyi, Yang Jinzhi, Cai Yugao (2006, May 30). Zeguo shiyan: zhengfu shang xiangmu, gongmin lai paiban [The Zeguo experiment: the citizens decided the government's infrastructure projects]. Retrieved July 10, 2009, from http://news.xinhuanet.com/politics/2006-05/30/content_4619571.htm.

Gao Fang (2006). *Zhongguo zhengzhi gaige de xinsheng [My voice for China's political reform]*. Chongqing: Chongqing Publishing House.

Gao Xinmin (2007). Dangdaibiao renqizhi yunhan de zhidu kongjian [The institutionalisation of the system of the permanent tenure of the party's congress delegates]. Retrieved March 18, 2008, from http://www.chinaelections.com/NewsInfo.asp?NewsID=120631.

Gao Yingxiong (2004, November 25). Quanguo zuida guimo xiangzhen zhixuan zai Yun'nan Honghezhou qidong [The largest scale of direct elections at township level were started in Honghe Municipality, Yunnan Province]. *XinzhouBao*.

Gou Ye (2003, April 22). Tie haibao jingxuan ju renda daibiao [Putting up campaign posters and competing for district congress seat]. *Nanfangdushi Bao*.

Government of Buyun Township (1999). Suiningshi Shizhongqu Buyunxiang xuanmin zhijie xuanju renminzhengfu xiangzhang de shixing banfa [The trial method of directly electing government executive at Buyun Township, Shizhong District, Suining City]. Retrieved March 3, 2007, from http://www.chinaelections.org/newsinfo.asp?newsid=54835.

Government of Xinhe Township (2007). Erlinglingqi nian caizheng yusuan xihua shuoming [The detailed annual financial budget for the year 2007]. In Li Fan (Ed.), *Zhongguo Jiceng Minzhu Fazhan Baogao 2008 [Grassroots Democracy in China 2008]* (pp. 39–41). Beijing: Zhishichanquan chubanshe.

Government of Yangji Township (2003). Yangjizhen haitui zhixuan chengxu [Open nomination method in the election held in Yangji Township]. Retrieved October 27, 2006, from http://www.chinaelections.org/NewsInfo.asp?NewsID=83345.

Guo Xiaojun (2006, April 27). Beijing shiliu ming tingzheng daibiao tongyi dishi zujia shangtiao [Sixteen participants approved to increase taxi fare in a consultative meeting in Beijing]. *Xinjingbao*.

Gutmann, Amy, and Thompson, Dennis (2004). *Why Deliberative Democracy*. Princeton, NJ: Princeton University Press.

Han Lei (2006). Dangdaihui zhidu de zhang'aixing yinsu jiqi duice [The disadvantageous points of the party congress system and the solutions]. In Xiao Lihui (Ed.), *Zhongguo Gongchandang Dangnei Minzhu Jianshe Yanjiu [The research of the CCP's inner-party democracy construction]* (pp. 96–135). Chongqing: Chongqing Publishing House.

Hao Wang (2005). Guomindang de zhuanbian: taiwan zhengdang zhengzhi zhi fazhan jingyan [The transformation of KMT: the experience of the political party's evolution in Taiwan]. Retrieved April 17, 2008, from http://www.tecn.cn/data/detail.php?id=6015.

He, Baogang (2006a). Intra-party democracy: a reivsionist perspective from below.In Kjeld Erik Brodsgaard & Yongnian Zheng (Eds.), *The Chinese Communist Party in Reform* (pp. 192–209). New York: Routledge.

He, Baogang (2006b). Participatory and deliberative institutions in China. In He Baogang (Ed.), *Search for Deliberative Democracy in China* (pp. 175–196). New York: Palgrave Macmillan.

He, Baogang (2007). *Rural Democracy in China*. New York: Palgrave MacMillan.

He Baogang (2007). Zeguizhen erlinglingliunian chengzhen jianshe yuxuan xiangmu minzhu kentan [The deliberation conference on the infrastructure projects in Zeguo Township in 2006].Retrieved June 6, 2009, from http://www.chinesedemocratization.com/item1.html.

He Baogang (2008a). Zeguozhen de erlinglingba nian caizheng yusuan minzhu kentan hui [The deliberation conference on the government's annual budget of 2008 in Zeguo Township]. Retrieved June 3, 2009, from http://www.chinesedemocratization.com/item4.html.

He Baogang (2008b). Xieshang minzhu canyuzhe de queding jiqi fangfa [The method of selecting participants in deliberative democracy experiments]. Retrieved August 6, 2009, from http://www.chinaelections.com/NewsInfo.asp?NewsID=121034.

He Baogang, Lang Youxing (2002). Buyun kunjing: zhongguo xiangzhenzhang zhijie xuanju kaocha [The hardship in Buyun reform: a survey on the direct election for twonship government head in China]. Retrieved Octomber 12, 2006, from http://www.chinaelections.org/NewsInfo.asp?NewsID=57557.

He Baogang, Lang Youxing (2008). Xieshangminzhu zai zhongguo jiceng de shenhua [The further development of deliberative democracy in China]. Retrieved July 3, 2009, from http://www.china.com.cn/xxsb/txt/2008-03/10/content_12193440.htm.

He Jianping, Zhu Shuiqing, Ren Xueping (2007). Shanghai xiangzhen dangdaihui changrenzhi de shijian [The practice of the permanent tenure party congress in the townships of Shanghai]. Retrieved June 23, 2008, from http://www.chinaelections.com/NewsInfo.asp?NewsID=109673.

Hong Qihua (2008). Canyushi yusuan gaige:Wenling moshi suyuan [The participatory budgeting reform: the origin of the Wenling model]. In Li Fan (Ed.), *Zhongguo Jiceng Minzhu Fazhan Baogao 2008 [Grassroots democracy in China 2008]* (pp. 85–90). Beijing: Zhishichanquanchubanshe.

Hu Jiajia (2006). Xiangzhenzhang zhixuan de shehui jichu wenti yanjiu [A research of the social conditions of the direct elections for township executives]. Retrieved September 21, 2006, from http://www.xbnc.cn/Article_Show.asp?ArticleID=191.

Hu Jintao (2007). *Gaoju zhongguo tese shehuizhuyi weida qizhi wei duoqu quanmian jianshe xiaokang shehui xin shengli er fendou—zai zhongguo gongchandang di shiqici quanguo daibiao dahui shang de baogao [Hold High the Great Banner of Socialism with Chinese Characteristics and Strive for New Victories in Building a Moderately Prosperous Society in all Respects—Report to the Seventeenth National Congress of the Communist Party of China]*. Retrieved December 21, 2007, from http://cpc.people.com.cn/GB/104019/104099/6429414.html.

Hu Kui, Wu Peishuang, Zhang Lan (2003). Shukexin de geren jingxuan zhilu [The way of Shu Kexin's electioneering]. Retrieved February 12, 2009, from http://www.chinaelections.org/NewsInfo.asp?NewsID=78206.

Hu Nianfei (2006). Zhejiang Wenling shiyan xiangzhen zhili xinmoshi [A new township governance experiment in Wenling Township, Zhejiang Province]. Retrieved May 3, 2009, from http://www.chinaelections.org/NewsInfo.asp?NewsID=46919.

Hu Ping, Wang Juntao (1990). *Kaituo — Beida xueyun wenxian [Pioneering — the Documents of the Democratic Movements in Beijing University]*. Hong Kong: Green Field Bookstore.

Hu Qiaomu (1982, September 13). Huqiaomu tongzhi jiu dangzhang xiugai wenti da xinhuashe jizhe wen [Comrade Hu Qiaomu replied Xinhua News Agency about amending the Party's Constitution]. *The People's Daily*.

Hu Wei (1999). Zhonggong dangnei minzhu yu zhongguo de zhengzhi fazhan [The CCP's inner-party democracy and China's political development]. In Lin Jialong, Qiu Zeqi (Ed.), *Liang'an Dangguo Tizhi Yu Minzhu Fazhan [The party-state regime and democratic development across across the Taiwan Straite]*. Taipei: Yuedan Publishing House.

Hua Yangsheng (2007). Zhongguo zhenggai xinlujing shiqida qian baoguang [The new political reform path exposed before the 17th CCP's National Congress]. *The International Chinese Newsweekly, 21*(20).

Huang Shunxiang (2007, January 11). Hainansheng renda huanjie xuanju xuanchuan gongzuo shoudao xinwenju kending [The NPC's press bureau praised the work of promoting the local people's congress elections in Hainan Province]. Retrieved February 22, 2009, from http://npc.peop le.com.cn/GB/15017/5272473.html.

Huang Weiping, Zou Shubin (2003). *Xiangzhenzhang Xuanju Fangshi Gaige: Anli Yanjiu [Reform the Elections for township government heads: case studies]*. Beijing: Social Sciences and Documentation Publishing House.

Huang Weiping (2000). Shenzhenshi longgangqu dapengzhen sanlun liangpiao tuixuan zhenzhang quancheng shilu [The record of the whole procedure of the three round two voting for township head of Dapeng Township, Longgang District, Shenzhen City]. In Huang Weiping (Ed.), *Zhongguo Jiceng Minzhu Fazhan De Zuixin Tupo [The Latest Breakthrough in Chinese Grassroots Democracy]* (pp. 17–22). Beijing: Social Sciences and Documentation Publishing House.

Huang Weiping, Zou Shubin, Zhang Dinghuai, Yang Longfang (2001).Zhguo dalu xiangzhenzhang xuanju fangshi gaige yanjiu [The research of the reformed elections for township heads in Mainland China]. *Modern China Studies* (4).

Huang Xiaomei (2008). Zhongguo xuanju:sanshinian de fazhan yu weilai zouxiang yantaohui huiyi jiyao [The record of the conference on Chinese elections: development in the past thirty years and its future tendency]. Retrieved February 12, 2009, from http://www.chinaelections.org/NewsInfo.asp?NewsID=143385.

Jacobs, J. Bruce (1991). Elections in China. *The Australian Journal of Chinese Affairs*, 171–199.

Jacques, Martin (2009). *When China Rules the World: The End of the Western World and the Birth of a New Global Order.* New York: Penguin Press HC.

Ji Shuoming (2009). Zhengxie weiyuan zeren bi rongyu geng zhongyao [A CPPCC member's responsibility is more important than his fame]. Retrieved August 12, 2009, from http://www.yzzk.com/cfm/Content_Archive.cfm?Channel=ag&Path=3157217821/06ag2.cfm.

Ji Zhilong (1999). Zai Dapengzhen di shiyijie renmindaibiaodahui diyici huiyi hou jizhe zhaodaihui shang de jianghua [The speech at the press conference after the 1st meeting of the 11th Dapeng Township people's congress]. In Huang Weiping (Ed.), *Zhongguo Jiceng Minzhu Fazhan De Zuixin Tupo [The latest breakthrough in Chinese grassroots democracy]*(pp. 38–43). Beijing: Social Sciences and Documentation Publishing House.

Jiang Xiaowei (2005). Tingzhenghui biaoda minyi haishi xinwen fabu [Shoul a consultative meeting be a press conference or a public opinion collection]. Retrieved June 5, 2009, from http://www.chinaelections.com/NewsInfo.asp?NewsID=43443.

Jiang Xun (2008). Xunhui Sunzhongshan—zhonguo fanlanlianmeng xianxiang beihou [Bring Dr. Sun Yet-Sun back—the background of the Union of the Chinese Nationalists]. *The International Chinese Newsweekly* (18).

Jiang Yun (2007). Xinhe: xiangzhen caizheng de "yangguang shiyan" [Xinhe Township: an experiment of exposing the annual budget in the sunshine]. Retrieved July 1, 2009, from http://wlnews.zjol.com.cn/wlrb/system/2007/09/03/010046870.shtml.

Jiang Zemin (1997). *Gaoju Deng Xiaoping Lilun Weida Qizhi, Ba Jianshe You Zhongguo Tese Shehuizhuyi Shiye Quanmian Tuixiang Ershiyishiji —Jiang Zemin Zai Zhongguo Gongchandang Dishiwuci Quanguodaibiaodahui Shang De Baogao [Hold High the Great Banner of Deng Xiaoping Theory for an All-round Advancement of the Cause of Building Socialism With Chinese Characteristics Into the 21st Century—Jiang Zemin' report to the 15th National Congress of the Communist Party of China]*. Retrieved November 1, 2007, from http://news.xinhuanet.com/ziliao/2003-01/20/content_697207.htm.

Jiang Zemin (2002). *Quanmian Jianshe Xiaokangshehui, Kaichuang Zhongguo Tese Shehuizhuyi Shiye Xinjumian—Zai Zhongguo Gongchandang*

Di Shiliuci Quanguodaibiaodahui Shang De Baogao [Build a Well-off Society in an All-round Way and Create a New Situation in Building Socialism with Chinese Characteristics—Report to the Sixteenth National Congress of the Communist Party of China]. Retrieved November 1, 2007, from http://news.xinhuanet.com/newscenter/2005-01/16/content_2467719.htm.

Jiang Zhaohua, He Baogang (2005). Xieshang minzhu kentan: canyushi zhongda gonggong shixiang de juece jizhi [Deliberative polling: a participatory policy-making mechanism for important public affairs]. Retrieved July 10, 2009, from http://www.china.com.cn/xxsb/txt/2005-10/25/content_6009665.htm.

Lao Gu (2006). Zhongguo fanlanlianmeng canxuan renda de zhanlue he celue [The strategy and tactics of the Union of Chinese nationalists in Chinese people's congress elections]. Retrieved April 9, 2009, from http://boxun.com/hero/2006/fanlan/46_1.shtml.

Legal Daily (2006, April 25). Tingzhenghui yao jianshou minzhu dixian [Consultative meetings must be democratic]. *Legal Daily.*

Leib, Ethan J., & He, Baogang (Eds.). (2006). *The Search for Deliberative Democracy in China.* New York: Palgrave Macmillan.

Li Changhong (2006). Tingzhenghui bixu chongfen fanying minyi [Consultative meetings must represent people's will]. *The People's Forum* (12).

Li Changping (2002). Muji buyun huanjie xuanju [Witness the election in Buyun]. Retrieved April 12, 2007, from http://www.chinaelections.org/NewsInfo.asp?NewsID=66921.

Li Dongming (2008). Tuijin dangnei minzhujianshe de xinyaoqiu [New requests for pushing forward the inner-party democracy]. Retrieved April 26, 2008, from http://www.chinaelections.com/NewsInfo.asp?NewsID=125913.

Li Fan (1999). Sichuansheng Suiningshi Shizhongqu Buyunxiang xianzhang zhixuan de diaocha baogao [Survey Report on the Direct Election for the Township heads in Buyun Township, Shizhong District, Suining City, Sichuan Province]. Retrieved October 1, 2007, from http://www.world-china.org/newsdetail.asp?newsid=461.

Li Fan (2007). Jinyibu gaige Wenlingshi Xinhezhen gonggong yusuan gaige de chengxu an'pai [The procedure of the further reform experiment in budget examination in Xinhe Township]. In Li Fan (Ed.), *Zhongguo Jiceng Minzhu Fazhan Baogao 2006–2007 [Grassroots Democracy in China 2006–2007]* (pp. 57–62). Beijing: Zhishichanquan chubanshe.

Li Fan (2008). Jiceng renda daibiao huanjiexuanju zhong de yixie caozong xingwei [Some manipulations in the local congress elections]. In Li Fan (Ed.), *Erlinglingliu Zhi Erlinglingqi Nian Zhongguojiceng Renda Daibiao Xuanju Shilu [The Memoir of the Chinese Local Congress Elections in 2006–2007]* (pp. 22–27). Beijing: World-China Institution.

Li Jiajie (2007). Gongtuizhixuan yu deng'er xuanju bijiao [Comparing open nomination direct election with equal candidatures and seats election: a new approach to push inner-party democracy]. In Wang Changjiang, Zhou Hongyun, Wang Yongbing (Ed.), *Zhongguo Jiceng Minzhu Fazhan De Zuixin Tupo [The Latest Breakthrough in Chinese Grassroots Democracy]* (pp. 104–125). Beijing: Central Compilation and Translation Press.

Li Jianjun (2006, September 13). Wuhan ju rendadaibiao dulihouxuanren Wenyan bei xiongtu wei'ou [An independent candidate in Wuhan was assaulted by people unidentified]. Retrieved September 30, 2008, from http://www.rfa.org/cantonese/news/china_dissident_election-20060913.html.

Li Jie (2006, October 25). Kuoda dangnei minzhu xuyao jiaqiang zhidujianshe wanshan dangnei jiandu [To expand inner-party democracy, we need to improve the inner-party inspection system]. Retrieved June 21, 2007, from http://news.xinhuanet.com/lianzheng/2006-10/25/content_5247682.htm.

Li Junru (2005). Zhongguo nenggou shixing shenmeyang de minzhu [What kind of democracy can be realised in China]. Retrieved July 11, 2009, from http://www.chinaelections.org/NewsInfo.asp?NewsID=1013.

Li Junru (2006a). Xieshangminzhu:zhongyao de minzhu xingshi [Deliberative democracy: an important form of democracy]. Retrieved July 14, 2009, from http://www.chinaelections.org/NewsInfo.asp?NewsID=93493.

Li Junru (2006b). Zhongguo minzhu zhengzhi xingshi he zhengzhitizhi gaige [The forms of the democratic politics in China and the Chinese Political reform].Retrieved July 15, 2009, from http://www.chinaelections.org/NewsInfo.asp?NewsID=128465.

Li Junru (2006c). Xieshangminzhu yu xuanjuminzhu yao jiehe tuijin [The deliberative democracy and electoral democracy should be pushed ahead together]. Retrieved July 15, 2009, from http://politics.people.com.cn/GB/1026/4624844.html.

Li Junru (2006d). Zhonggongzhongyangdangxiao fuxiaozhang zuoke Qiangguo tan xieshangminzhu [The central party school's deputy president Li Junru talking about deliberative democracy with netizens at Qiangguo Forum]. Retrieved July 18, 2009, from http://www.people.com.cn/GB/32306/54155/57487/4622931.html.

Li Junru (2006e). Yingdui yansegeming zhongguo zhengxie juyou dute youshi [The unique advantage of the CPPCC in the struggle against the colour revolution].Retrieved July 23, 2009, from http://www.chinanews.com.cn/news/2006/2006-03-10/8/701319.shtml.

Li Junru (2006f). Zhongguoren zai minzhu wenti shang buyao wangzifeibo [The Chinese people don't need to feel self-contempt in democracy].Retrieved July 24, 2009, from http://news.xinhuanet.com/politics/2006-07/27/content_4883798.htm.

Li Junru (2008). Zhongguo zhengzhitizhi gaige de chengguo jiqi zoushi [The achievements and future tendency of the Chinese political reform]. Retrieved July 22, 2009, from http://theory.people.com.cn/GB/49150/49

152/7861579.html.

Li Ling (2006). Sichuan dangdaihui changrenzhi shidian diaoyan de sikao [Some thoughts based on the reseach of the permanent tenure party congress experiment in Sichuan Province]. Retrieved May 12, 2008, from http://www.chinaelections.org/NewsInfo.asp?NewsID=46990.

Li Meiling (2007). Pingchangxian gongtuizhixuan yu dangnei minzhu fazhan—bijiao de shijiao [Development of inner-party democracy and the open recommendation and direct election for township party committee members in Pingchang County, Sichuan Province—from a comparative perspective]. In Wang Changjiang, Zhou Hongyun, Wang Yongbing (Ed.), *Zhongguo Jiceng Minzhu Fazhan De Zuixin Tupo [The Latest Breakthrough in Chinese Grassroots Democracy]* (pp. 65–89). Beijing: Central Compilation and Translation Press.

Li Shenming (2006). Fazhan dangneiminzhu bixu zhengque chulihao jige guanxi [Make well some relations to improve the inner-party democracy]. Retrieved April 19, 2008, from http://myy.cass.cn/file/2006121526539.html.

Li Yajie (2006). Zhongyang xianjinxing jiaoyu huodong lingdao xiaozu youguan lingdao da jizhe wen [The officer of the Central CCP's leading team of 'advanced party education' answering journalists' questions at press conference]. Retrieved June 16, 2007, from http://cpc.people.com.cn/BIG5/47816/4156971.html.

Li Yuanchao (2007). Tuijin dangnei minzhu jianshe zengqiang dang de tuanjie tongyi [Pushing forward the inner-party democracy and strengthen the unification of the party]. Retrieved December 11, 2007, from http://www.chinaelections.com/NewsInfo.asp?NewsID=118070.

Lin Hui (2009, November 4). Cunzai zhi wei buyong zai cunzai zhuan fang chuanmei gongzuozhe Zhu Tianyun [Existence for the future non existence—story about a journalist Zhu Tianyun]. *Mingpao.*

Lin Jialong (1999). Bijiao liang'an de zhengti zhuanxing [A comparison of the political transformation across the strait]. In Lin Jialong, Qiu Zeqi (Ed.), *Liang'an Dangguo Tizhi Yu Minzhu Fazhan [The Party-State Regime and Democratic Development across the Taiwan Straite].* Taipei: Yuedan Publishing House.

Lin Jialong, Qiu Zeqi (Ed.). (1999). *Liang'an Dangguo Tizhi Yu Minzhu Fazhan [The Party-State Regime and the Democratic Development across the Taiwan Strait]*. Taipei: Yuedan Publishing House.

Lin Long, Hu Guoqiang (2008). Yusuan gaige zhi zeguo shiyan [The experiment of budgeary reform in Zeguo]. Retrieved July 29, 2009, from http://news.mzyfz.com/mag/a/20080530/142355_6.shtml.

Lin Shangli (2006). Xieshang minzhu: dui zhongguo minzhu zhengzhi fazhan de yizhong sikao [Deliberative politics: a thought on Chinese democracy development]. In Cheng Shengyong, He Baogang (Ed.), *Xieshang Minzhu De Fazhan [The Development of Deliberative Democracy]* (pp. 68–78). Beijing: China Social Sciences Press.

Linz, Juan J (1999). Dui minzhu zhuanxing de yixie sikao [Some thoughts on the democratic transformation]. In Lin Jialong, Qiu Zeqi (Ed.), *Liang an Dangguo Tizhi Yu Minzhu Fazhan [The Party-State Regime and Democratic Development across the Taiwan Straite].* Taipei: Yuedan Publishing House.

Liu Binglu (2004, September 15). Yichang yushe jielun de gongre tingzhenghui [A consultative meeting on the heating price with the preset decision]. *Xinjingbao.*

Liu Shengmin (2008). Canjia Pudongxinqu renmin daibiao jingxuan de jingli [My experience of standing for the congress election in Pudong District]. In Li Fan (Ed.),*Erlinglingliu Zhi Erlinglingqi Nian Zhongguojiceng Renda Daibiao Xuanju Shilu [The Memoir of the Chinese Local Congress Elections in 2006–2007]* (pp. 220–230). Beijing: World-China Institution.

Liu Shixin (2004a, September 3). Beijing jumin dianjia tingzhenghui butaolun zhangbuzhang zhi taolun zhangduoshao [A consultative meeting in Beijing on increasing power price: discussing how much should do rather than if should do]. *China's Youth Daily.*

Liu Shixin (2004b, July 14).Tingzhenghui ying cong gongshi zouxiang kangbian [Consultative meeting's function should be changed from publishing to debating]. *China's Youth Daily.*

Liu Yawei (2002). Jianjinshi minzhu zhongguo xianxiang de zhijie xuanju [The gradual democratization: China's township and county direct elections]. Retrieved September 30, 2006, from http://www.chinaelections.org/NewsInfo.asp?NewsID=22391.

Luo Liwei (2003, June 14). Shui shi shoupi duli houxuanren [Who are the first group of independent candidates]. *Nanfang Zhoumo.*

Ma Shengkang (2002). Buyunxiang liangci xuanju de gaikuang, bijiao ji sikao [The comparative studies of the two elections in Buyun Township]. Retrieved April 22, 2007, from http://www.chinaelections.org/newsinfo.asp?newsid=53711.

Ma Ya (2004a). Haineiwai gejie guanzhu Pingba zhixuan fengbo [Reviews of the Chinese and Overseas scholars on the Pingba direct election]. *Phoenix Weekly, 139.*

Ma Ya (2004b). Liangzhong bamian, yizhong youlu [Two kinds of recalling, one worry]. *Phoenix Weekly, 146.*

Mao Fei (2004, September 16). Meiyou zhongli de caipan jiu zhiyou "tingzhengxiu" [A consultative meeting without an impartial mediator is just a "show"]. *The Guangming Daily.*

Mao Zedong (1956). Zai zhonggong zhongyang zhengzhiju kuoda huiyi shang de zongjie jianghua [The summary speech at the CCP's Political Bureau (enlarged) meeting]. Retrieved April 29, 2008, from http://www.cnread.net/cnread1/zzzp/m/maozedong/mx7/008.htm.

Miller, David (1992). Deliberative democracy and social choice. In David Held (Ed.), *Prospects for Democracy.* Cambridge: Polity Press.

Naisbitt, John, & Naisbitt, Doris (2010). *China's Megatrends: The 8 Pillars of a New Society* New York: HarperBusiness.

National Bureau of Statistics of China (2004). *Erlinglingsinian zhongguo tongji nianjian [Statistic Yearbook 2004]*. Retrieved April 27, 2009, from http://www.stats.gov.cn/tjsj/ndsj/yb2004-c/indexch.htm.

NPC (1983). *Quanguo Renmin Daibiao Dahui Changwuweiyuanhui Guanyu Xianji Yixia Renmin Daibiao Dahui Daibiao Zhijie Xuanju De Ruogan Guiding [Regulations by the NPC's Standing Committee for the People's Congress Direct Elections below the County Level]*. Retrieved June 3, 2010, from http://www.law-lib.com/law/law_view.asp?id=2580.

NPC(2004a). *Dishijie Quanguo Renmin Daibiao Dahui Changwuweiyuanhui Di Shi'er'ci Huiyi: Zhonghuarenmingongheguo Difang Geji Renmin-daibiao dahui He Difang Geji Renminzhengfu Zuzhifa [The 10th NPC standing committee the 12th meeting: the PRC Organization Law for Local People's Congresses and Local Governments at All Levels]*. Retrieved July 3, 2009, from http://www. peopledaily.com.cn/GB/14576/28320/39838/39842/2947955.html.

NPC (2004b). *Zhonghurenmingongheguo Xianfa [The Constitution of the People's Republic of China]*. Retrieved September 4, 2006, from http://news.xinhuanet.com/ziliao/2004-09/16/content_1990063.htm.

NPC (2004c). *Zhonghuarenmingongheguo Quanguo Renmin Daibiao Dahui He Difang Geji Renmindaibiao Dahui Xuanjufa [The Electoral Law of the National People's Congress and Local People's Congresses of the People's Republic of China (2004)]*. Retrieved February 18, 2009, from http://www.people.com.cn/GB/14576/28320/39838/39842/2947944.html.

NPC (2010). *Zhonghuarenmingongheguo Quanguo Renmin Daibiao Dahui He Difang Geji Renmindaibiao Dahui Xuanjufa [The Electoral Law of the National People's Congress and Local People's Congresses of the People's Republic of China (2010)]*. Retrieved April 8, 2010, from http://www.gov.cn/flfg/2010-03/14/content_1555450.htm.

O'Brien, Kevin J., & Li, Lianjiang (2001). Accomodating "democracy" in a one-party state: introducing village elections in China. In Larry Diamond & Ramon H. Myers (Eds.), *Elections and Democracy in Greater China* (pp. 101–125). New York: Oxford University Press.

Ouyang Song (2007). Sound progress of the new and great project of party building since the 16th National Congress of the CPC. Retrieved March 3, 2008, from http://english.people.com.cn/90001/90776/90785/628528 0.html.

Pastor, Robert A., & Tan, Qingshan (2001). The meaning of China's village elections. In Larry Diamond & Ramon H. Myers (Eds.), *Elections and Democracy in Greater China* (pp. 126–148). Oxford University Press: New York.

Peng Jianjun, Mao Zhengxiang (2007). Changrenzhi:quebao dangdaihui qu-anlijiguan diwei de zhidubaozhang [The permanent tenure system: the system guaranteeing the leading position of the party congress]. Retr-ieved March 16, 2008, from http://www.chinaelections.com/NewsInfo.a

sp?NewsID=109646.

Peng Lanhong (2008). Du Quanbing ji Li Haishun de canxuan jingli [The experience of Li Haishun and Du Quanbing standing for local congress elections]. In Li Fan (Ed.), *Zhongguo Jiceng Minzhu Fazhan Baogao 2008 [Grassroots democracy in China 2008]* (pp. 283–286). Beijing: Zhishichanquan chubanshe.

People's Congress of Hubei Province (2006). *Hubeisheng Xianxiang Liangji Renmindaibiaodahui Daibiao Xuanju Shishi Xize [The Rules for Implementation of the Elections for People'sCongress Delegates at the Township and County Levels 2006]*. Retrieved October 18, 2008, from http: http://www.chinabaike.com/law/df/hbei/1409025.html.

Perry, Elizabeth J., & Goldman, Merle (Eds.). (2007). *Grassroots Political Reform in Contemporary China.* MA: Harvard University Press.

Przeworski, Adam, Alvarez, Michael E., Cheibub, Jose Antonio, & Limongi, Fernando (2000). *Democracy and Development: Political Institutions and Well-Being in the World, 1950–1990.* Cambridge: Cambridge University Press.

Qian Gang (2007). Zhengzhi tizhi gaige zai nali [Where is the political reform]. *The International Chinese Newsweekly, 21* (43).

Qian Liqun (2008). Buneng yiwang de sixiang—yijiubalingnian zhongguo xiaoyuan minzhu yundong pingshu [Unforgettable ideas—comments on the university democratic movements in 1980]. *Modern China Studies* (100).

Qiu Jiajun (2008). Rendadaibiao zhijiexuanju zhong zhengzhi baguanquan de yunxing weidu [The power holders' interference in the direct congress elections]. In Li Fan (Ed.), *Erlinglingliu Zhi Erlinglingqi Nian Zhongguojiceng Renda Daibiao Xuanju Shilu [The Memoir of the Chinese Local Congress Elections in 2006–2007]* (pp. 35–53). Beijing: World-China Institution.

Ramo, Joshua Cooper (2004). *The Beijing Consensus.* London: Foreign Policy Centre.

Renmingwang (2004, November 25). Shiping shiyan: xuanmin zhijie xuan zhenzhang [Experiment in Shiping: voters direcly elected township heads]. Retrieved April 3, 2007, from http://www.people.com.cn/GB/pa per447/13474/1207070.html.

Renmingwang (2006, October 25). Yiyi liudong xuanmin quanli ruhe luodi [How to guarantee the voting right of the one-thousand-million migrant voters]. Retrieved October, 2009, from http://npc.people.com.cn/GB/15 037/4956077.html.

Renminwang (2008, March 5).Xinyijie zhengxieweiyuan you "wuduo" jingtou buzhuo "mingren weiyuan" [Members of the new term CPPCC who are celebrities]. Retrieved July 24, 2009, from http://culture.people.com.cn/GB/22226/116301/116311/6958277.html.

Research Institute of the Beijing Municipality Party Committee (2004). Dang de daibiaodahui bihui qijian fahui daibaio zuoyong de tujing, xing shi wenti yanjing [The research on how to fulfill the party congress delegates' duties during the period when the congress is not in session]. Retrieved May 1, 2008, from http://www.bjdcyj.gov.cn/swyjs/dykw/cx/wqsh/wtdy_2004/shjj_2004_6/t20040714_113003.htm.

Research Institute of the Huizhou Party Organization Department (2004). Shixing dangdaibiaodahui changrenzhi yaobawo de ruogan wenti [Some key points in the reform of the permanent tenure party congress system]. Retrieved June 12, 2008, from http://www.chinaelections.com/NewsInfo.asp?NewsID=106736.

Research Team of the Organization Department of the CCP Committee of Sichuan Province (2003). Guanyu gongxuan, zhixuan xiangzhen lingdaoganbu yu dangde lingdao wenti de diaocha yu sikao [The survey and thoughts on the direct elections for township government and party heads]. *Marxism and Reality* (7).

Rosenberg, Shawn (2006). Human nature, communication, and culture: rethinking democratic deliberation in China and the west. In Ethan J. Leib & Baogang He (Eds.), *The Search for Deliberative Democracy in China* (pp. 77–112). New York: Palgrave MacMillan.

Ruan Siyu (2007). Dangnei minzhu zhiduhua de tansuo: difang dangdaihui changrenzhi de jingyan yanjiu [Research on the institutionalisation of the inner-party democracy: the case studies of the permanent tenure local party congress system]. Retrieved March 10, 2008, from http://www.chinaelections.org/NewsInfo.asp?NewsID=105600.

Shao Daosheng (2006). Tingzhenghui: an' liyijituan de jidingfangzhen ban [Consultative meetings: follow the interest groups' instructions]. Retrieved August 12, 2009, from http://www.wyzxsx.com/Article/Class4/200605/6358.html.

She Jiao (2004, August 13). Tingzhenghui zhidu qineng chengwei zhexiubu [How can the hearing system beome the curtain to hide bad governance]. *The Legal Daily*.

Sheng Huaren (2006). Yifa zuohao xianxiang liangji renda huanjie xuanju gongzuo [Work well for the people's congress elections at township and county levels according to the laws]. *Qiu Shi* (16).

Sheng Ruowei (2008). Dangnei jiceng minzhu shiyantian:sichuan ya'an dangdaihui changrenzhi shidian diaocha [An experiment of inner-party democracy: research of the system of the permanent tenure of the party congress in Ya'an, Sichuan Province]. Retrieved March 19, 2008, from http://politics.people.com.cn/GB/30178/6893182.html.

Shi Weiqin (2003). Muji linyi de xiangjian minyidiaocha [Witness the opinion poll in the villages of Linyi]. Retrieved May 5, 2007, from http://www.world-china.org/book/chuangxin/fulu4.htm.

Social Science Academy of Sichuan Province (2004). Dangdaihui changrenzhi shidian diaoyan de sikao [Thoughts on the experiments of the permanent tenure party congress system]. Retrieved May 1, 2008, from http://www.chinaelections.com/NewsInfo.asp?NewsID=110970.

Sui Binbin (2007). Lu Banglie tan ziji de rendadaibiao xuanju jingli [Lu Banglie's talk on his candidate experience in the congress election]. In

Li Fan (Ed.), *Zhongguo Jiceng Minzhu Fazhan Baogao 2006–2007 [Grassroots democracy in China 2006–2007]* (pp. 203–207). Beijing: Zhishichanquan chubanshe.

Sui Binbin (2008a). Wenlingshi Xinhezhen er'linglingqi nian gonggongyusuan'an tiaozheng guocheng [The procedure of amending the annual budget plan of 2007 in Xinhe Township, Wenling City]. In Li Fan (Ed.), *Zhongguo Jiceng Minzhu Fazhan Baogao 2006–2007 [Grassroots democracy in China 2006–2007]* (pp. 19–31). Beijing: Zhishichanquan chubanshe.

Sui Binbin (2008b). Yao Lifa tan er'linglingliunian Qianjiangshi renda daibiao huanjie xuanju [Yao Lifa's talk on the local congress election in 2006]. In Li Fan (Ed.), *Erlinglingliu Zhi Erlinglingqi Nian Zhongguojiceng Renda Daibiao Xuanju Shilu [The Memoir of the Chinese Local Congress Elections in 2006–2007]* (pp. 118–125). Beijing: World-China Institution.

Sun Wenguang (2007). Sun Wenguang canxuan riji [The diary of Sun Wenguang regarding the election]. Retrieved April 9, 2009, from http://news.boxun.com/news/gb/pubvp/2007/11/200711200812.shtml.

Takungpao (2009, February 14). Yue: fang didui shili jie "weiquan" gaoshi [Guangdong: guard against the enemy power under the veil of maintaining rights]. Retrieved April 3, 2009, from http://www.takungpao.com:10000/gate/gb/www.takungpao.com/news/09/02/14/tp-1032475.htm.

Tan, Qingshan (2006). *Village Elections in China: Democratizing the Countryside.* New York: Edwin Mellen Press.

Tang Hao (2006, May 8).Tingzhengzhidu kaoyan zhizhengweimin de chengyi [The consultative meeting system tests the sincerity of the people's government]. *The Nanfang Daily.*

Tang Jianguang (2002). er'linglingyi nian Buyunxiang xiangzhang xuanju xin shiyan [New experimental election for Buyun Township Executive in 2001]. Retrieved October 28, 2006, from http://www.chinaelections.org/xjzl/readnews.asp?newsid={3F06FA7D-AB02-4619-B870-C39B64E7FCE7}.

Tang Jitian, Cheng Hai, Zhang Lihui (2008). Shunying lishi chaoliu shixian luxie zhixuan—zhi quanti Beijing lushi, shi sifaju, shi luxie de huyu [Follow the historical trend and hold the direct election for the lawyer's association—an appealing letter to all lawyers in Beijing, the Justice Bureau of Beijing and the Beijing lawyer's association]. Retrieved April 12, 2009, from http://www.gongmeng.cn/sub_r.php?zyj_id=1924.

Tang Juan, Zou Shubin (2003). *Er'linglingsan nian Shenzhen jingxuan shilu [The Memoir of the Elections in Shenzhen in 2003]*. Xi'an: Xibeidaxue Chubanshe.

Tang Xiaoqing (2006). Dangnei minzhu yu dang de xianjinxing shi hudong gongjin guanxi [Inner-party democracy interacts with the party's advanced characteristics]. Retrieved June 21, 2007, from http://theory.people.com.cn/GB/49150/49151/4388817.html.

The Beijing Lawyer's Association (2008). Beijingshi lushixiehui guanyu shaoshu lushi huyu suowei "Beijing luxie zhixuan" de yanzheng shengming [A formal statement of The Beijing Lawyer's Association on the so called "appealing letter for direct electing the lawyer's association" made by a small group of Beijing lawyers]. Retrieved April 12, 2009, from http://www.bmla.org.cn/bjlawyers2/news/show_content.jsp?infoID=IC02000024280.

The State Council Law Office (2008). *Zhonghuarenmingongheguo Quanguo Renmindaibiaodahui He Difang Geji Renmindaibiaodahui Xuanjufa Zhujie Yu Peitao [The explanation of the electoral law of the National People's Congress and Local People's Congress of the PRC]*. Beijing: China legal Publishing House.

The State Council of PRC (2008). Guowuyuan guanyu jiaqiang shi xian zhengfu yifa xingzheng de jueding [The decision by the state council to enforce laws in the governance of the city and county governments]. Retrieved August 12, 2009, from http://politics.people.com.cn/GB/1026/7399651.html.

Tian Qizhuang, Wang Weixing (2007). Zoujin heli shi shuishen—jingxuan renda daibiao jishi [To test the river depth by walking into the river: the memoir of a participation in a congress election]. Retrieved April 12, 2009, from http://crd-net.org/Article/Class55/200708/20070826132137_5448_3.html.

Tian Shubin, Li Ziliang, Wang Yan (2004).Yun'nan Honghezhou dadan gaige zhitui zhixuan xiangzhenzhang [The bold reform of direct elections for township heads in Honghe Municipality, Yunnan Province]. *China Comment* (19).

Valadez, Jorge M (2000). *Deliberative Democracy,Political Legitimacy, and Self-Determination in Multicultural Societies*. Boulder: Westview Press.

Wang Changjiang (2009). Dangdaibiao changrenzhi de zuofa zhide kending [The permanent tenure system of party congresses should be supported]. Retrieved December 11, 2009, from http://theory.people.com.cn/GB/9960580.html.

Wang Feiling (2000). Dangnei minzhu he dangnei paibie de hefahua [Inner-party democracy and legitimisation of the inner-party rival factions]. Retrieved April 26, 2008, from http://www.chinaelections.org/NewsInfo.asp?NewsID=75843.

Wang Kongrui (2008). Wenling minzhu kentan: jujushou shige da wenti [Deliberations in Wenling: if it is a big issue raise your hands]. In Li Fan (Ed.), *Zhongguo Jiceng Minzhu Fazhan Baogao 2008 [Grassroots Democracy in China 2008]* (pp. 78–84). Beijing: Zhishichanquan chubanshe.

Wang Na (2008). Wenling yusuanminzhu shidian niannei tuiguang [Wenling budgeting democracy will be expanded in this year]. In Li Fan (Ed.), *Zhongguo Jiceng Minzhu Fazhan Baogao 2008 [Grassroot Democracy in China 2008]* (pp. 70–74). Beijing: Zhishichanquan chubanshe.

Wang Xiugui (2002). Zhengzhi tizhi gaige weihe buneng huanxing [Why political reform cannot be delayed]. Retrieved April 11, 2008, from http://www.chinaelections.org/NewsInfo.asp?NewsID=73897.

Wang Xuejiang (2009). Beijing gugong deng menpiao tingzhenghui daibiao zhongkouyici nairenxunwei [High support rate in the consultative meeting on increasing the ticket price of the Forbidden City is suspicious]. Retrieved August 11, 2009, from http://www.chinaelections.com/NewsInfo.asp?NewsID=68384.

Wang Yi (2003). Xiangzhen de zizhi he xianzheng [The self-governance and power-restriction of townships]. *Modern China Studies, 83*(4).

Wang Yongbing (2006). Xiangzhen dangweishuji gongtui zhixuan xu wanshan de wenti [Some problems concerning the open nomination and direct election for township party secretaries]. Retrieved March 21, 2008, from http://theory.people.com.cn/GB/49150/49151/4314305.html.

Wang Youjin (2009, February 25). Zhongguo lushi weihu ziji de quanli dou nan [Chinese lawyers find it hard to maintain their own rights]. *Mingpao.*

Wen Jiabao (2005). Talking about direct elections at press conference. Retrieved September 28, 2006, from http://www.number-10.gov.uk/output/Page8133.asp.

Wen Jiabao (2006). Wen Jiabao zaitan xiangzhen zhixuan [Premier Wen talked about direct elections again]. Retrieved September 22, 2006, from http://www.chinaelections.com/NewsInfo.asp?NewsID=95188.

Wen Jiabao (2007). Guanyu shehuizhuyi chuji jieduan de lishi renwu he woguo duiwaizhengce de jige wenti [Some issues about our tasks and foreign policies at the initial stage of socialism]. Retrieved March 4 2007, from http://politics.people.com.cn/GB/1024/5418093.html.

Wong, John, & Wang, Gungwu (2007). *Interpreting China's Development.* Singapore: World Scientific.

Wu Guoguang (2000). Zhongguo dalu de xuanju zhidu jiqi biange [The electoral system in Mainland China and its evolution]. Retrieved October 4 2007, from http://www.chinayj.net/StubArticle.asp?issue=000104&total=68.

Xi Xuchu (2006). Tingzhenghui meiyou minzhu henzao dan jiaminzhu ye haobudao na'er qu [Consultative meetings: fake democracy is worse than no democracy]. Retrieved July 10, 2009, from http://www.chinaelections.com/NewsInfo.asp?NewsID=97108.

Xiao Gongqin (2004). Cong zhengzhi fazhan jiaodu kan dangneiminzhuhualun [Viewing the theory of inner-party democracy from the perspective of political development]. *Zhejiang Academic Journal* (2).

Xinhua News Agency (2010, March 14). Amendment to Electoral Law adopted. Retrieved June 8, 2010, from http://www.chinadaily.com.cn/china/2010npc/2010-03/14/content_9586601.htm.

Xinjingbao (2006, May 20). Meiyou gongzhong canjia de tingzhenghui tuyouxuming [A consultative meeting without real citizen representatives is deceptive]. *Xinjingbao.*

Xinjingbao (2007, June 3). Hefei tingzheng daibiao xinxi bei wujiaju baomi [The price bureau in Hefei kept secret of the consultative meeting participants]. *Xinjingbao.*

Xu Jiling, Guo Bensheng (2008). Nanjing shixing dangdaihui changrenzhi jihuo dangdaibiao ziyuan [The reform of permanent tenure system of party congresses adopted in Nanjing activates the delegate resources]. Retrieved June 5, 2008, from http://www.chinaelections.com/NewsInfo.asp?NewsID=123451.

Xu Jiqing, Ma Bingjun (2007). Dangdaihui changrenzhi de lishi youlai [The origin and development of the permanent tenure party congresses]. Retrieved March 2, 2008, from http://www.chinaelections.com/NewsInfo.asp?NewsID=118702.

Xu Xing (2006). Xuan'ge xiaoxiangzhang ye buzhun [It is not allowed to elect even the township chiefs]. *Open Magazine* (11), 44.

Xu Yaotong (2005). Yi dangnei minzhu daidong renminminzhu [Let inner-party democracy motive people's democracy]. Retrieved June 21, 2007, from http://www.china.com.cn/xxsb/txt/2005-11/02/content_6017450.htm.

Xu Zhiyong (2009). Beijing luxie xuanju xiangmu zongjie [A summary of the election for the Beijing Lawyer's Association]. Retrieved April 12, 2009, from http://blog.sina.com.cn/s/blog_4aa8956f0100cobn.html.

Yan Yuxiang (2008). Er'linglingliu nian Wuhanshi Wuchangqu renda huanjie xuanju zhong wo de tiyan yu guancha [My observation and experience in the local congress election in Wuchang District of Wuhan City in 2006]. In Li Fan (Ed.), *Erlinglingliu Zhi Erlinglingqi Nian Zhongguojiceng Renda Daibiao Xuanju Shilu [The Memoir of the Chinese Local Congress Elections in 2006–2007]* (pp. 147–154). Beijing: World-China Institution.

Yang Jisheng (2007). Xianggang yanjiang zhengzhi gaige [Speech on the political reform at the University of Hong Kong]. Retrieved April 23, 2008, from http://221.10.254.25/chinacddb/News_View.asp?NewsID=203.

Yang Lin (2007). Jinkan dangde quanguo daibiaodahui zhidu [Have a close watch at the Party's national congress system]. Retrieved March 21, 2008, from http://news.xinhuanet.com/politics/2007-10/10/content_6862372.htm.

Yang Xiaohong (2004, July 14). Meishijian peizhe zuoxiu [No time to play with you]. *Nanfangdushibao.*

Yang Xuedong (2003). Xiangzhenzhang xuanju fangshi gaige: liuzhong leixing [Six models of election experiments for township executives]. Retrieved October 24, 2006, from http://www.china.com.cn/xxsb/txt/2004-04/19/content_5547640.htm.

Yao Lifa (2006). Yao Lifa dengren zhi zhongguo zuigaoceng "sidajia" lingdaoren de gongkaixin [An open letter to China's four top heads from Yao Lifa]. Retrieved March 19, 2008, from http://www.bowenpress.com/cn/2006/china/143_3.shtml.

Yao Lifa (2008). Wode jingxuan "yiyuan" zhilu jiqi zaoyu [My competition for a congress seat]. In Li Fan (Ed.), *Erlinglingliu Zhi Erlinglingqi Nian Zhongguojiceng Renda Daibiao Xuanju Shilu [The Memoir of the Chinese Local Congress Elections in 2006–2007]*. (pp. 126–137).Beijing: World-China Institution.

Ye Chuan (2009). Zhejiang Wenlingshi Zeguozhen fangmin you dao Beijing jubao [The petitioners from Zeguo Twonship, Wenling City, Zhejiang Province appealed for help in Beijing again]. Retrieved August 20, 2009, from http://news.boxun.com/news/gb/china/2009/05/200905310913.shtml.

Yu Jianrong (2009).Lizhi duidai butong xingzhi de quntixing shijian [Handle the different kinds of mass incidents sensibly]. Retrieved October 3, 2009, from http://news.xinhuanet.com/theory/2009-04/09/content_11153708.htm.

Yu Jindong (2004, February 2). Jiangsu Suyang cha'e zhixuan zhen dangwei shuji [Differential quota elections for township party secretaries at Muyang County, Jiangsu Province]. *The Beijing Youth Daily.*

Yu Keping (2006). Minzhu shige haodongxi [Democracy is a good thing]. Retrieved January 1, 2007, from http://theory.people.com.cn/GB/49150/49152/5224247.html.

Yu Meisui (2006). Bailizhouzhen xuanqu toupiaori, Lu Banglie bei jingfang diaoli xuanju xianchang hou [What happened after Lu Banglie was taken away from the voting station]. Retrieved October 11, 2008, from http://www.peacehall.com/news/gb/china/2006/12/200612142140.shtml.

Yu Ping (2004, December 6). Tingzhenghui daibiao yijian weihe yu minyi jieranbutong [Why the opinions of the consultative meeting participants are different from public opinion]. *Xinjingbao.*

Zha Qingjiu (1999, January 19). Minzhu bu'neng chaoyue falu [Democracy cannot overstep laws]. *The Legal Daily.*

Zhang Boshu (2007). Zhongguo xianzheng gaige: beijing, mubiao, shishibuzhou yu yueshu tiaojian [Constitutionalist reform in China: background, targets, procedure and conditions]. Retrieved April 22, 2008, from http://www.ccdtr.org/index.php/docs/1233.

Zhang Jun, A Ji (2006). Wangluo daxia canxuan renda daibiao [A cyber-celebrity will compete in congress elections]. *Democracy and Legal System* (7).

Zhang Shulin (2007a). Dangnei minzhu de zengliangshi fazhan yu yilai lujing [The incremental development of the inner-party democracy and the path to achieve it]. Retrieved February 2, 2008, from http://www.chinaelections.com/NewsInfo.asp?NewsID=109762.

Zhang Shulin (2007b). Dangdaihui changrenzhi yanjiu: jiazhi, lujing, yuzhenglun [Research on the permanent tenure system of party congresses: value, route and debate]. Retrieved March 19, 2008, from http://www.chinaelections.com/NewsInfo.asp?NewsID=109485.

Zhang Xiaoshan (2008, May 17). Wenling yusuan minzhu gaige zouxiang zongshen [The reform of deliberation on government's final budget goes further]. Retrieved July 27, 2009, from http://news.xinhuanet.com/politics/2008-05/17/content_8195441.htm.

Zhang Yuke, Zhang Haiyan (2007, April 25). Guotaiban: suowei de "zhongguo fanlan lianmeng" zuzhi shi feifa de [Taiwan Affairs Office of the State Council: The Union of Chinese Nationalists is an illegal orgnisation]. Retrieved February 3, 2009, from http://tw.people.com.cn/GB/148 10/5663993.html.

Zhao Lei, Tang Huimei (2006). Beijing zhengxieweiyuan huyu tingzhenghui jilu ying quanbu gongkai [A member of Beijing CPPCC proposed to publish all information of the consultative meetings]. Retrieved July 2, 2009, from http://www.chinaelections.com/NewsInfo.asp?NewsID=956 74.

Zhao Xiaoli (2004). Jiaqiang renda xuanju de chengxu jianshe—jiedu xuanjufa xiugai [Improve the procedure of the people's congress elections—interpreting the amendment of the electoral law]. Retrieved July 24, 2008, from http://www.fatianxia.com/paper_list.asp?id=3856.

Zhao Xin (2006). Wei fanlan xiongdi canjia renda daibiao xuanju gu yu hu [Boast for the union members' participation in the people's congress elections]. *Beijing Spring 160*, 11–12.

Zhen Xiaoying, Li Qinghua (2003). Yi dangnei minzhu tuijin renminminzhu [Push forward political democracy by improving inner-party democracy] *Qiu Shi* (12).

Zhongguowang (2007, March 7). Quanguo rendadaibiao: xingzhengjingfei yusuan meiyou tixianchu jieyuexing [The NPC member said the government budget indicated it was not economical]. Retrieved August 4, 2009, from http://big5.china.com.cn/2007lianghui/2007-03/07/content_79162 24.htm.

Zhou Hongyun (2007). Sichuansheng Pingchangxian xiangzhen gaige qingkuang jiqi sikao [Introduction of the township reform in Pingchang County, Sichuan Province]. In Wang Changjiang, Zhou Hongyun, Wang Yongbing (Ed.), *Dangnei Minzhu Zhidu Chuangxin [The breakthrough to Inner-Party Democracy]* (pp. 3–35). Beijing:Central Compilation and Translation Press.

Zhou Hucheng (2003, May 23). Wang Liang bushi shouwei renda duli houxuanren [Wang Liang is not the first independent candidate]. *Nanfang Dushibao.*

Zhou Ruipeng (1999, November 4). Tamen qiongpale, suoyi zhixuan xiangzhang [Poverty led to a direct election]. *Lianhe Zaobao.*

Zhou Tingyu, Hou Lijun (2010, March 8). Mimi Xiepiaochu youwang bei xieru woguo xuanjufa [Establishing voting booth was expected to be written into the electoral law]. Retrieved June 8, 2010, from http://news.xinhuanet.com/politics/2010-03/08/content_13123380.htm.

Zhu Ling (2006). *Wo fandui: yige renda daibiao de canzheng chuanqi [I Oppose: The Legend of a People's Congress Delegate]*. Haikou: Hainan Chubanshe, URL: http://www.bookfm.com/book/bookdetail.html?bid=103288.

Zou Shubin (2003). Yige lixiangzhuyizhe de zhengzhi jiqing [The political passion of an idealist]. In Tang Juan, Zou Shubin (Ed.), *Er'linglingsan nian Shenzhen jingxuan shilu [The Memoir of the Elections in Shenzhen in 2003]* (pp. 68–83). Xi'an: Xibeidaxue Chubanshe.

Zou Shubin (2004). *Er'linglingsan nian Beijing shi qu xian rendadaibiao jingxuan shilu [The Memoir of District and County Congress Elections in Beijing in 2003]*. Xi'an: Xibeidaxue Chubanshe.

Zou Shubin, Huang Weiping, Liu Jianguang (2003). Dapengzhen yu Buyunxiang xiangzhenzhang xuanju gaige zhi bijiao [A comparative study of the election reforms in Buyun Township and Dapeng Township]. *Modern China Studies* (1).

Index

additional candidate, 104, 105, 119

Beijing Consensus, 3. *See also* Chinese model
Buyun Township, Sichuan province, 12, 13, 19

Central Party's Organisational Department, 35
Chen Caiqiong, 114, 139
Chen Huibin, 127
Chen Shengyong, 77–8
Chi Haiping, 120
Chinese model, 3
Chongqing Municipality, 20, 26, 39, 52, 71, 106, 108, 112, 118, 120
consultative meeting, 79, 92–4,
competitive election, xiii, 3, 23, 34, 35, 49, 50, 77, 117. *See also* non-competitive election
CPPCC. *See* People's Political Consultative Conference

Dapeng Township, 12, 14, 19
deliberative democracy, x, xiii, 2, 4–6, 9, 23, 26, 50, 73–81, 85–96, 98–100, 103, 144, 103, 104, 146–49
deliberative polling, 80–3, 85, 99, 100
Deng Xiaoping, 57
direct elections: for township executives, xiii, 2, 4–6, 23, 24, 141, 144, 147; for township party secretaries, xiii, 2, 4–6, 23, 24, 38, 69, 147, 149; of township government executives, ix; of township party secretaries, x
Du Peng, 115–8, 129
Du Quanbing, 113, 119, 125

efficiency of democracy, 77

Fan Jianmin, 120
formal candidate, 104, 105, 113, 118, 119, 124, 126, 131, 136

Handan, Hebei Province, 112, 119, 122, 124, 125, 139
He Baogang, 79, 81, 82, 84, 88–92, 96, 97, 98, 100
Hengnan, Hunan Province, 116, 121
Hu Guojian, 117, 119, 124, 125, 129
Hu Jintao, 33, 35, 48, 51, 58, 80, 100
Huizhou City, Guang Dong Province, 63, 64, 66, 71
Hukou, 26, 113, 115, 138

independent candidate, x, xiii, 2, 4, 5, 6, 103–41, 145, 146, 147, 148
informal candidate, 104, 105, 113, 131, 136
inner-party democracy, x, 23, 29–35, 48–51, 55, 56, 58, 68, 73, 143, 144, 147. *See also* intra-party democracy; people's democracy
inner-party election, 31, 33, 35, 37, 38, 45–9
inner-party reform, 9, 29, 30, 32, 33, 34, 35, 38, 49, 50, 68, 69, 144
intra-party democracy, 33, 51

Jiang Shan, 113, 123, 124, 140
Jiang Zemin, 20, 51, 58
Jiaojiang, Zhejiang Province, 63, 64, 66, 70, 71
Ji'nan, Shandong Province, 121, 124, 125, 126, 127

Kan Ke, 107

Legal Daily, 21
Li Fan, 81, 87, 88, 89, 91, 92
Li Junru, 77, 94, 95
Lianhua Township, Sichuan Province, 38
liberal democracy, 3, 5, 6, 23, 50, 74, 75, 145
Lin Shangli, 95
Liu Shengmin, 113, 116, 119, 122, 124
local political reform experiments, 1, 2, 3, 5
Longxin Township, Chongqing Municipality, 39, 52
Lu Banglie, 113, 116, 122, 123, 124, 125, 127, 130, 132
Lu Jin, 116, 117, 139
Luo Qiulin, 116, 121
Luotian County, Hubei Province, 63, 65, 66, 71
Luoyang, Henan Province, 115, 116, 117, 118, 119, 129
Luxi County, Yunnan Province, 31, 39
Luzhou, Sichuan Province, 106

Ma Jianhua, 114, 122
maintaining rights, 111, 131, 138
Mao Zedong, 57, 70
Mulan Township, Sichuan Province, 39
multi-party cooperation and political consultation, 50, 75. *See also* People's Consultative Conference
multi-party politics, xiii, 3
multi-party system, 23, 50
Muyang County, Jiangsu Province, 39

Nancheng Township, Sichuan Province, 38
National People's Congress, 21, 97, 107, 140.
non-competitive election, 121
NPC. *See* National People's Congress

open nomination, 12, 15, 64; and direct election, 35, 51
organisation-nominated candidate, 104, 105, 116
organisation-preferred candidate, 104, 105, 112, 114, 115, 118, 121, 128, 132, 133, 134, 139
Ouyang Song, 35, 70. *See also* Central Party's Organisational Department

party congress reform, xiii, 2, 4, 5, 6, 55, 65–70, 72, 143, 147, 149
participatory budgeting, 81, 98, 99, 100, 103
People's Political Consultative Conference, 42, 43, 46, 65, 75, 76, 77, 95, 97, 101, 147, 149
People's Daily, 30, 31, 56, 70
people's democracy, 30, 31, 33, 34, 35, 49, 50
permanent tenure system of party congresses, 55–8, 62, 67–70. *See also* permanent tenure system of party congress members
permanent tenure system of party congress members, 57
Pingchang County, Sichuan Province, 39
Pingba Township, Chongqing Municipality, 20, 39, 52

Qianjiang, Hubei Province, 106, 112, 115, 117, 119, 121, 123, 125, 126, 127, 129, 135
Qiushi, 21, 22, 30

Renminwang, 31, 80
representative democracy, 32, 60, 62, 74, 78, 94

Rongcheng, Hubei Province, 127
sannong wenti, 11
self-nomination, 13, 16, 17, 26, 36, 37, 40, 41, 42, 47, 63, 64; and test, 12, 16
self-nominated candidates, 104, 105, 115, 121
Sheng Huaren, 21
Shenzhen, Guangdong Province, 12, 71, 107, 109, 113, 114, 115, 116, 117, 118, 119, 120, 121, 122, 123, 124, 125, 126, 127, 128, 129, 135, 136, 139, 140
Shiping County, Yunnan Province, 12, 14, 25
Shu Kexin, 112, 121, 123, 128
single-party system, xiii, 3, 4, 5, 23, 144, 145, 148
socialist democracy with Chinese characteristics, xiii, 3, 4, 23, 27, 50, 74, 76, 147, 149
soft authoritarianism, 3
Study Times, 31, 35, 36, 38, 80
Sun Wenguang, 116, 121, 124, 125, 126

three ballot system, 12, 14
Tian Qizhuang, 112, 122, 124, 125
two ballot system, 12, 15

Union of the Chinese Nationalists, 111, 137

village election, 4, 5, 21, 78, 130
voter-nominated candidate, 104, 105, 115, 116, 118, 134

Wang Guoqiang, 122, 125
Wei Shengduo, 20, 26
Wen Jiabao, 22
Wu Haining, 115, 120, 121, 125, 127, 128, 139
Wu'an, Hebei Province, 113
Wuhan, Hubei Province, 107, 112, 116, 117, 119, 120, 122, 124, 125, 129

Xiao Shuixiang, 122
Xiao Youmei, 121
Xiangshui Township, Shaanxi Province, 39
Xie Xiaoying, 115, 116, 118, 119, 121, 125, 126, 128
Xingjing County, Sichuan Province, 63, 64, 65, 66, 68, 71
Xinhe Township, Zhejiang Province, 81, 84, 87, 89, 90, 91, 92, 95, 96, 98, 99, 100
Xinhuawang, 80
Xu Bo, 118, 121
Xu Yaotong, 31

Yan Yuxiang, 116, 117, 119, 122, 125, 129
Yangji Township, Hubei Province, 12, 15, 25, 38
Yao Lifa, 106, 112, 115, 118, 121, 123, 125, 126, 127, 129, 132, 135, 140
Yao Shaofan, 118, 120, 132
Ye Yuanbai, 114, 118, 121
Yidu City, Hubei Province, 63, 65, 66, 71
Yongxing Township, Sichuan Province, 39
Yucheng District, Sichuan Province, 63, 64, 65, 66, 67, 68, 71

Zeguo Township, Zhejiang Province, 81, 89, 90, 91, 95, 97, 99, 100
Zeng Jianyu, 106, 132, 135
Zhen Xiaoying, 30
Zhijiang, Hubei Province, 113, 116, 122, 123, 124, 125, 127, 130
Zhou Changqing, 112, 121, 127
Zou Jiajian, 121, 125
Zou Tao, 113

About the Author

Zaijun Yuan received his PhD in politics from Monash University, Australia. His research interests include China's local politics, political development in Hong Kong and Taiwan, and cross-strait relations. Before he moved to Australia, he was a PhD candidate at the School of Public Administration, Nanjing Normal University, China. He got his MEcon in policy analysis from Nanjing University of Science and Technology, and got his BA in English language from Beijing International Studies University.